城都行

LOOKING for CHENGDU

A volume in the series
Anthropology of Contemporary Issues
EDITED BY ROGER SANJEK

城都行

Looking for Chengdu

A WOMAN'S ADVENTURES IN CHINA

HILL GATES

CORNELL UNIVERSITY PRESS

ITHACA AND LONDON

First published 1999 by Cornell University Press
First printing, Cornell Paperbacks, 1999

Printed in the United States of America

Library of Congress Cataloging-in-Publication Data
Gates, Hill.
    Looking for Chengdu : a woman's adventures in China / Hill Gates.
        p.   cm. — (The anthropology of contemporary issues)
    ISBN 0-8014-3646-X. — ISBN 0-8014-8632-7 (pbk.)
    1. Gates, Hill—Journeys—China.   2. China—Description and
travel.   I. Title.   II. Title: Woman's adventures in China.
III. Series: Anthropology of contemporary issues.
DS712.G37   1999
915.104'58—dc21   99-28430

Cornell University Press strives to use environmentally responsible suppliers and
materials to the fullest extent possible in the publishing of its books. Such materials
include vegetable-based, low-VOC inks, and acid-free papers that are recycled,
totally chlorine-free, or partly composed of nonwood fibers. Books that bear the logo of
the FSC (Forest Stewardship Council) use paper taken from forests that have been
inspected and certified as meeting the highest standards for environmental and social
responsibility. For further information, visit our website at
www.cornellpress.cornell.edu.

Cloth printing   10   9   8   7   6   5   4   3   2   1
Paperback printing   10   9   8   7   6   5   4   3   2   1

FSC   FSC Trademark © 1996 Forest Stewardship Council A.C.
        SW-COC-098

城都行

CONTENTS

城都行

PREFACE

Anthropology is an exhilarating vocation, if an exhausting one. Living in Taiwan and China, I eat extraordinarily well, meet marvelous, unlikely people, and shop for silk socks or dogskin blankets, accumulating weight, good karma, and exotic soft furnishings along with serious research notes. Contrapuntally, I lose sleep, illusions, and all track of American time. Fieldwork is important to an anthropologist, though not its ultimate goal. I work hard at it, interviewing until my assistants plead for holidays; expanding the day's scribbled notes on my laptop every night; pestering bureaucrats to give me a longer investigative leash.

But Chinese evenings spent far from the big cities of the coast are long, especially if one fails to find much joy in TV, dance halls, or low-stakes gambling. I wrote this journal on those nights—to push back loneliness, but also from the narcissism all journal-keepers share. Choosing words to fix the minutiae of my days promises insightful distance, a chance to better see myself as I peer and pose and watch for sharks. Only some years after I had begun this after-hours writing did I squarely face that I might be writing for other readers as well. Would those readers be as charmed as I with my supple honesty, my wise perceptions?

Of course not. They would want to learn about China, which they know both exists and matters in this world, not about the mid-life crisis of a jumpy unknown lady don.

Can one write a book about one's self as that self urgently seeks to understand China *without* including something useful about the Chinese themselves, if only as a byproduct? The layperson might think not. As a hardened professional, I assure you that it can be done. In recent years, some disciplinary colleagues have published volumes about their experiences in the field that filter out nearly all information about the people they were ostensibly studying. An e-mail joke describes the end of a two-year field trip: An anthropologist is talking incessantly with her local informants on an intense final day. At last, reluctantly, she dusts the sand off her pareu, and says, "Well, that's enough about me. Let's talk about *you*."

Is this such a book? When it began as a catalog of field uncertainties and triumphs, it was intended to be a journal, just me on me. Friends now tell me that the navel gazing is interrupted by substantial close-range sightseeing into Chinese daily life. I can no longer tell. Large parts of my life happen in China; when writing in this mode, I cannot disentangle what I am from where I have been, or what I know from where I have eaten and cried and been surprised, or who I am from the others who have traveled with me. Although it is easy to pretend it is so, the self is not inside.

This journal has kept me company on two adventures to remake my life: a search for fuller knowledge of what is happening to Chinese women; and my own passage from a time of trouble to a sunny stretch of health, confidence, and love. Though I wrote for private reasons, making that writing public now seems important. A hundred years after Isabella Bird Bishop gave us her views on the Chinese, and despite energetic documentation by thousands of later and better-prepared visitors, Chinese are still often presented as flat and alien to Westerners. Our popular press especially urges us to see them as well-drilled school of sardines or—worse yet—guided in their lives by an unfathomable culture, "the Wisdom of the East." It is rare to read or see an account of particular Chinese people acting—as they do when I'm around—like perfectly ordinary people, very varied, responding as you or I would if we lived among their constraints and opportunities.

If I were a novelist—Maxine Hong Kingston, perhaps, or Timothy Mo—I might try to offer portraits of Chinese who are both real and plausible to my readers. But I know my literary limits. Learning limits is what these adventures have largely been about. I bump into knowledge, or a veil of secrecy, or "the country's regulations" at every step. I want simply to detail a bit of the blundering that has taught me what people can and cannot do, will and will not think, in Chengdu, though I can do this only as myself.

At the end of this dual journey into Sichuan and my fieldnotes, I realize that I ought properly to thank all one hundred and ten million Sichuanese, and perhaps a few million people from outside this province as well. But I will focus my gratitude on the women of the All-China Women's Federation, Sichuan Provincial Branch, Propaganda Department. They have been close collaborators on the two academic projects in the interstices of which this book was written. Out of modesty, senior cadres prefer to go unnamed in this account, and, in accordance with anthropological canons of privacy, I have tagged all my interviewees with anonyms. By being named, Teacher Jiang Yinghong, Ms. Hua Xinghui, and Ms. Li Jufang were persuaded to take at least this much credit for all that they have done for the projects, and for me. Professor Qin Xuesheng too appears in his true guise, with his permission, and has my deepest thanks.

Although they may puzzle at how I used part of the resources with which they entrusted me—grantsmanship is a subtle game, after all—I acknowledge with gratitude the funding supplied by the Rockefeller Foundation's program on women's status and fertility, and by the Harry Frank Guggenheim Foundation's program for the study of violence and aggression. I hope they will not object to this small lagniappe over and above the professorial productions that their lovely money made possible.

These adventures were played out under a lucky star. As the reader will quickly see, I am not much of an impresario; I must credit fortune's favor as well as the integrity and good will of my many associates for the success of my quest. Rarely, anywhere, can one expect to begin a complex new project, with unknown colleagues, in an unfamiliar setting, and not come some sort of a cropper. Unmanageable messes bubbled up almost weekly in separate fieldwork in Fujian and Shanghai, as they always have in Taiwan. In Sichuan, magically, nothing awful happened to any of us, and the work got done. We have brought in a fine haul of enduring friendships and of solid evidence outlining the shape of Chengdu women's lives, some of it now listed at the end of this Preface. We are planning to do it again.

Polishing up these notes was a pleasure; handing the manuscript round for others to polish further was unsettling. My mother, Vera Neill Gates, edited me with a firm hand, maternally elevating my often-deplorable tone. Arthur Wolf, my husband, laughed in all the right places. An anonymous reviewer for Cornell Press praised parts, giving much-needed encouragement, but also ticked me off intelligently for structural laxities still insufficiently corseted. Wang Min chose the Chinese title; Melissa Brown, Colette Plum, John Rohsenow, Shih Chuankang, Terry Sulyma, Helen Young, and Zhang Haiyang read, commented, and corrected. I thank them all.

1991. "'Narrow Hearts' and Petty Capitalism: Small Business Women in Chengdu, China." In *Marxist Approaches in Economic Anthropology*, edited by Alice Littlefield and Hill Gates, 13–36. Society for Economic Anthropology Monograph no. 9 (Lanham, Maryland: University Press of America).

1991. "Eating for Revenge: Consumption and Corruption under Economic De-reform." *Dialectical Anthropology* 16:233–241.

1991. "Taibei Family Businesswomen: Experiences with Commoditization." In *Taiwan: Economy, Society, and History*, edited by E. K. Y. Chen, Jack F. Williams, and Joseph Wong, 327–338. Hong Kong: University of Hong Kong.

1992. "Small Fortunes: Class and Society in Taiwan." In *Taiwan: Beyond the Economic Miracle*, edited by Denis Simon and Michael Y. M. Kau, 169–185. Armonk, N.Y.: Westview Press.

1993. "Cultural Support for Birth Limitation among Urban Capital-owning Women." In *Chinese Families in the Post-Mao Era*, edited by Deborah Davis and Stevan Harrell, 251–274. Berkeley: University of California Press.

1994. "Labors of Love? Family Businesswomen in Chengdu and Taibei." In *Papers from the Harvard Taiwan Studies Workshops*, edited by William Kirby, 125–165. Cambridge, Mass.: Harvard University, Fairbank Center for East Asian Studies.

1996. "Owner, Worker, Mother, Wife: Taibei and Chengdu Family Businesswomen." In *Putting Class in Its Place. Worker Identities in East Asia*, edited by Elizabeth J. Perry, 127–166. Berkeley: University of California Press.

1996. "Buying Brides in China—Again." *Anthropology Today* 12 (4):8–11.

1997. "Footbinding, Handspinning, and the Modernization of Little Girls." In *Constructing China: Economy and Culture in China*, edited by Ernest P. Young, 177–194. Ann Arbor: Association for Asian Studies Monographs.

1997. "On a New Footing: Footbinding and the Coming of Modernity." *Jindai Zhongguo Funu Shi Yanjiu—Research on Women in Modern Chinese History* no. 5: 115–136.

CHAPTER ONE

城都行

Facing China

In 1965, through love and accident, I stumbled into Chinese studies at the University of Michigan, after five years of preparing to do anthropology of the South Pacific. In spite of the difficulties of China's Bronze Age script and multiple languages, I struggled through basic sinology because I was still a woman who followed her husband—even into his puzzling profession.

China had inherent attractions, of course. By its own claim, it was the new leader of the Third World, cutting a different path to industrialism, feeding, employing, and educating its massive population, scaring the bejesus out of the United States. The Chinese of the 1960s were experimenting with their society in a way that would change history. Their momentum would mobilize Southeast Asia and who knows how many other of the world's poor regions from Peru to Pakistan, confirming to students in Paris and Mexico City, as well as in Berkeley and Ann Arbor, that *the* revolution had begun. Much of this I longed to believe; my considerable skepticism about the imminence of socialism was based more on the fear of disappointment than on distaste.

In the 1960s, the United States forbade its citizens to visit China, and neither side was prepared to have social investigators living there. Instead, I did fieldwork in Taiwan, and wrote about its peculiar oppressiveness for a doctorate in 1973. The sense of Chineseness I learned there strengthened both my doubts about China's revolution and my hope that they were misplaced. I yearned for socialism to succeed both because it seemed necessary and because I wanted to spend my working life engaged with positive, humane development. I had neither the stomach to chronicle the ever-deepening misery of Africans and Latin Americans nor the eyes to blind in needlepointing fussy cultural inter-

1

pretations, as more resigned anthropologists began to do after the Vietnam War.

In 1978, just as I was perfecting an updated-Marxist explanation of China's extraordinary end run around capitalism, Chinese leaders began to dismantle collectivism in agriculture, encourage small-scale private industry and commerce, and permit foreign capital investment. The Chinese barged into the 1980s on currents that, to my Taiwan-trained eyes, looked appallingly familiar.

For China-studies lefties like me, the early 1980s were ghastly. Suit-wearing colleagues who had always wanted to go to Washington smirked from TV screens, pontificating on China's return to the free-market fold. Obnoxious relatives explained in painful detail why human nature was designed by God, if not Darwin, to truck, barter, and exchange, and that they had long told us so. Opportunist academics deserted the movement in droves, taking up export-import jobs or burying themselves in "traditional Chinese culture" and political reaction. Sincere comrades stoically completed research that was now unpublishable or spent a year or five under the bed. I remarried in haste, disposed of my academic library, taught well, grew enough potatoes for yearly consumption, tried every cure for depression known to medicine and the *National Enquirer,* repented at leisure of trying to settle forever in a small Michigan college town, divorced, finished my first book, and returned to Taiwan to meet Mr. Qin. Through him, in the mid-1980s, China—and life—gave me a second chance.

After two decades of depression, my energy was back, and I was ravenous to begin the China anthropology that had so long eluded me. China was more open to outsiders than it had been since the 1949 revolution; fieldwork in Taiwan had polished my Mandarin and my cultural expertise. All I needed was a project, some money, and a Chinese connection to smooth the bureaucratic obstacles. With suitable contacts in China to guarantee cooperation, funding would be easy, for American foundations were eager to sponsor studies in a country that made a habit of rejecting Western curiosity. My project was obvious: Economic reforms after 1978 had enabled many Chinese to establish the small family firms that I had studied in Taiwan. Now in China, I would investigate how people—especially women—had geared up for business after a generation of socialist constriction. The best possible place to ask this question was the region where reform began—the huge inland province of Sichuan. There, little influenced by the foreign investment that was transforming the east coast, business was resprouting from indigenous roots.

How could I persuade authorities in Sichuan to sign the documents to get the grant to interview the locals who built this boom?

Fate intervened, in its usual random fashion, through Mr. Qin. This old friend, a Taiwan taxi driver, has an elder brother who was "some kind of professor" in China. The brothers had lost touch since the Maoist crackdown on intellectuals in the mid-1950s. In 1986, Mr. Qin located Professor Qin, and began a roundabout correspondence with him. It was not then possible for them to write directly to each other; China and Taiwan, still officially at war, had no postal links. Could I transmit their letters through the United States, asked Mr. Qin? Of course I could. Adding selfish delight to pleasure in my friend's joy was the Professor's address: Museum of Archaeology, Chengdu City, Sichuan.

Like most Chinese scholars, Professor Qin had been starved for years of new academic materials. I cleared my and my colleagues' bookshelves of anything that might fill the forty-year anthropological gap since he had studied at Northwestern University. When the six mailbags of books reached Chengdu, I followed them with a request to visit and discuss research possibilities. Professor Qin, a Chinese Saint Peter, opened the pearly gates. With his chop-bespangled letter and my newly stable health, I was going to the promised land. After years of reading, of talking to émigrés, and of peering at Chineseness through Taiwan's distinctive lens, would I recognize heaven when I got there?

Anthropologists like the exotic; we prefer new terrain. Experiencing people as "others" is the occupational vice, once openly proclaimed and now forsworn or closeted as dehumanizing to them and us. I cannot help liking unfamiliar, delicious, mental pickles on the palate. I hope China will be "different" from Taiwan, will slip undreamed-of cultural flavors into my daily rice. Taiwan, by now, has lost its capacity to surprise me; it is a second home. Knowing its surface quirks of fashion and its stable architecture of enduring social relations is a pleasing accomplishment—and should make China, when I get there, more transparent.

This apparent familiarity might be deceptive, however. Taiwan has been separated from China proper since the last century and has been busy building its own history over those years. Besides the knowledge I can transpose from Taiwan, what I know about China comes from a brief month's touring in 1980 and from books. That knowledge is not great, but it is enough to hint that Westerners know remarkably little about either the new People's Republic or the old China that gave it birth.

Although some "scientific" anthropology was done in China in the 1930s and 1940s, much of it looks very dated now, and much was of dubious value even when published. One account, presenting itself as a description of ideal Chinese kinship, in fact documented a minority people who had taken on Chinese culture only in the previous generation. Many of their elders still spoke an indigenous, non-Han language, and their customs blended Han with obviously non-Han elements. Another key study focused tightly on the writer's home village. Except for a single pregnant sentence about a barbed-wire perimeter, the author ignores the reality that the villagers were living in the middle of a revolution. Today's anthropologists would make much more of the ethnic and political contexts of such communities, explaining their cultures as ongoing local reactions to the there and the then. The timeless and highly idealized visions of China set out by such early anthropologists now seem quaint, mixtures of useful information, innocence, and deviousness. For good or ill, anthropology in the first half of this century produced only a few major works to record how ordinary people lived in China before the revolution.

The Chinese themselves, of course, have been avid and indefatigable chroniclers of their own society for over four thousand years. The quantity of written materials for later centuries particularly is overwhelming. The uninstructed might imagine that Westerners could simply read Chinese sources to learn what China is about. These texts—on bronze, bamboo, silk, stone, porcelain, and even paper—are treasures of immense value, but they are by no means easy to use. Apart from formidable language difficulties and their sheer volume, they were written by and for Chinese. We must understand the minds that wrote them before we can truly translate what the words mean; yet we must gain that understanding of the intentions of the writers, at least in part, from the texts themselves. It is a slow and contentious undertaking.

The Chinese, when they have had peaceful moments in the last two troubled centuries, have sometimes tried to explain themselves to Westerners. They are, however, as stubborn in their insistence on explicating matters in their own terms as we are in converting them, somehow, into our own. The handy English translation on the back of a box of Chinese cold medicine shows what I mean. *Banlangen* is said to be especially good for "common colds of the wind heat type" (along with a great many other afflictions). What in the world is a cold "of the wind heat type"? As a literal translation, it is perfect, but it yields little information to the Western reader. One must understand Chinese medical categories to give these everyday English words a meaning which, in our own medical terminology, makes sense. Analyses of Chinese life in terms of such native concepts as "the mandate of heaven," "traditional Chinese culture," or "feudal superstition" do not mean much to contemporary Western social scientists who do not perceive heaven as an agent, who see "tradition" as a way of manipulatively extending the present into the past rather than the reverse, and who find "feudal" too broad, and "superstition" too narrow, to be of much use in describing anything. It is not that the Chinese are wrong in their views, only that they divide up the world and interpret causality in human affairs very differently from the way these things are currently done in the West. A few academic specialists on each side attempt to read and make use of the others' insights, but this interchange too is slow and contentious. I was saddened to learn from Professor Qin that the anthropological work from Western languages that is now being translated for scholarly use is mostly that of the 1930s and 1940s, of interest to people like myself only as historical footnotes.

After the 1949 revolution, Western-influenced social science fell into official disfavor and was dropped from university curricula and academic agendas. Marxism took its place. Marxism, or historical materialism, is in principle an extremely broad intellectual framework capable of holistically interpreting and connecting a wide range of phenomena. This is one of the signs of a powerful theory. Contemporary Western anthropology would be gutted if the insights derived from Marxism were to disappear, although pusillanimous careerists regularly plagiarize its insights without crediting their sources.

But Chinese Marxism turned intellectually rigid in the late 1950s, perhaps from Soviet influence, perhaps from an increasing rigidification of Chinese society itself after the initial successes of the revolution. Solipsistically focused on the Chinese experience, it learned nothing from the cross-cultural perspective that rejuvenated European Marxism when it learned from peoples of the colonial world. While French academics responded to their government's outrages in Algeria and Vietnam, and American academics to theirs in Vietnam and Central America by learning Marxist lessons, the Chinese, concerned only with China, forgot what a flexible and innovative tool Marxism could be for analysis and policy.

Most Chinese, from overexposure to rigid Marxism, have lost all taste for any. I once lectured on Chinese folk religion as a means of popular resistance to students being trained to be leaders among their own, minority, peoples. They liked the lecture (laughed at the jokes, buzzed among themselves at the unexpected points) until I mentioned Marx.

Then one-third of them got up and walked out. Friendly Chinese intel-lectuals are sometimes patient with my attempts to sharpen Marxist the-ory against the stubborn facts of Chinese history, but I rarely meet one who sees what might be gained from such an exercise. It is as if the Marx that I and my anthropological generation rely on and contend with had never been heard of.

China after 1949 has been as difficult of access physically as it has been intellectually. Its government fears that outsiders will report only China's failures and supervises travelers with centuries'-old expertise. Visitors travel through an elegant gulag of well-managed "sights," pre-cluded not only by attentive supervision but also by their own linguistic insufficiencies from breaking through into ordinary life. Often quite unaware of how little they have seen, such tourists have written an enor-mous amount about this vast country since more outsiders were permit-ted entry after the mid-1970s. Much of it is drivel, the worst of it written by people who spend their time with officials and academics in the extremely atypical cities of Beijing, Shanghai, and Guangzhou. The pro-tective devices of educated Chinese are not easy for Westerners to pene-trate. Officials take seriously their task of making China look good to outsiders; Chinese politeness and hospitality are powerful codes for manipulating people into indebtedness and self-censorship. Short-timers leave cheerful, fatter, but not much the wiser.

Ignorance is not the only reason that our apparent familiarity with China is deceptive. Many Westerners who went to China during the later stages of the Cultural Revolution wanted to believe a new utopia was being achieved; they swallowed (and published) some astonishing lies. Many of those who have visited since want to use China for the opposite, rightist reason: to prove that capitalism is based on human nature and that China's economic difficulties demonstrate the worthless-ness of socialism. Such writers, some of whom know better, have pre-sented pan-Chinese behaviors as examples of Communist wickedness and deviousness.

A well-known journalist shows us how this is done in his anecdote about how difficult it is to get Chinese to identify themselves on the phone. For the edification of the American public, he attributes this apparent paranoia to suffering under Communist rule. In fact, however, the journalist spent some years in Taiwan during a time when the Tai-wanese had few telephones. He must have been as familiar as I with the evolution of Chinese telephone manners. In both Taiwan and China, people are habitually cautious with strangers, and, when or where phones are still a novelty, are generally loathe to give any information out to the faceless voices they produce. A long string of "Wei?" "Wei?" "Wei?" exchanges initiates conversation as each party tries to recognize the other. Unsophisticated phone users often greet me on the phone with a "Shi wo"—"It's me," assuming they will be recognized as quickly as if we were face to face. Thus "Communist paranoia" is better seen as "Chinese culture," or maybe just "getting used to telephones." Those who learn about China from a distance must constantly cope with such petty perversions of truth.

I am proud of the small store of expertise about Chinese life that I have (painfully) garnered through fieldwork in Taiwan, and often find it transferable to the understanding of China proper. I am delighted when I can interpret, for example, the arcane symbolism of folk religion in Chengdu through analysis developed in Taibei. But I am skeptical of that transferability, too. Old ladies praying in Chengdu are doing something very different from those who pray in Taibei, even when the rituals they perform are nearly identical. Ceremony and social action of all kinds take their fullest meaning from the social context in which they are performed. In Chengdu, folk religion is carried on in the teeth of strong official disapproval by a tiny minority of people who know well they are doing something faintly subversive and disapproved. In Taibei, folk religion is part of the normal background of life that the Guomindang government has long ceased to try to eradicate and now exploits as a tourist attraction. For many Taiwanese, participation in folk ritual claims membership in a truly Taiwanese society. When I commence work in Sichuan, I must remember that others' books and my own Taiwan field experience may draw misleading parallels, that there is little about "being Chinese" that I can take for granted.

I will travel to Chengdu not just as an anthropologist. Inevitably, necessarily, I travel as a woman, to understand women's lives. I am— inevitably, necessarily—a feminist, but wanting to study Chinese women grows for me as much out of my subject as out of ideological commitment. One cannot understand an economy without researching the activities of all its participants, and the processes through which they are born, taught, and defended by their families. To try to do so is, quite simply, stupid. That Nobel laureates and entire economics departments pretend to, and that policy in great countries is sometimes made on such pretenses makes it no less stupid. Once that reality is faced, the choice is simple. One may do stupid work on men and individuals only, or do the job right and study women, households, and classes too.

Besides—not to be too self-righteous about it—for a woman, studying other women is both easier and more fun. Among Chinese, still an androcentric people, this may be even more true than elsewhere. In Taiwan, many Chinese men are as convinced of women's inferiority as they are of the hardness of metal and the fluidity of water. Such men do not see me. If they are brought, somehow, to focus on my face, they forget what I have said, they rush me out of their offices with pleasantries, they occasionally manifest symptoms of sexual embarrassment ("What is this foreign woman *up to!*"). In interviews, they mouth politically correct answers and seem unable to describe the reality that surrounds them. A woman researcher cannot easily invite them out to the dinners that smooth the path from introduction to friendship without raising a host of anxieties, and she invites trouble if she invites them to her rooms.

Chinese women, by contrast, are wonderful company, easy to entertain, and far more straightforward than men in their views and descriptions of their worlds. They hold my purse in the toilet, struggle to understand my odd views, and are, if anything, too sympathetic toward the discomforts of dislocation from hearth and home. A Taiwanese matriarch may not want me to interview her, but she will generally be pleasant about it. If she does give the interview, I can count on learning a lot. In Sichuan, where clear differences and illusory similarities might complicate my research, working with women will supplement and illuminate the usual males-only vision of China's changing economy.

To talk to Sichuan women, however, I had first to find a way to explain my plan to some influential Chinese who could assist me in getting permission to do research. In December 1987, Professor Qin's invitation in hand, I set out for Chengdu to arrange a field study. The trip to Sichuan was to be the first of seven I have now taken to that spectacular province: large as France, poised between an economically primitive Tibet and China's richest heartland, speeding from the sixteenth to the twenty-first century, home to fashion designers, yak milkers, the world's best cooks, and now, ten years later, a third home for a woman who has already had too many.

城都行

December 1987–January 1988

Guangzhou, Wuzhou, Liuzhou, Kunming, Yunnan, The Burma Road, Lijiang, Dali, Chengdu

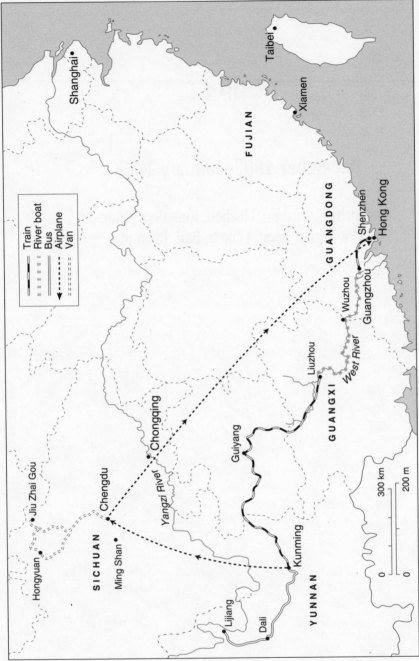

1. Exploring Southwest China

CHAPTER TWO

城都行

A Journey to the West

DECEMBER 20, 1987. GUANGZHOU

On the basis of a Chinese map, which I have no reason to believe is a good analog of its territory, I have planned a month-long trip alone across southwest China to Chengdu. Friends look unhappy when I tell them this, but I, who cannot go to a movie by myself, pooh-pooh all difficulties. I am in Guangdong, a good beginning. Attending the conference that paid my way here—a hundred seedy sinologues at a matching off-season beach resort outside Shenzhen—I am beginning to feel easy in spoken Putonghua again. I will take the slowest, most local forms of transport and one small bag. The famous Victorian traveler, Isabella Bird Bishop, did it in 1896 with no Chinese and a broken heart; I can, too.

For a few initial days, I travel with an old and dear friend. John knows the China-hand tricks I failed to learn on my brief stay in 1980, filling me in as fast as my time-warped mind can function. We spend a day in Shenzhen, looking for a "talking watch" for his blind Chinese in-law. In the unrelenting messiness of this new industrial town, buildings sprout in a weekend, postmodern bamboo. Its chop-suey denizens are flat cartoons in my jet-glazed gaze: a shop-soiled woman running a dance hall, a tableful of Shanghainese bitching about the over-sharp Cantonese (!), the unpredictably helpful manager of the talking watch factory. I should be more curious—how business gets done in China is my academic forte—but I want to be on my way. The comfortable train that China deceptively offers to the newly arrived dumps us early the next day in Guangzhou's chaotic main square. I am seriously on the road again.

The Liuhua Bin'guan across from the railroad station is unrecognizable as the hostelry that sheltered me in 1980. It was then a cheap, Overseas Chinese hotel where I was the only Westerner: low, sprawling, primitive. New towers have shot up fore and aft, with glitzy mirrored restaurants and waitresses to be plucked like fruit. I paid 30 *renminbi* (RMB) a night in 1980 (about $6 U.S.), and meals were almost free. Rooms in the new Liuhua range from 90 to 800 FEC! The street rate for FEC, the special currency foreigners are supposed to use, is close to one and a half to one RMB, cautious but persistent money changers inform me. A pricey room is thus worth either $100 U.S. or about $67 U.S., depending on which currency you are permitted to pay in. John waves documents, and gets my room for 90, payable in RMB; twenty dollars U.S., more or less. It is clean (although [inoffensive] water runs from odd places in the plumbing), well supplied, and unheated.

Here in the warm southeast, lack of heat is no problem. Further inland, I can expect snow—and no heat. At the Friendship Store, I find a cheap, cheerful, angora sweater, thick enough to stop bullets. A more lurid pink than it appeared in the fluorescent store, it at least is big enough to encompass all the layers of long underwear that I will need in Chengdu.

You can fly to Kunming, in Yunnan, the next place I have a real reason to pass through, but I don't want to fly. You can go there by train, via one of two long detours. More appealingly, my map shows a railhead at Liuzhou, in the neighboring province of Guangxi, from which I could take the train to Yunnan. I know a man in Taiwan who had grown up in Liuzhou, or somewhere nearby. Mr. Su had been a peddler to mountain tribespeople before he joined the Guomindang army in the late 1930s. He had liked it; why not me?

How to get there? Asking around at the hotel produces my first pleasant surprise of the trip. You go up the Liu River on a passenger boat to Wuzhou and "maybe" from there to Liuzhou by a second boat. Wuzhou sounds fine for starters.

Off to the number thirteen dock. No line for tickets, 10.5 RMB for a guaranteed numbered bunk with quilts, food available on board, arrive in Wuzhou in twenty hours. Be here tomorrow at five thirty. Nothing to it.

I spend the rest of this day and the next walking around the area near the wharf. It is quiet, clean, orderly, basic. Is this the old or the new China? Hard to tell; the tidiness seems overdone. Chinese neighborhoods, left to their own devices, are more unbuttoned. The older dwellings are very small, dating to before the revolution, but a good deal of new and varied building is in progress, part of the privatization program. In the dark evening lanes, open doors frame domestic altars honoring gods and ancestors, small incense holders near thresholds twinkle, propitiating ghosts. Local markets burst with "ten thousand things" including paper spirit money, pigs' feet, and the heavenly tangerines that perfume a street.

A daycare / kindergarten seems immense in that crowded quarter— the central courtyard bigger than dozens of dwellings. Children have to be pulled away from teachers and small companions when parents come to shepherd them to homes with no playmates. The center has no study fees, a teacher tells me, but charges 40 RMB a month for food, half of mama's likely salary. The narrow, stone-paved streets lead me gently into the Chinese memories and mindset that will keep me comfortable as I drift toward my destination. By the end of two slow-paced, quiet days, I have seen my friend off to his train, bought the towel and screw-lidded cup necessary on Chinese journeys, and headed for the wharf.

As easily as the daydreams that brought me here, I find the boat at berth, buy toilet paper and fruit (fruit is for drinking, when you are tired of tea), wave away the peddlers wanting to sell me things I can't carry and the porters who want to carry the things I already have, find my bunk on the upper deck, eye my fellow-travelers, and check with three independent sources that this boat goes to Wuzhou. The vessel is a sixty-foot iron bucket, designed for drudgery. Its decor of crew laundry and potted plants gives me confidence that it will make one more run.

I am only a little surprised that my bunk is simply a two-by-six segment of an open platform. If I stretch out my arms, I can embrace the sleeping spaces of my neighbors to the left and right. The slumber party will include a hundred guests. For a long half hour after our eleven thirty scheduled departure, the boat rumbles and clanks alongside the same crowded quay. Then, for no particular reason, it lurches purposefully upriver. I lie blissful, head out the porthole, watching the flotsam of Guangzhou vanish astern, and the river life of domestic sampans and industrial barges swim into view. Banana and tangerine skins flutter from the ports like jumbo-colossal confetti. Stifling the ecological impulse, I strip a banana and throw its peel to drift with the rest.

An hour or two past Guangzhou's dirty suburbs, the river-borne traffic jam recedes, but we are never out of sight of ferries, barges, houseboats, police cruisers, and rafts. From the blackened stone wharves of smaller towns, boats pay calls on us, bringing freight, passengers, and the vegetables for our dinners. A steward offers choices, takes payment, and, in due time, brings the tray of rice and side dishes to my bunk. He is nervous, worried that I will not want to, or be able to, eat what is prepared, that I will be sick, or cross, or make what Chinese call "a foreign appearance"— a scene. Can I use chopsticks? I reassure him—and the whole deck of bunks, all covertly eyeing the foreigner—by tucking in with greedy pleasure to river fish full of tiny bones, to one of the hundred versions of cabbage southerners have been breeding since the Neolithic, and to the phallic eggplant on which Chinese impale coarse jokes. Grit in the grain reminds me to be tender of my teeth; I will be a long way from both top-grade rice and painless dentistry for some weeks.

In Chinese trains and boats at night, lightbulbs are left glaring to deter thieves and rats. Travelers thus play out their repertory of intimate scenes on a brilliant stage. Even the narrow privacy that one is due in a Chinese home broadens to a luxurious space worth anticipating at journey's end. My deportment, from luggage placement to sleeping style, will be on view till Wuzhou. Each of us in this boatload of journeymates is part of everyone else's furnishings. So much the better for me, curious by nature and a snoop by profession.

A young family of three sharing the two bunks aft of me are, perhaps, new to this first-class stuff. She has a broad, rosy face and braids, wears buttery 24-karat earrings. He's monkeywiry, the sort of skinny, indefatigable southeasterner who makes himself at home in London or Trinidad or Mauritius. Travel means nothing to him. The boy is a spoiled five-year-old in a child-sized Army uniform—bile green, with theatrical scarlet patches, like the originals. His fear of me won't last, I fear.

When they embarked, the father, young but work-roughened to an ambiguous middle age, removed the three-inch-high bundling board separating their allotted pad-mattresses. The woman arranged their impedimenta: quilts supplied by the boat, snacks for the little boy, and everybody's shoes, which she cautiously tucked under the mat for safekeeping. (Thanking her silently for the tip, I do the same with my irreplaceable walkers.) During this nest-building entr'acte, the five-year-old entertained himself and his parents with his attempts to crawl through the portholes into the river.

With everything tidied to her satisfaction, the broad-faced woman begins to wonder about the foreigner in the next bed. We fall into conversation, each curious about the other's motives for the trip. They are peasants, she says. She is very hard to understand, but comes closer to standard Mandarin than her completely uneducated spouse. They have been on vacation to Guangzhou.

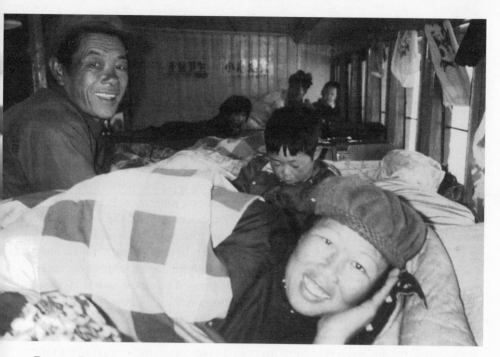

Peasant Family on Vacation, 1987

I must have misunderstood: "You were doing business in the city, perhaps, or visiting relatives?"

"No, we don't know anyone in Guangzhou. We made a lot of money this year, and my husband said that he'd never seen Guangzhou. Why didn't we just open our hands and spend a little? So we came traveling. We were in Guangzhou for a week. We stayed in a hotel, went everywhere, and saw everything."

"We saw a fire engine," said the little boy.

"Peasants" and "vacations" historically have not fit into the same sentence, certainly not in China. Was the responsibility system, the post-1980 subcontracting of formerly collective land to households really this successful? How delightful! Though Westerners love to stereotype Chinese as loving-the-good-earth stay-at-homes, they are surely the world's most enthusiastic travelers. When they have the chance and the money, they are off: on pilgrimages, to Disneyland, to see famous scenery or urban marvels, at home or abroad. They know how to travel, too, comfortably spending six weeks on the road with a small bag weighing five pounds. They layer on loose, comfortable clothes, and, these days, wear their money round their middles in the funnily fashionable belly bags that make everyone look like a train conductor on a busman's holiday.

The self-declared peasant holiday-makers in the next bunk, now near the end of their trip, are laden with an obligatory burden of gifts for those who stayed at home. But even so, with their sensible equipment and single child to manage, they are still having fun. When we run out of words in common, they reenter the little family world that Chinese carry about with them, and proceed to talk, eat, play, and sleep with unabated gusto till I lose sight of them in Wuzhou.

After dinner, well-fed smokers take up their repellent refreshment, and I briefly resent the Chinese ability to sleep among nuisances. When the draft from yawning portholes brings me only river smells and the woodsmoke from passing settlements, though, I wallow, discreetly, in sensuousness, as everyone else is doing. Never warm enough in chilly weather, like most women, I am grateful for the thick, wadded quilts, grateful to the women who picked and spun and wove for this journey. I recall the words of one of Taiwan's preeminent feminists, descanting on the exquisite contradiction between well-warmed body and icy nose-tip. And more—*this* embracing cocoon has cut the moorings of a quotidian bed to go a-roving, moving, rolling on the river. Bedding down in a boat tunes one's heartbeat to the thumping silence of Tina Turner and the cosmos.

DECEMBER 22, 1987. WUZHOU

We arrive in Wuzhou unexpectedly early, just before six A.M. In befuddling darkness, I march up the long stone ramp, across the street, and into the nearest thing that looks like a bus station. Locals on the boat had assured me I couldn't go upriver to Liuzhou, but must try for a twelve-hour bus ride. I conclude that, after a dreamy eighteen hours aboard the boat, I might as well catch the damned bus.

Finding what seems to be the right queue, I line up. Eventually, the man behind enlightens me that we are queueing for the boat for Liuzhou. As so often happens in my battles with the written Chinese word, the appropriate characters then resolve themselves into an unambiguous affirmation of known fact. The sign says plainly that a bunk in the boat to Liuzhou costs 10.7 RMB, stops at fifteen intermediate places, and takes about thirty hours. We wait for the ticket window to open, perhaps at dawn.

Wuzhou is dark still; the tiny, deep, ticket windows will not open for an hour. The importance this river-town once enjoyed is clear from its pre-revolution and once-handsome waiting room. A complex chiaro-scuro dramatizes a greenish terrazzo floor, streaky marble walls, elaborate arches of no known order. Hopper / Hapsburg, perhaps, or van Gogh / Victoria and Albert. The light picks out the blue- and green-jacketed ticket-buying majority, turning their dull twills metallic, washing out the warmer colors of younger people's western styles. The crowd shuffles restlessly in this eclectic opera-set, waiting for the overture.

A centimeter of water lies over part of the floor. During the hour I inch toward my ticket, a woman station attendant pushes it around with a mop. There is no drain; she doesn't slosh it out the door; she doesn't wring out the mop or in any way reduce the quantity of water. She merely transfers it from place to place, through the lines of waiting ticket purchasers and their bundles. After a while she stops. It is reassuring, after the surprise of encountering vacationing peasants, to see that the workstyle of those employed by the state has not changed since I was last in China. Every society needs some sense of continuity.

The lines are orderly. When five young toughs start to push in at the window, a cop appears and yells loudly at them. They jump to, fade out. The policeman stands by (near my bag, I am glad to note) looking military and reassuring. Earlier, I had stashed my single, but significantly over-five-pound bag on a bit of floor that seemed to stay above the flood. Unnecessarily, I keep turning to check on it. A man across the room says, loudly, angrily,

"Foreign miss! Don't worry about your bag so much. We Chinese have fine things of our own. We don't want your foreign things!"

Probably. But for a moment, I remember that I am now a hundred miles up the creek, in the dark, the only foreigner in town.

Ticket sellers are notoriously nasty in China. They have something people want badly, and they take full advantage of that fact. Perhaps this one is an exception—she seems genuinely pleasant—or she wants no trouble from my foreign face. She answers all my questions, sending me on my way at seven to find Wuzhou's best hotel. Wandering into another, nearer one, I surrender 46 FEC for the pleasure of a bed, bath, toilet, and luggage room till six in the evening. I neglected to note its name, but you go right out of the port office to the first red / green light, turn right at the bus station, and it's about two blocks on.

Before I check in, I have chicken noodle soup in a tiny restaurant carved out of the corner of the hotel. The other customers are young schoolgirls, abacuses slung at the ready, eating noodles for breakfast. When I ask about the local sights, they are pleasant and helpful, and don't stare, follow, or make rude noises. Throughout this journey, I am impressed by the civility of children whom I automatically compare with Taibei kids in the 1960s and 70s, when shrieks of "hello," *da bizi* (big nose), *a-toka* (protruder—another reference to noses), and *yang guizi* (foreign devil) were the *obbligato sostenuto* of my public life. The courtesy of these ten-year-old Wuzhou girls warms me as much as the soup.

The hotel is a long cut below Guangzhou standards—the public rooms are littered with cigarette butts and spit; alien substances lurk in the chandeliers. The bed is clean, however, and the staff accommodating. I show my Sichuan Provincial Government document to try for a lower rate, but the gaggle of young clerks waves it away, amused. Money is the dominant document in the coastal southeast, and Sichuan might as well be Saskatchewan.

Already regretting I have committed myself to a same-day departure, I realize I have only eight hours to explore. Wuzhou was a treaty port in the late nineteenth century, an inland station for foreign trade. It is now a city of 100,000 people, a major center for hundreds of miles of crumpled landscape, and a perfect jumble of old and new. At a tiny shop, I buy a black velvet headband-hat of a sort I had previously seen only in old photos; in Wuzhou, elderly women still wear them. The town clock, memorializing Scottish imperialists of yore, plays "Auld Lang Syne" on the hour. A shy student asks me to write her letters ("Lots of letters, please. It is so boring in Wuzhou"), sounding just like my overstimulated niece. Off the main streets, lanes of old brick rowhouses guide the eye to distant factories and a large new wharf under construction.

In a tiny park, grannies watch fat bundled toddlers act out their every whim. Like the grannies, I find a patch of sun for warmth, and start a conversation. Are there any temples about? There are two: one up on the mountain ("take that little alley, and go straight on up"); the other, Lung Mu Miao, the Temple of the Dragon Mother ("not far, but not easy to explain, either"). I set off for the first.

Folk temples, when their management is left to local initiatives, are China's only real "civil society," encompassing state hierarchy, market logic, and the moral imperatives through which ordinary people try to reconcile them. Before the revolution, the recreational, cultural, and ritual life of producer-class people centered in the fragrant gardens and cool halls of temples. Small businesspeople, farm families, and artisan households supported wide-reaching networks of ritual organization based in these holy headquarters; temples imply an invisible polity based on fantasy and trust. Good Communists, like good Confucians before them, monitor and fear the florescence of this public, but nonofficial space. For a few years of high Maoism, the Earth Gods and the Birth Goddesses, the apotheosized local heroes and the martyred maidens, were liquidated. Now, with the return of the private production that formerly supported community life, communities are rebuilding the outward and visible signs of this out-of-plan sphere of power. Temples are always worth a look.

A well-paved path leads up the side of a hill and round the inner curve to a rocky point overlooking the city; excellent geomantic orientation for house, grave, or temple. The building is square, brick, undistinguished, a simple convent built in the 1880s. Convents then and now are women's refuges, rarely endowed abundantly enough to pay for elegant roofs and elaborate carvings. Yet this one is busy, with dozens of women, old and young, burning the incense and paper spirit money they have bought from elderly female stall-keepers along the path. In orthodox fashion, worshippers pay their respects outside (to Heaven), inside (to a boring Buddha of recent manufacture, no artistic quality, and none of the folk adhesions that are grist for the anthropologist's mill), and behind the building (against a rock wall—to earth spirits? They would not say).

Visiting temples with early-rising old women is my best cure for jet lag. In their dim cloisters, the fiery buds of incense sticks bloom and drift, the smoke of burning spirit money smudges even the crudest religious art into eerie vitality. Worshippers circle from god to god, attracting divine attention with their burning bouquets, identifying themselves and their families to the gods in mumbled invocations. If you sit quietly, you catch the words of entreaty—for health, for grandchildren, for a break on wholesale prices. No bumptious clergy interfere between a woman and her deities, and even foreigners are welcome in these most perfectly public of places.

Here in Wuzhou, the temple's day has fully begun. With more light, the peeling walls and workaday clothes show the ritual equipment as commonplace, poorly made, recent replacements for what may have been ruined during the Cultural Revolution. The absence of subsidiary gods, with which folk-managed temples swarm, argues for the limits which "feudal superstition" may not transgress. I talk to the temple manager, a curt woman with whom I have little language in common, learning only the temple's age and conventual origin.

On the way down the hilly path, a seventy-year-old with grandchild on her back catches me up, wanting to chat. How odd for a local elder to speak so much standard Chinese; perhaps Wuzhou is a grander place than I imagine. She especially wants to know my salary, and is not impressed when I offset the royal sum with recitations of how much things cost in the United States. She grumbles about the taxes and the rising cost of living, as everyone always does. With four sons and some daughters-in-law working, however, she must be doing well. She wants to keep me company for the rest of the day, offering to guide me about the town to anywhere I care to go. Perhaps this is so that I can meet her son, who has hopes for foreign travel? She seems both kind and honest, but it is not what I want to do with my brief time in Wuzhou. I need my eyes free of the demands of guestly courtesy to see this prosperous town so as to better evaluate those further upriver.

Anthropologists must constantly tack between what people tell us, and what we can see, count, and interpret for ourselves. Indigenous insights are wonderful, surprising sometimes by their obscurity, but just as often by their pounding platitudinousness or stubborn denial of the obvious. What I need now is not my helpful companion's narratives, but a quick and dirty walkabout equivalent to a statistical handbook of economic development.

I beg off, we part, I look for lunch.

Instead, I find the Dragon Mother Temple. It is being refurbished by the Wuzhou Cultural Relics Preservation Committee, a local branch of the museological work unit that Professor Qin heads in Sichuan. This national institution preserves cultural sites and materials—tombs, temples, archaeological discoveries and the like, funding most of this work with ticket receipts from places of pilgrimage or historical significance. The Dragon Mother isn't much, but she is local.

An academic-looking woman, formerly of the Wuzhou Museum gives me the tour. The Dragon Mother herself was a virtuous person of the Song, epitome of Chinese triteness, loved by the people for her uprightness. The general on her right (on his own, separate altar) was similarly a real person. The Dragon Prince on her left is said in folk story to have emerged from the last of a clutch of five eggs the Mother laid—all of which hatched dragons. This scaly scion is mischievous, and a special protector of Wuzhou people. My guide makes the distinctions with careful Communist orthodoxy: history, created by real people, who contributed to society, versus feudal superstition, based on folk imaginings that embody the unlettered masses' aspirations for a good life. The Dragon Prince stands just inside the pale that excludes feudal superstition from official recognition for the rickety reason that he is Wuzhou's favorite god. What determined negotiations secured his present place? I wish I knew some pious open-handed Overseas Chinese, provenance Wuzhou, to be his angel. She would be warmly welcomed.

The building is sadly shabby, gutted during the Cultural Revolution and rebuilt, grudgingly, by the city in the past few years. My Taiwan-trained eye registers the minuscule inner courtyard, the absence of any open space nearby on which an opera stage could be erected to energize a folk festival. The Dragon Mother may continue to receive her widow's mites, but it is hard to imagine her cult ever amounting to much, with such unpropitious real estate as the revolution has left her.

My hostess, Director Chen, rarely has the opportunity to explain the history of the temple to strangers. In fact, she has nothing at all to do here, and wishes she were back in the Museum, where at least she had colleagues to talk to. There are hardly even any worshippers, she complains.

"Why was it necessary to rebuild the temple, if no one wants to come here?" I ask.

"This is really unclear. It's all feudal superstition anyway."

The temple overlooks a bluff down to the river, the far shore of which is aboil with heavy industry, shipbuilding, and quarries. A boat bridge to the other shore swarms with stevedores and punts. One imagines the Dragon Mother as having had much the same place in the life of these river folk as Mazu, goddess of the sea, had for the ocean-going Taiwanese. Her temples too stand by the docks, protecting the lives of poor sailors and the fortunes of rich merchants. It is just these old Daoist gods, so often associated with commerce, that Confucians and Communists find offensive to hierarchical moral order. They are, however, exactly the symbols that newly rich peasants and urban shopkeepers have always turned to for help in obtaining sons and money. For centuries, waterborne merchant adventuring enriched the Cantonese and Fujianese, giving them the dreams of social mobility and change that Chinese rulers to this day find alien and subversive. And, for centuries, gods such as Mazu and the Dragon Mother, like real mothers in the Chinese patriarchy, slipped them goodies that their strict father-authorities would have forbidden them.

Perhaps there is hope for the Dragon Mother yet. Where Director Chen sees only solitude and waste, I see astonishing regrowth of custom after the revolutionary decades. Not a few worshippers have picked their way through carpenters' debris while we sit drinking tea. These visitors sometimes comment critically on the disorder of their place of worship and glance sharply at the quality of the construction. If this temple is like others in the Chinese world, the Dragon Mother's regular wor-shippers are also the financial sustainers of a local organization they will ceaselessly seek to expand. Does Director Chen agree?

"The common people's cultural level is terribly low. They should be building schools and libraries, not resurrecting these old folk temples. But there's really nothing we can do about it; they just keep doing it."

She gives me her card, lets me pee (on the floor in a clean little room, with a hose to wash it out to a drain), and reluctantly sends me on my way.

I return to my doss-house slowly, through small residential streets that hairpin down the steepish hill. Ugly and traffic infested as their main streets may be, the main part of most Chinese cities is made up of back alleys which are often village-like in comfort and neighborliness. In the warming sun, women wash babies and their hair in doorstep tubs. Old people play cards and mahjong, caged birds preen and twitter, laundry dries nicely, and even the chickens seem cheerful. Individual things are very clean—fresh clothes, scrubbed chopping boards, scoured granite stairways—even though the overall effect of laissez-faire construction and overcrowding is not cleanly. One has to have lived in a rainy, hot place with thick industrial pollution, far too many people, and expensive soap and water to realize what a struggle it is to keep a potted plant's leaves shiny, to send a son to school tidy.

Wuzhou markets are full of a strange substance, looking like coconut fiber, all lined up in little bricks: fine cut tobacco, as the smell soon teaches me. *Huge* quantities of dried mushrooms are for sale, too, along with vegetable seeds and medicinal oddities trekked in from the hilly hinterland. People look comfortable in this town.

I begin to daydream about doing fieldwork in these neat lanes, in this highly local market only two easy days from Hong Kong. I would spend the first, difficult months observing, mapping, talking to people like Direc-tor Chen. Books, to be read lazily in a chair, perhaps even in comfort, would tell me useful things about this commercial cluster on one of the nation's vital arteries. Children, shopkeepers, astute elders with time on their hands would drop their defenses and begin to let me hover on the fringe of their discussions, tell me family tales, point out where change is most sharply figured in their landscapes. As I ask directions back to the hotel, the sharpness of the language problem punctures this fantasy. I would have to learn standard Cantonese, as different from Mandarin as Portuguese from French, then confront Wuzhou's distinctive local dialect thereof. Horrified by the thought of subtracting three more years of my life in grinding, mindless language study, I let the dream dissipate.

This boat is a smaller iron bucket, neatly green and white like its larger sister, its disreputability stopping well short of dilapidation. Yet it seems worryingly overloaded with goods and heavy smokers. Trepidation comes too (dare I say it?), from the increasingly peasanty style of the passengers. I am as ardent a supporter of subaltern classes as any good leftist, but I am also realistic in another way: the value of my bag goes up exponentially at each move down the central place hierarchy. This is a milk run, with dozens of anonymous getters on and getters off. Not to worry. With the vast wealth and passport I keep strapped to my body, I can replace whatever the light-fingered night crawlers might take. And here, unlike at home, I am not a candidate for mugging.

Here, the ranks of bunks stand only a meter apart, so the luggage has to stay in bed with its owner's sleeping feet. The mattresses are thinner, but the quilts are thick and clean. A sleazy young sprat is bedded down on my left. He smokes, of course, but that is too normal for complaint. His sleaze quotient derives from an untended head of wildly sprouting hair. In my early years in Taiwan, I grew used to forced haircuts except on hooligans. This man, who will sleep six inches from my shoulder, looks as if he has overstayed his parole. Still, he is doing a very creditable job of housekeeping in his five-by-two allotment. He smiles shyly, and like a movie werewolf in reverse, metamorphoses into a nice young man. On my right, a couple have settled in so swiftly that they are both already asleep.

Excellent neighbors, all; the Chinese, after all, insist that nearby neighbors are much better than far off kinfolk. Only one fly spoils this ointment. I'm in the bow, four bunks from a forward-facing wide open window. The river-damp will be as bad as the smoke tonight. Hmm. Maybe they'll close it? Maybe I'll just snuggle down and wait.

Someone closes the window. The man next to it has a wonderful new boombox with separate (and powerful) speakers. The evening passes pleasantly. People open windows often enough to alternate warm fug with cool river secrets. I am warm, and the public address system dribbles its musical trivia softly around great reefs of whiny Hong Kong pop rock from the boombox. Why have I not spent more of my life sleeping on boats?

A lot of stops are printed on this ticket, but as far as I can tell, the night only once brings us to a dock where we actually anchor. Maybe people are put on and off in midstream at other places, where small craft swarm out around us in the dark.

The Qiping stop comes about seven. The loudspeaker comes alive, the lights go out. Should I get off at Qiping, just to see? No, I have achieved oneness with my quilt. I have remembered the Chinese trick of dozing indefinitely, as my companions do, and still not missing much.

Dawn colors the river valley narrowing to rocky shores, steep slopes, and no visible agriculture. The water is full of boats, however, taking timber in rafts, bamboo, and undeterminables up- and downriver. We have left China, a real place of fields and villages, and swum into this strange, deserted country where the only life is afloat.

Last night, a sailor came to chat me up and use his English. When he finished his watch, he invited me to join him and his off-duty mates for a drink and to talk (he said "report") about Taiwan. Like a fool, I declined. The categorical imperative that nice girls don't go off with strange sailors has no relevance here. Silly of me to miss this chance of seeing the boat through their eyes. Ruefully, I remember a similar missed chance in Taiwan, when I missishly refused a meal from six bored Taiwan marines who were guarding their lonely beach against invasion by Communist frogmen.

Luck is with me, though. The sailor invites me to lunch with his messmates again the next day. It is a hearty and delicious feed, but the best part is the long, difficult, enjoyable discussion of political economy, neo-Marxism, and what is wrong with the country that we have for dessert. Their state-paid jobs are secure—people will always need to ride the river—but things have changed since the reforms. It seems uncontrolled, disorderly, to have people moving about the way they do now. Men younger than themselves go to Guangzhou and take jobs; they come home and start businesses; nobody has a clear path ahead any more. The peasants sometimes surprise them with their worldliness. Proletarians don't expect that.

Talking about class with these sailors does not make them uneasy, even fearful, as it does with working-class people in the States. Plying their river, these young men see a lot more of their world than most Chinese. Some were in the merchant marine, and one has been to New York. Still, I do not expect this better-than-grad school grasp of political economy from river swabbies, though perhaps I should.

Their sophistication certainly does not come from frequent foreign contacts. They had a foreigner on board a year or two ago, one remembers. He couldn't talk, though, unfortunately; no hands-across-the-sea for him.

CHAPTER THREE

城都行

Mr. Su's Hometown

DECEMBER 23, 1987. LIUZHOU

Liuzhou swims out of the darkness, the broad stone steps of the wharf its welcome mat. The only other woman getting off gravitates toward me, burdened with a fat year-old boy and an immense, lumpy bundle. Women stick together in the strange dark. Cai is a dressmaker, coming home from a buying trip to Wuzhou. And where am *I* going? she wants to know.

I have not the faintest idea of where I am going, except that I should aim for the city guesthouse for those traveling on government business. Does she know where that is? Oh yes, but it's not easy to find.

She eyes me kindly, as I pick my way up the steep landing.

"I'd better take you. You'll never find it alone, and—well, it's dark, and you're a stranger."

It is two hours until dawn. When I leave the lights of the waterfront, I—or my chubby bag—will have advertised my singleness to everyone in the untidy straggle of disembarking men. I repress all decency and accept her offer. As we walk, she tells me with amazing good humor that she has had too fine a time in Wuzhou, and spent every cent. She could not pay for the hot meals that were brought on board from the towns we passed, and so has been twenty-four hours hungry.

"The sailors took pity on the baby, and gave him noodles," she laughs.

Mold-blackened stone buildings of four stories make dank canyons of the first kilometer. These streets are as silent as Chinese cities ever are. In the few hours between when a night worker's return home ignites the sizzle of a hot meal, and when the early riser stifles her beeping alarm, Liuzhou is a necropolis, and every footfall sounds. We reach a broader street, lined with the concrete block apartments of the 1950s. It too is like the grave. The Liuzhou Hotel main gate stands open, and we pound determinedly on the front door. At last, a girl in pajamas leaves her concierge's bed behind the registration desk to take me in.

The next few minutes are a little nightmare of weariness, anxiety for the yet wearier Cai, and the tension of the usual struggle with the desk clerk to allow me to stay. The electricity is off, so my carefully packed travel documents are hard to read until, amazingly, an emergency light cuts in over the desk.

"This says Sichuan Province! We're in Guangxi Province! We don't ever have people from Sichuan here. And you're a foreigner; we don't usually have foreigners, either. I don't know if I can let a foreigner stay here."

I move to the Argument Irrelevant: "This woman has traveled all night with no food, and she has a baby! She must go home, and she won't leave until I have a room. Consider the baby! Besides, these documents are from the provincial level in Sichuan. They make it clear that I am to be given a room."

The clerk is tired too; she gives in easily.

They are pressed for rooms and can put me up for only that day and night. Eventually, a payment of 26 RMB elicits vague directions to a building far back in the compound. My traveling flashlight helps its attendant to find a key and then my room—grubby but well supplied. I get Cai's address, see her to the gate, and let her set off on what the next day I learn is a two-mile walk. There is no way even to send for a car to take her home—although she rejects the notion in genuine horror.

I am awakened at eight by a phone call asking if I am going down for breakfast. Assuming it is the service person being extra helpful, I mumble a negative and fade out. At nine thirty, another call. The man says he has been waiting for me to come out since eight. He wants to meet me.

Is this the sailor with whom I chatted so companionably about historical materialism and how all societies have to pass through the stage of capitalism before they can reach socialism? After that conversation on the boat, he had tracked me down rather insistently. To avoid any further contact, I deliberately disembarked after I noticed him go below. In the prissy voice my generation employed to answer dormitory phones at Radcliffe I ask my caller:

"How have we met?"

There has, alas, been no such good fortune in his life; he has seen me (when? where?), and wishes to make my acquaintance. The phone rings for some time after I hang up, and then my admirer is silent.

Awake, I face an important truth: no electricity means no hot water. Fortunately, the drinking thermos is large enough for a sponge bath, and I am soon clean enough to inquire about railway tickets.

This morning's desk clerk opines that they can help with tickets, but not until two, when the person who does them returns. Yes, it will be very hard to get one at this season. So I ride their train-meeting van, line up for half an hour in Liuzhou Railway Station, and buy the ticket myself. Less grandeur equals greater efficiency, another useful lesson. 156 RMB gets me a soft sleeper to Kunming. I had wanted to stop over in Guiyang, capital of Guizhou Province (and reputed armpit of the known universe), but decide not to push my luck. The satisfaction I feel over this transaction is only slightly tarnished by the train's departure time: it will pass through Liuzhou at one A.M.

It is a lovely, crisp, sunny day for walking back from the station, wandering through the south bank market just off the big bridge. Here is what I had come to see: foodstuffs, handmade brooms and brushes, plastic basins, brilliant synthetic clothes, medicine, tobacco, and occasional furs. A local favorite is bobcat skins; I even saw a marmalade housecat pelt stretched to cure. In a region not yet ready for ready-made, stalls carry regiments of bolts of gray to blue synthetic fabrics. These make up into the now near-universal western coats and trousers the better-off urbanites all wear. As I stroll about in my Chinese padded jacket, I feel quite a hick. Still, my blue silk *mian'ao* is warm, light, and a lot easier to sleep in than a tailored coat. It also semaphores my good intentions. Old people observe pleasantly that the foreign miss is wearing one of our Chinese jackets, and everyone smiles.

Liuzhou overflows with the picturesque. Surrounded by the sugarloaf hills beloved by Chinese painters, bisected by its green river, it is the biggest town for thousands of square miles of difficult landscape, a Han enclave in a region of outrageously colorful tribal folk. A dozen sellers spread arrays of bear bones between the railway station and the main bridge. They are minority people, their accent hard to understand. The better-stocked display a skull or two, some of the bigger long bones, vertebrae, a foreleg with paw still attached. A few curly sheep / goat horns and other delicatessen make up the pharmacopoeia. A lot of this stuff is only barely bare; a good deal of the bear himself clings to the bones. A seller keeps up a patter as he saws rings from a femur. One man, wearing a string of big wooden beads, is accompanied by a silent, squatting woman. Her features are lovely—a far-western face from Tibet—fairer and rosier than anyone in my family. She wears an elaborately folded square headdress, lots of semiprecious stone bead jewelry, and a complicated, appliqué-edged tunic. She looks scared. Too many strangers.

There are monkey acts, too—straight out of Song paintings. Maybe they are the same monkeys, for they are very much the worse for wear. Also out of China's past is a boy of about fifteen who is reviving (if indeed it was ever lost) the fine old act of begging with fake injuries. His puffy, inflamed looking wax hand with a bloody dagger through the wrist is a fine specimen. He has come to the end of his shift and is taking it off with the help of a younger apprentice. The patent falsity of the dagger and the oleaginous blood make one wonder: are people fooled, and if so, how credulous can they be? Nobody old enough to have money to give away could mistake this gruesome artifact for reality. Or are such things seen as an act, an amusement, paid for like the monkeys?

Liuzhou's department stores carry an impressive range of light industrial goods. The cheapest washing machine is marked at 300 RMB or $60 U.S., and there are lots of bikes. Guitars, badminton sets, and toys for sale mean that younger people have a little money to spend—or that Jianxi Provincial Department Store marketing researchers are behind the curve in Liuzhou. There are more browsers than buyers, and the guitars are dusty.

I check out the New China Bookstore—the only bookstore in Liuzhou, and the biggest (it claims) in the province. Not a single English book, even of English lessons, is on offer. Nor are foreign-language newsmagazines or periodicals available anywhere. I still have plenty to read in English, but a chill passes over me as I realize I might be reduced to fighting my way through *People's Daily* or duck-raising manuals for entertainment.

Among the bigger shops perch shoe repairers, key makers, and numberless little restaurants, with occasional bakeries, hair dressers, and coffee shop / bars. Later, pushcart food and drink stands now nesting in alleys will set up for the evening paseo, just as they do in Taiwanese towns. Shops sell sheets of plywood, linoleum and tile, and even paint; I remember how hard it was in the 1970s to find the simplest do-it-yourself household goods in Taiwan. Liuzhou people must be fixing up their houses—discreetly, inside, where strangers will not see.

I buy the largest, handsomest tin of cookies I can find, and plunge into the maze of old-city streets to find Cai. Her brother is pressing pieces of pants in front of the barbershop that occupies the first floor of their house. At first, he is grimly reluctant to have anything to do with this apparition; his sister is "out." I am used to Chinese anxiety disguised as rudeness, and have perfected some rudeness of my own as a way of getting tough Taiwanese to see I mean no harm. I persist, telling him how indebted I am to his sister's kindness. Absorbing the amicable implication of the cookies, he leads me up two flights of stairs to where his mother is rocking the baby.

Each of the three floors of this newly built house is about ten feet by eight, poured concrete, completely unsurfaced. It would be unwise to infer poverty from its drab grayness. People add the refinements later, if at all. Perfectly unadorned concrete is greatly superior in point of cleanliness and absence of vermin to adobe and thatch, or to rough brick and tile. This is a modern house, one to be proud of. The two upper floors hold double beds draped with mosquito netting and a few pieces of new, industrial furniture. The third has a balcony and door leading to another room or rooms, connected in architecturally mystifying fashion to the house behind. As in such workshop homes in Taiwan, the family keeps its capital for productive purposes, eschewing show on home decor.

Amazingly, Cai's mother too speaks some Putonghua, and we chat a bit: about the baby, about Cai's good nature, about the fact that I am just passing through and will be gone tomorrow, about the attractiveness of the town. Cai never comes, but her mother is so much like an old Taiwan acquaintance that I stay longer than I should, and leave with a pang. I am a very long way from my own near and dear.

Recrossing the bridge that spans the Rong River, I pass into a different city. The constantly mentioned Southside and Northside segments of town are symbolic as well as geographic. South of the river is local, the old city, though the old commercial waterfront where my boat landed is also on the north bank. Most of the steeply rising Northside, however, is dense with the government organizations that have expanded the city far beyond its pre-revolution limits. The roads back to the hotel—itself a government organ—are lined with hospitals, schools, factories, and hives of administrators for both province and city. Northside housing is mostly inside the walled compound of one of these units, and may be marginally better (at least in space and quietness) than that in the commercial town.

Walking the Northside streets, the speech of passersby indexes a surprising number of people from outside the province living in Liuzhou. These folks with north-China faces and accents sojourn here much as the post–World War II Nationalists have lived in Taiwan: segregated in state housing, longing for homes in distant, cooler places. The Liuzhou aliens came with the government, hold most state jobs, and have filtered into all local sinecures that the party has in its gift. Retired northerners get the door-keeping jobs in parks and public buildings, and form a substantial proportion of the railroad station drunks. When I asked for help in finding the street address Cai had written for me, the hotel people, Northsiders all, were baffled, hadn't heard of such a place. "I don't know much about Southside; I live over here."

The hotel complex is made up, mostly, of 1950s and 1960s guesthouses for traveling cadres. Its new wing is as yet finished on only a few floors. As often happens in Taiwan, the workers pour the concrete first. They then decide what they *really* want, chisel and hammer it roughly into final shape, cover it with tile, and dump the refuse in the yard. Both old and new wings are classically bureaucratic—while there are lots of personnel, all tasks fall between actual individuals. Nobody has the same story for anything:

"Can I get a car at one A.M. to the railroad station?"

"Of course, we'll help you arrange it tomorrow at six."

"No, we don't do that."

"Yes, but it's too late now at six."

"You'll have to go out and find one yourself."

Et cetera. Still, the desk clerk kindly has found me a room for a second night's stay (they are obviously practically empty, but it is kind anyway).

For dinner I choose a quite dreadful "package meal," turning down both the overfamiliar dishes and the several endangered species from a zoologically flamboyant menu. The giant salamander I never ate still haunts my curiosity. Well trained in the petty snobberies of academic life, but against the advice of the server, I order local beer. A bottle of dead flat Fish Hill Beer, brewed right there in beautiful Liuzhou is the perfect accompaniment to several plates of fat pork fried in pork fat. (I try a second bottle of Fish Hill the next night, thinking that perhaps the sister from another planet who waited on me had slipped me an old opened one that was just lying about. Bottle number two was equally still, and neither had enough alcohol to fuddle a kitten.)

And so to bed, where I very comfortably watch color TV (programs on primate research in Yunnan, vegetable oil production in a northern province, and Islamic minorities in Kashgar) until ten, when the electricity goes off again.

On the morrow, I will visit famous local sites, and I will drink Qingdao.

DECEMBER 24, 1987. LIUZHOU

Liuzhou stands in karst country. Great limestone fingers spike the horizon around the city, and measureless underground rivers lick out caverns beneath its fragile streets. My map takes me to the right bus stop, and the Number Nine whisks me the six kilometers to Duke Cave Park where I can trace this three-dimensional landscape's hidden topography. Alas, the park has excellent intentions but insufficient resources, and is suffering from one of its frequent electrical failures. Eating sunflower seeds and watching other people wait for the power to come on in The Fairies' Cave, I doze on a warm stone bench, have lunch by the dry pond, and, finally, bus back to town in disappointment.

The road is lined with state industries that appear to produce nothing. The large, quiet factories are barnacled with buzzy little businesses— roadhouses, casters of fanciful concrete blocks, dim workshops—in the city-style shotgun houses that people build as they tear down their less compact farm compounds. Between them stand fields not yet industrialized, waiting for the agricultural year to start with spring rains. The land is too dry to be worth ploughing in midwinter. This whole region is desiccated—no water in canals, ponds dry or nearly, and dust on everything. No one is in the fields, but someone has been working. I see a *very* large field, acres, looking as though it were being double-dug for perennials. It is gridded with two-by-two foot ditches, neat and square, with the dirt heaped on the intervening ridges, the scale and regularity suggesting a major collective effort.

Liuzhou's other main attraction is a park that one would like to admire wholeheartedly, but can't. I am reminded vividly of visiting the densely populated University of California at Los Angeles after a decadent stay at wealthy Stanford. In Liuzhou's park, as at UCLA, heavy use of this rare amenity leaves it scuffed and shiny, and ill-considered architecture distracts from the breathtaking setting. I push away my country-club perspective; from ever-more-valuable urban land, the city has reserved several acres for tired urbanites and visiting country folk— roundabouts and climbing bars for children, boats on a pond (it has water, and an almost equal quantity of orange peel), flower beds, winding paths, trees, and a monument to the liberators of Liuzhou in 1949. I smell osmanthus, the sweet olive, and listen to the quiet.

Like many Chinese urban parks, this one is built around history lessons. One is a post-revolution memorial to a Song dynasty worthy who freed women bond slaves. His bronze image—a cranky-looking Confucian scholar, plainly tired of having to cope with the problems of petty people and birds—focuses its grounds. More interesting is the collection of dozens of inscribed stelae. A billboard summarizes these into a useful potted history of the town, which dates from the Han. Chinese poet–officials have been coming here since Roman times, leaving bureaucratic and aesthetic mementos of the beauties and administrative frustrations of their exile.

The other feature of the park, an affectionately kept old mansion, warrants much more time than I can spend. I have come in very late, literally through the back door, and fear I will be thrown out if I seem to linger. Nipping smartly through its rambling rooms and courts, I almost cry with frustration. For range and quality of low-key, Ming-style architectural ornament I've never seen its like. The gray tile and white plaster rooms are timeworn, inviting, not yet renovated into living color. Indoor and outdoor spaces need little spatial distinction in this mild climate; a walker glides between house and garden on currents of light, of temperature differentials, of changing fragrances. The mansion's brilliant gardeners have punctuated its courts and corridors with displays of bonsai and tray gardens, commenting wittily on the "real" mountains outside.

Usually when I explore Chinese elite architecture, I think grumpy leftist thoughts about how far the maidservants must have had to carry bathwater and slops for their petted mistresses. Here, I am seduced. Despite my hasty steps and dirty Nikes, I become a wealthy woman cooling my erotic pulse in graceful gardens, catching fireflies in gauze sleeves, playing the zither among my mountains, great and small.

I am caught at last, and gently ejected by the head gardener. He speaks almost no Putonghua, but understands my effusions of pleasure at his skill. Before he throws me out, he lets me photograph him in one of his creations, and teaches me the Chinese for osmanthus.

Sybaritic ladies take cabs rather than trudging dustily back through town. The car I commandeer, driven by a man who is vastly amused at the idea of traveling for pleasure without companions, deposits me at the sparse Friendship Store. I buy my lover a long, silky-headed brushpen, acquire mooncakes and oranges for the train journey, and return to the hotel for more up-to-date luxuries.

Reality quickly supervenes. Ordering a cab for the middle of the night takes much coming, going, phone calls, and anxiety on my part, and seriously drains the limited patience of six of the hotel's workers. The best we can do is to have one come at midnight; this not decided till 9:30. I get a good *hot* shower (hard stream from high on the wall onto the bathroom floor, just like the University of Chicago faculty club), into my clean clothes, and a rest in front of the TV.

The programs are more than usually bizarre. I channel-surf into a fantasy about a terminally cute little girl who lives alone with Daddy because Mama loves her work too much and won't come home. This princess is pampered beyond belief—*what* do the Cais of the world, let alone little peasant girls, think about this ninny's very-own all-pink bedroom? Or does she share it with Daddy? There's some funny stuff in this film. The child, a creepy miniature grown-up, wears makeup and flirts with every male in sight, including an elderly streetsweeper. She pouts and prisses at him as Chinese maidens are supposed to treat importunate lovers. Finally, this unlikely couple have an ecstatic meeting of minds, but not before the plot is complicated by an imaginary little girl-friend with golden hair and blue eyes—much is made of these—whose role in the plot remains obscure.

This pre-Freudian scenario is followed by a Chinese Cagney and Lacy, two pretty women cops who arrest people, break up family fights, and have impenetrable (and pouty and prissy) relationships after work with bland, high-minded boyfriends. I prefer the next program, a socialist fantasy in which a wholesomely gorgeous girl plays with her lover in the snow (fully dressed—no hanky-panky in that climate) and thinks about him a lot as she goes about her job as a train conductor. She scrubs the train (Under the seats! On the backs! This train looks like Tiffany's!) and serves the most obnoxious travelers with a smile. She breaks up family fights. In the end, she gets an award and an opportunity to give the most trite speech I have ever heard, even in Chinese. I slide into sleep, hoping she will appear on my train with her pigtails and steaming kettle, a convenient referee for altercations that may break out among my fellow-passengers.

All expectations to the contrary notwithstanding, the cab comes at midnight. In five minutes, I am settled on a wooden bench under a galvanized tin shelter in front of the railroad station. No one even faintly resembling the heroic train attendant is visible. Opinions circulate both that the train will be much later than its scheduled one o'clock passthrough and that it has already come and gone. A few obnoxious Chinese tourists arrive, then vanish. Eventually, I locate a station employee who tells me that I am waiting in the wrong place. Inquiring after the right place, she waves me impatiently into the station's pitch-dark interior.

The Liuzhou train station is not an ideal place to spend a cold night unless one has, as I do, rather low tastes in entertainment. There are punks and drunks—no monks—as well as lots of respectable citizens monstrously burdened by bundles on carrying poles, babies, and traveling bags. Among them wander military men in comic opera uniforms, a blind man getting around efficiently but to no apparent purpose, and, for a hallucinatory moment after a short doze, a tribal woman wearing a tutu of short, shiny, black layers and brilliantly beribboned leggings. I spot several other tribal costumes on women, none on men, and none so dramatic. A sweet old lush with a distinctive northern snarl to his speech keeps the waiting-room crowd amused with songs. The station is partially lighted after all, the low wattage enhancing the staginess. It is like being at the pantomime for the first time; I wait for Mother Goose or Father Christmas to appear and the story to begin.

In the local waiting room, there are no tourists, and no signs indicating my train. After half an hour of the floor show, I seek out a better waiting room, empty except for the tourists, and stretch out on a bench. My midnight blue, Romanian worsted trench coat comes into its own as blanket; my fat bag is a fine pillow. Anxious as I am about missing my train, I am incapable of resisting sleep at bedtime. When the train is announced, I am too fuddled to find the Chinese tourists. A nearby man says my train has already gone, when it was supposed to, an hour or more ago.

Increasingly uneasy as three o'clock approaches, I again beg instruction from station workers. One brusquely orders me out of doors, where people are lining up under sharp official eyes to march onto the platform. We wait another quarter of an hour.

With a rush, the train screeches in, and I am efficiently popped into compartment six, car eight, lower berth, by a woman conductor. She reminds me of the female warden-cum-flight attendant on the long-ago New York to San Juan flight that initiated me into overseas travel, and I am pleased to see she looks much more powerful around the shoulders than her television representation. Thus encouraged, I ignore my three male roommates, strip off my heaviest layers, pull up the down quilt, and pass into a coma. Bliss is assured, because the compartment's ashtray is full of pits and skins, *not* cigarette butts.

DECEMBER 25, 1987. SOMEWHERE IN GUANGXI

Five o'clock brings cheerful music over the PA. One of my roomies turns on a light to read, enabling me to find the volume control. I return us to silence. I doze till seven, when the warden insists I rise and tidy my bed.

"It doesn't matter that you have this bunk all day. We can't have people in bed when it's daytime!"

I fold my quilt, eat her offered bowl of noodles, try to stay awake, and slowly, sneakily, rewrap myself in bedding. For several hours, the view is spectacular—karst needles like a seismographic record of all the geo-logical strain this earth has ever felt. No one having seen them could deny the assumption built into traditional geomancy that the earth lives, coiling and stretching like huge, slow tigers and dragons. Seen at train speed, these movements unroll themselves even more vividly than they did to China's great painters. The limestone strata, at first absolutely ver-tical, recline like relaxing muscle to horizontal layering. By late after-noon, they have pushed upright again, gorgeous to look at, unspeakable to build train tracks through.

In this rugged country, people raise little horses that pick their way neatly among the rocks. We glide past gray limestone villages, lime-burning ovens for cement, rice stubble and strawcocks on chalky-white soil, fields cut directly into stone beds or on tiny terraces among the rocks. There are towns that look mostly official / industrial and villages that look like the Song dynasty. Out of Guangxi into Yunnan, the lime-stone disappears and is replaced by rounded hills and red soil. Still lots of ponies.

After a morning of courteous silence and eye avoidance, my room-mates realize I can speak. One is a TV filmmaker from Chongqing, returning from making a series on Hainan Island, a development hot spot. We talk about political economy. What else is there, really? Its structures are the jungle gyms through which we all must wriggle to our life goals, and China's are particularly apparent in the current clash between maintaining a planned economy and letting capitalism rip. Although this man is a certified intellectual, our discussion is not very different from the one I pursued with the sailors. Everyone knows the basic Marxist language, though no one sees it through the nimbus of rea-sonably democratic and prosperous western European institutions that the words imply to me. When we get down to cases, the filmmaker is the kind of Jacksonian democrat who believes that the contemporary equiv-alent of forty acres and a mule per family would solve most of China's problems, except for those generated by inimical foreigners. Forty years of revolution to make a nation of far-eastern rednecks.

Another roommate turns out to be a member of the sociology section of the Shanghai Academy of Social Sciences. *He* only wants to talk com-parative academic salaries. His section is researching "opinions" of the birth control and development policies, but from his vagueness I realize they aren't really doing anything but building cases for the program's tighter management. We dine in a jolly, beer-drinking group, they wish me Merry Christmas, we sleep, nobody smokes: amazing grace.

CHAPTER FOUR

城都行

Eternal Spring

DECEMBER 26, 1987. KUNMING

The train deposits me in Kunming at seven on a morning rimed with frost. The city is on my itinerary not only for its fame as a beauty spot with a fine climate. My lover's graduate student's friends, Mssrs. Wang and Zhao, local anthropologists, have volunteered at long distance to show me around. Having introduced me to Kunming, they will get me on a bus to the Yunnan border where Toby, the graduate student who links us all, is doing his doctoral fieldwork. Toby's friends are not there to meet me, as it later emerges, because the message I sent from Liuzhou was garbled. Given the state of the phone lines, and that operators in the two regions have no language in common, I am not surprised, nor even entirely sorry. I pick the Kunming Hotel randomly off a list at the station because it is downtown rather than on the touristic shores of Dianchi, largest lake in southwest China. It will be lots cheaper and insulate me less from a city I know I will have little enough time to inspect. Hospitable notions of sightseeing are rarely congruent with my own.

My Sichuan letter gets me a room at 45 RMB; Sichuan is becoming a real place, from which government documents might legitimately emanate. I will have to wait two hours in the stone-cold lobby for it to be cleaned. Noticing my shivers, the clerk graciously assigns me to a southside room—I must ask for that henceforth—because it warms up well in the day and radiates in at night.

"We Chinese call this the city of eternal spring because the weather is always beautiful. You foreigners complain about the weather a lot, though. You like to have heaters indoors and so forth. *We* think that's bad for the health," instructs the clerk.

I refuse to be beguiled into a discussion of how temperature affects the human body. Food warms; I will seek food, read all the old English-language *China Dailies* in the lobby, examine the dusty minority embroideries that compete for space with mystical medicines in the hotel's department store–style displays. After I have checked in, I will write letters, and I will explore Kunming alone. I anticipate the help and companionship Toby's friends will provide, but I am reluctant too to give up my solitude.

Luck steers me to a big outdoor clothing market on Youth Street where I can add a finishing fillip to my wardrobe. As a child, I was fascinated by hoboes, who were reputed to travel with everything they needed packed into a kerchief tied to a stick. The light, sturdy, expansible duffel my brother and sister-in-law have found for my trip is as close to this impedimentary ideal as I am likely to get. I can strip naked and get everything I have brought into it—minimalist overkill, but shopping must be factored in. Half the volume of this fine piece of luggage is required to house my trench coat, purchased to impress my potential Sichuan colleagues. With its belts, epaulets, sleeve straps, and dignified midnight color, I hoped it would make me, too, look like a cadre—like anything but a flighty, crazy foreigner. As it turned out, it was perfect— for a man. In Kunming, I didn't know that yet. I did know, however, that if my grand coat were to remain clean, and I to continue cozy, I should not wear it into Toby's mountains. At the Youth Street market, I find a gray padded affair long enough to insulate me from freezing benches, and voluminous enough to zipper up over all my clothes at once (except the trench coat). It is made in Yunnan, sartorial perfection.

Around the hotel, Kunming's new commercial district offers shops, street life, an air of comfort and provincial superiority. The old Muslim quarter near the principal city temple, Yuantong Si, is tidy and neighborly. Joints and strips of the beef that proclaim Muslim presence like a flag hang outside its many butcher shops. Unlike the situation with many minority peoples, it is the men who identify themselves with caps; women Muslims dress like everyone else. This neighborhood is locally considered undesirable compared to the newer housing from the 50s, 60s, and 70s that rebuilt the city. Indeed, while the quarter is picturesque, I note the crumbling wattle-and-daub walls and the crumbling ceilings with the eye of a wary housewife. I see almost no construction dating from the 80s, though housing is sorely needed.

Official Kunming is extremely handsome, full of parks, lakeshore, and expensive old government guesthouses. As the provincial capital, the city center flourishes on the multitude of institutions states build in order to rule, to produce, to heal, and to educate. Did Beijing not see fit to keep a government here, Kunming would be a tiny caravanserai for the trickle of long-distance trade in preciosities that first seduced the Chinese into this chaos of mountains, each long-defended by its autochthonous people.

Yunnan Provincial Museum, an impressive colonial building, houses a striking collection of minority costumes, textiles, and archaeological finds. In this deep south, where patriarchal Han culture is raggedly interspersed with Southeast Asian hill tribes, a more gender-equal past is memorialized. Bronze makers who invented their metallurgical techniques long before China's Shang ancestors once cast treasured drums that found their way from here to Borneo. The museum's versions show the drums as stages for tiny tableaux of women rulers receiving tribute from male and female alike. A rich display of glorious textiles honors more recent, and more ordinary, women as artists and citizens of their kinder polities.

The provincial university is appalling—it looks as though no one has cleaned or repaired anything since the war. But then, students are more troublesome tenants than the ghosts of minority matriarchs. The Cultural Revolution hit Yunnan intellectuals hard, and little of their former status has been yet returned to them. Dropping in on a woman scholar for whom I have an address reveals that she and her colleagues still live in slum conditions, having camped for over a decade in a crowded, filthy firetrap built in the last century. Climbing splintering wooden stairs to her third-floor room, I pass the open doors of a dozen families, each with a stark bedroom or two, sparsely furnished, who cook, store fuel, and wash clothes and dishes in the common hall. It is my first view on this trip of the kind of state-employee poverty that so shocked me in Shanghai and Hangzhou in 1980, a politically induced condition I thought the eighties were beginning to remedy. I am sorry to have embarrassed her—she is plainly horrified that I have sought her out in this undignified dwelling—and slink back to my now-luxurious hotel. We meet again later, at her insistence, but my intrusion into her humiliating backstage spoils the pleasure we should have had in sharing her expertise. We graciously decline each other's patently insincere invitations to a meal, and I flee a ruined opportunity.

DECEMBER 27, 1987. KUNMING

Now to find Wang and Zhao, my hosts. Bearing yesterday's contretemps in mind, I am glad the address I hold is to Wang's office and not his home. Heading for the Yunnan Academy of Social Sciences on a local bus, I extract from my seatmate, a member of the Minorities Institute, that I have hopped on the wrong one. Slowly, kindly, he instructs me, speaking the deep-south version of Putonghua used locally, of which I understand virtually nothing. Smiling grateful thanks, I catch a bicycle-pedaled trishaw. It rapidly becomes evident that the trishaw man has no idea where to look for the Academy either, and—does this come on the Y chromosome?—is unwilling to ask directions. After a fine tour of the quarter, he abandons me in relief before a silent, rundown building. My luck holds. The only person at the office this Sunday is kind enough to answer my knock and give me a written home address for my contact. Bracing myself for interpersonal disaster, I find the university's main gate. Asking directions, I learn that even college students speak little Putonghua beyond simple courtesies.

At last, down the garden alley of a block of small university flats, up several dark flights of stairs, is Mr. Wang, mystified that he had not found me alighting from the morning train. Wang is Muslim, which in China counts as an ethnic community; his wife is Yi minority; their bub-bly baby counts as Yi, following his mother; their babytender is a teenager from a nearby village. They speak lovely northern-accented Putonghua, having been trained in, and fallen in love at, the Beijing Minorities Institute. The five of us crowd their tiny sitting room, from which I can see the even tinier bedroom and kitchen. It seems fair that they pay the University only 2 RMB a month for this and a closet-sized bathroom. They have a color TV and a cassette player, but separate stud-ies, even separate desks, let alone word processors, are distant dreams.

Wang has recently transferred from history to ethnology to sociology, looking for a more open and stimulating work environment. We are soon joined by Toby's other friend, Mr. Zhao, of the Minorities Institute. He's planning anthropology fieldwork among the Dai people of south Yunnan, where he spent some years during the Cultural Revolution. *He* wants to do straight descriptive work with no theory to get him into trouble. They show me the university, their neighborhood, the Muslim streets with Arabic inscriptions and beef-and-lamb restaurants, the mosque and the temple. They brush up my vague knowledge of Mongol troops taking Kunming as the southeastern outpost of Genghis Khan's great mediaeval empire, then settling in for the long haul as other dynas-ties come and go. We eat, and drink, and talk anthropology until late, though Wang's wife slips away early to do what needs to be done. Zhao will take me round the city tomorrow.

December 28, 1987. Kunming

At midmorning, Zhao and I begin a leisurely spiral around the older parts of the city. He is funny and informative, switching easily between the Putonghua he speaks to me and the impenetrable street Yunnanese he uses with his countrymen. We see the museum again, this time with a counterpoint of academic gossip about the archaeologists. Zhao makes sure I don't miss the treasured drums, using them as Friedrich Engels would have to illustrate a feminist prelapsarian Eden in the origin of the family, private property, and the state.

We lunch, we stroll, we chat up the imam. Beginning to be sore-footed, we return to my hotel, dine early, and continue our conversation in my room. Side by side, with the usual small table between us, we try to figure out what books might be most useful to him in planning his next fieldwork. Zhao stands, stretches, closes the bedroom door. I am immediately alert and, in a few minutes, rise casually, get a tissue, and open the door. Zhao blandly starts another cigarette, and closes the door. I seek a hospitable cup of tea for him, and open it. He looks disgusted, gathers himself, and takes his leave.

I'm an American woman who grew up in that crystalline moment of history between easily accessible contraception and sexually transmitted diseases. Sex comes easily to my mind. Yet two principles guide my conduct during fieldwork: I am culturally overstimulated in this department and should not incautiously attribute my thoughts to Chinese associates; and most Chinese men find most western women aggressive, lumpish, hairy, and undesirable. I have almost certain imagined a problem that is not there. At the same time, in Taiwan I once took this consciously innocent attitude and found myself jumped by a colleague. He appeared to see the latter of these two rules of thumb less salient than the former, and we were both thoroughly embarrassed.

December 29, 1987. Kunming

Despite his teaching salary at the university and research stipend from the Academy, like many low-ranked state employees, Wang finds it hard to make ends meet. His knowledge of history and good Putonghua allow him to moonlight several days a month as a tour guide. This pays him 5 RMB a day (and lunch). Today he will take me along in the minibus with two dozen Hong Kong tourists to see Kunming sights. The

Hong Kong travelers are late middle aged with a few grandkids in tow. To everyone's amusement, I supply an occasional translation from Putonghua to English for some of the older people, who know Cantonese and English, but no Putonghua.

With this cheerful crew, full of good Chinese breakfast and ready for fun, we drive out beyond the industrial suburbs and their peculiarly lifeless air. We see few people working, no products ready for shipment in factory yards, a general sense of Sunday, though the smokestacks work. For a few miles, we ride the Burma Road, my leftish brain complaining silently about the egregious expenditure of human effort that building this improbable route required. Quite peaceful now, the roadside is piled with tons of potatoes, a food Yunnanese eat with reluctance. (They are very good potatoes; the hotel makes delicious french fries of them, and the vinegar that my British heritage demands as a sauce is also excellent.) Piled by the roadside too are the bony remains of a morning's butchering—a six-foot heap of pig and cow skeletons, waiting for their next incarnation. Meat and potatoes—the Road may have been worth it after all.

To my delight, older Yunnan rural women still wear the handsome peasant costume photographed by pre-war ethnographers. In bright blue pants and nunlike headscarf, side-closing blue jacket with a long, black velvet piping, and blue and black apron, they have a panache their daughters and granddaughters may never acquire from stretch pants and beaded sweaters.

Our Number One Beauty Spot of the tour is in the West Hills, a series of small temples and outdoor altars built into the face of a limestone cliff overlooking the valley's lake. The view is very fine, although the temples themselves are crudely built, carved, and painted. We climb the narrow, irregular stairs from one worshipping place to another, a miniature pilgrimage that enables the pious to have a word with several dozen gods in an hour and a half of comfortable strolling.

At each stopping place, money symbolism is strong—money tossed at the feet of religious images as offerings, floated on little vessels of water beside incense burners, dropped or thrown by gleeful tourists into the mouths of statues (dragons, lions) to ensure fortune. The money is real, not the bagasse-paper spirit money I am used to. Official two-inch notes worth a Chinese dime are the most abundant. I ask about spirit money, missing its color and shine, and am told its manufacture is not allowed. Also lacking are the customary fortune-telling devices, for which people find a rough substitute in a pair of coins.

The stairways and passages are densely crowded, and people take hair-raising chances of being accidentally shoved off the cliff by standing on railings to have their pictures taken. This complex is a popular suicide spot it seems: Every year a dozen or so people leap into nothing from its high wall-openings. The slender railings that guard the lively crowd from its own fecklessness remind me how fruitless would be the attempt to sue the temple, American-style, for maintaining an attractive nuisance.

At our next stop, Yunnan asserts its reputation as the origin of magnificent horticultural specimens. A huge and handsome temple, its pavilions trailing up a piney hill, has lovely and unusual plants in all its courtyards. A plum tree, reputedly dating from the Tang dynasty (over 1000 years ago!) is in full white blossom, with a fragrance finer than any I have ever smelled. Only knowing that I have no way to keep it alive on my journey restrains me from the enormity of nicking a twig to clone—that, and my perpetual "red-haired" conspicuousness.

These are temples on the grand scale that have been carefully protected during periods of iconoclasm. Their huge, old guardian gods are getting makeovers, having been recently repainted and temporarily propped up in odd places, such as the belly button, for support. Numerous and very workaday monks, worn offering boxes, and great piles of well-used straw kneeling pillows attest silently to the continuity of custom here. For centuries, with only brief closures in recent times, the temple has hosted the year's primary folk celebration, Lunar New Year, during which one can climb steep stone stairs through three massive gates, kowtowing at every step, if one is so inclined.

From there our cheerful busful rides to the tomb of a man named Nie Er, composer of the Chinese national anthem, who died young. The violin-shaped layout and socialist-realist statue are striking in their setting of tall, well-grown pines. My companions are plainly moved—less playful, quieter, attentive to the soft wind-music of the boughs. One of the Hong Kong couples wants to know what I think of the memorial. We agree that the place surprises us.

"I didn't think that these Chinese over here cared much for artists and musicians any more. We heard such a lot about what happened to intellectuals during the Cultural Revolution. I'm glad I came on this trip, but to tell you the truth, it's making me very confused. We Hong Kong people know we're Chinese by ancestry, of course, but the mixture of the familiar and the really strange leaves me wondering if I know what 'being Chinese' means. I suppose we'll find out when the Communists take Hong Kong back," a woman says, in easy English.

We break for lunch at the Begonia Hotel, Kunming's newest and finest. I eat with Wang, the China Travel Service guide, and the driver, and we have a nice low-key time of it, off-duty. The food is plain and good, served with a peculiar orange-flavored beer, which none of them will drink. "They're always dreaming up things to do with the surplus oranges here in Kunming," the driver complains. "No one's going to buy this stuff."

The hotel is so new that as yet there are no guest bathrooms in operation, so I have the opportunity to discover that the kitchen-staff toilet is equipped with neither toilet paper nor a hand-wash tap. After lunch, like sensible people, we all snooze in the astonishingly fashionable puce-and-lavender lobby till 2:30, belly bags rising and falling gently in the thin winter sun.

At last we reach a tangible manifestation of why Han Chinese have struggled up rough rivers and bad roads to Yunnan for millennia: the famous Jindian Si. This is a temple built by some mining magnate of the Qing dynasty around a twenty-by-twenty-foot structure made entirely of cast copper. Not very pure copper, perhaps, or it would have greened up a bit over the centuries, but metal, certainly, that hundreds of visitors have tested, slyly, with pins and coins. The nine-storied pagoda of solid money—copper cash were legal tender when it was built—flaunts Yunnan's metallurgical riches, which have been tapped for Chinese purposes since the great Southeast Asian Bronze Age began. Copper, lead, and silver have made this region worth the cost of supporting legions of northerners here. Emperors have exported waves of soldiers to marry with local women and to fight with their new brothers-in-law. But in Yunnan, the tiny lowlands that alone will bear the weight of wet-rice agriculture and Han population density are few and scattered. The mountains and their native cultures still win the ecological contest; the Han are still conquistadors in search of industrial bullion.

In the temples around the pagoda, the Buddhas and Guanyins are rough and recent. Though temple attendants are assiduous, and sweep up frequently, most images stand in a light scattering of thrown money, earnests of the sincerity of their many visitors. No ancient guardian images or temple paintings have survived what must have been fierce Cultural Revolution attacks. Two long, free-standing galleries, newly built along the central approach, house an exhibition of timeless landscape paintings, emphasizing that the complex is a cultural center more than a place of worship. Yet along with the gallery cases stand others housing the eight immortals and other such supernatural small fry. Here too, people have stuffed and thrown small coins and notes into the cases to reach particular images. As in taxi decorations of combined religious symbols and gold plastic ingots, the money links the mundane and supernatural planes in exchanges that are as much a part of the cosmos as hierarchy, or sex.

Further up the mountain, we enter a park, heavily trodden and grubby, but full of large trees, and centered on a tower supporting a fourteen-ton bronze bell. There is no arrangement to ring it, so young studs endanger their family line by leaning *way* out over the rails to whup it by hand. Its wonderful, unearthly sound surely communicates with the divine, but the lads seem to be motivated mostly by machismo. From the upper floors, the views are lovely—some of the hills badly cut over and starting to erode, but some still looking green. The park's protected trees, surely several hundred years old, are monsters in a country where planted timber is often cut at three inches in diameter. The park is a zoo for a botanical anarchy nearly vanished from the wild.

We end our sightseeing day back in the city, at the Yuan Tong Temple I saw yesterday, dedicated to a very Marian Guanyin, Goddess of Mercy. Unlike the carefully supervised establishments in the hills, this has the atmosphere of a real city temple, haven for neighborhood retirees, hope for families with intractable secular difficulties, hearth and home to several live-in households who keep the place up and running. Like most Yunnan temples, it is strong on potted plants and small gardens. An odor of divinity draws me to an other-worldly, yellow, flowering shrub that I learn later is wintersweet, or Hamamelis.

I invite Wang, Zhao, their wives, and one small son to a dinner in the hotel, where I do a spectacularly bad job of ordering from a wildly unfamiliar menu. I must order; I am the host, paying for the beanfest. The hotel prices are so outrageous by junior faculty standards that my guests would die before taking the responsibility of calling for anything but "a nice big bowl of soup." Zhao's wife giggles madly when I order a dish with salted vegetables. My interest in local preserved foods is absurd in the context: salted vegetables are what get you through hard winters in poor places. To compensate, I overorder by a factor of at least three, and command a torrent of the country's best beer, forcing them with toasts to drink more than they probably want. It's the best I can do.

As the meal winds down, I produce a pack of expensive Chinese cigarettes for the men. Zhao shoots me a look:

"My brand stinks so badly that Gates keeps airing out the room when we are talking. Well, I'll smoke these so you won't mind the smell."

Riding the Burma Road, 1987

December 30, 1987. The Burma Road

Wang insists on seeing me onto my bus to Lijiang before dawn this morning, and insists too on getting me one of the front-most seats. While this is generally sound practice—you don't bounce so much, get less fumes, and are not as likely to get stepped on—in this case, it is an error. My legs are so cramped that I cannot sit facing forward, and the window is stuck open to the frosty wind. So many travelers descend at the next large stop, however, that I change to marginally longer and more sheltered seating and am able to concentrate on my surroundings as the sun burns away the morning fog.

The highway has driven a ribbon of development through a sparsely settled and amazingly varied landscape. Mud villages give way to the wood-and-stone architecture of Bai people. Determined little towns with sawmills and cement-crushing plants spread a spatter of commerce and color along a few blocks, then we are back between dry fields and clear-cut hillsides, the bus jockeying for space with buffaloes, tractors, logging trucks, and lines of people carrying things to market on shoulder poles. Most of my traveling companions are old-before-their-time rural men, too shy or proper to talk to a strange woman. When words pass, we misunderstand each other, laugh, and fall silent. Deprived of my usual resource of eavesdropping, I peer at the passing scenes unblinkingly, trying to uncover the secrets that lie beneath the thatched roofs, below the misty cliffs.

After four hours, the bus stops for a hasty lunch at the roadside. I buy the most expensive lunch ticket, crowd into the crush around the kitchen windows, and hurry my main dishes onto a vacant table-corner. The server asks me how many ounces of rice I want. Looking askance at my tentative guesstimate ("Four?"), she enunciates carefully,

"Women usually eat two."

Two are ample, when accompanied with a dish apiece of cabbage and pork with onions. I ladle soup from the common vat into my empty rice-bowl, trying to calibrate my probable throughput for the next four hours. Yet by the time we stop for the night, I feel as though I have not eaten for days.

We stop at the bus route hostel, and I am installed in its fancier wing. This is a row of a dozen concrete rooms, side by side, and each opening onto the lot where the pale hulks of empty buses chew their cud in the gloaming. In my small room are a warmly supplied bed, a flask of boiled drinking water, a basin, a desk, a chair, and a light: the furniture supports the civilized inference of reading or note taking as well as merely sleep, and it assumes that one carries one's own cup, soap, and towel. The shy chambermaid points me to the women's latrine about a hundred yards beyond the ruminating buses and tells me I can draw hot bathwater from a roofed washing pavilion nearby. When I go to collect my basinful, I interrupt men—and all the travelers are men—stripped to the waist, scrubbing up along a communal trough in the chilly air. A man can, in decency, wash upper body, face, and feet in this public way, perhaps giving himself a lick and a promise with his wet towel when he changes his shorts behind closed doors. I return to my room, pin the curtains securely, and splash lavishly on the concrete floor.

Having dined and bathed in haste, I see it is still only 6:30. We leave in twelve hours, virtually all of which I shall spend in this cell, if only because they don't give out keys. If I want to go out, I must either leave the door unlocked and my worldly all in danger, or lock it at the cost of later having to roust out a service person to let me back in. The chamber pot-cum-spittoon that has been left discreetly under the bed removes one worry about this solitary confinement, but still leaves me with hours to fill.

A smoky bus, no exercise, the first day of a period: I feel grumpy, fractious, wanting to be entertained, guilty about losing an opportunity to see the town that mutters around the bus station, but not willing to deal with the hard stares and mild harassment I attract. Nor do I want to be conspicuous enough to draw night visitors to my locked and barred refuge. I have a nearly new English language paper, and my notes are way behind. The evening will be well enough spent indoors. As I slowly ease into the quilts, I take off all but the very last layer of long underwear—the smooth, silky ones—and settle into a sleep beyond peacefulness.

CHAPTER FIVE

城都行

Competing with Mrs. Bishop

DECEMBER 31, 1987. THE BURMA ROAD

Isabella Bird Bishop, already author of eleven accounts of her global travels during the 1870s and 1880s, began a twelfth on a journey to Sichuan in 1896. She did not get quite to Yunnan—the Burma Road was not built until World War II, and the border between Sichuan and Yunnan has some of the roughest terrain anywhere. My journey, a hundred years later, bears no comparison with hers in point of difficulty or danger. The sights along this unreeling road could easily be captured, though, in grainy black and white, and substituted for her photos, with no one the wiser. And, far oftener than one might think, the ideas that knowledgeable, thoughtful "Mrs. Bishop" brought to China are ideas that in the late 1990s, many Westerners still hold out as visions of the future.

Mrs. Bishop had already spent almost four years in East Asia, much of it in China, and was experienced enough to travel with only the absolute necessities: a Chinese (male) employee as translator and factotum, small supplies of curry powder and Indian tea, and a complete photographic outfit. Her translator and escort, Bedien, made all practical arrangements, leaving her free to observe and ponder her observations.

It was an inauspicious era for a foreigner of any kind, let alone a British woman, to travel in the interior. These years were the run-up to the Boxer Rebellion of 1900; there had been antiforeign riots in Sichuan in 1895; anticolonial demonstrations occurred in the mid-Yangzi city of Ichang only days before she arrived; and she herself was more than once attacked by crowds. In the county seat of Liangshan, the narrow street and then the inn yard filled with men throwing "mud and unsavoury

48

missiles," striking her as she passed, and attempting to set her room afire. When the local soldiery arrived—after two hours—and the crowd dispersed, the innkeeper's wife, in partial apology, asked "If a foreign woman came to your country, you'd kill her, wouldn't you?" Nothing daunted, Bishop finished her journey and wrote Sichuan up with much warmth and evenhandedness.

Capable as she was of seeing excellence in Chinese life, she was also convinced that the Chinese must eventually be obliged to end all restrictions on foreign trade. Central China appeared to her, as to so many other Westerners, as "the widest arena for commercial rivalries that the world has ever seen."[1] A fundamentalist free trader, she did not approve any more than the Boxers and the citizens of Liangshan of the formal "spheres of influence" that were slicing China up like a melon. She wanted "commercial rivalries" to operate unconstrained. At the same time, she readily recognized the superiority of Chinese methods that were "sweeping business out of foreign into native hands."[2] This trend was due in part, she opined, to the lavish-living laziness of Shanghai Westerners who did not even bother to learn Chinese, but it was due as well to the extraordinary productiveness and organization of indigenous institutions. Discussing the cotton trade as she rests at the river-port Wanxian, she observed that Sichuan

> does not produce much cotton; and cotton yarn from Japan and India comes in large quantitites into Wan to be woven there. In 1898 there were about 1000 handlooms. The cotton is woven into pieces about thirty feet long and sixteen inches broad, which take a man two days' labour, from daylight till 9 P.M., to weave. A weaver's wages with food come to about 600 *cash*, at present about 1s. 6d. per week of six days. Can Lancashire compete with this in anything but the output?[3]

I wish, very much, that I could discuss with Bishop the contradiction between her belief in dog-eat-dog competition, and her frequently stated opinion that the competition would have to be on Chinese terms. Surely she saw that this would lead to Chinese producers as winners in the competition for Chinese buyers? But Bishop was not the first nor will she be the last westerner to assume, with self-confident illogic, that they can make China play by illogical rules.

[1] Isabella Bird Bishop, *The Yangtze Valley and Beyond* (London: John Murray, 1899), 14.
[2] Bishop, *The Yangtze Valley and Beyond*, 64.
[3] Bishop, *The Yangtze Valley and Beyond*, 180.

Could I have liked this wise and kindly woman enough to spend months on the road with her? She must have read the feminism and socialism around which late-nineteenth-century intellectual life swirled; she never mentions them. Bishop is still worth a scholar's reading today because she *noticed* women and working people. But, though she broke many rules in her travels, she never questions the taboos of gender, class, and colonialism that more daring women were attacking back home.

After a solitary canteen breakfast of soymilk and steamed buns, I hunker down until daylight unwraps the villages from frosty mist. The boys on the bus smoke and snore uncompanionably, ignoring me as too strange even to contemplate. The dimness and jouncing make writing hard, but I scribble a bit, indulging in the lazy solipsism of writing about writing about writing until I am awake enough to see the real, outside my frowsy consciousness.

Journals of journeys are, at least in principle, unbuttoned in style and unstructured in analysis. In travel writing we conspire with the author to pretend that her lines fly from hasty pen to eager eyes without editorial interference or second thoughts. We accept that each turn in the road may bring inconsistency and surprise—the inherent disorganization of a purely chronological narrative is what makes the journey ours as well as the writer's.

This freshness, which after all is not wholly contrived, makes the genre a splendid source of naive frankness about how one sort of person views another. By the time of the Monroe Doctrine, two-thirds of the world's peoples were integrated into empires that were run from the east coast of North America and the west coast of Europe; and we Euro-Americans met those peoples, by and large, as figures in travelers' tales. What travelers said, and how they said it, came to form virtually the only "truth" about vast stretches of the globe. Read in retrospect, the various "natives" encountered along the way, and even the landscapes in which they are set, can be seen as inventions, figments constructed of a little swiftly captured detail and a great deal of un–self-conscious imagination. We now mine these books more for insight into our own culture than for that of their ostensible subjects, and have come to see travel writing as "in many respects a form of fiction."[4]

Scholars easily use this literature to illuminate colonialism and sexism, for those who journeyed were typically Euro-American men abroad in

[4] Christopher Mulvey, *Transatlantic Manners: Social Patterns in Nineteenth-Century Anglo-American Travel Literature* (Cambridge: Cambridge University Press, 1990), 7–9.

exotic empires, intermixed with a few "intrepid females," even more entitled than their men to preen themselves on their resilience in the face of the foreign. When I read Mrs. Bishop's peripatetic sisters, and when I revise the notes of *my* journey (as I shall surely do, gentle reader, before you see them), I am not much struck by their starchy colonialism and nit-picking genderedness; I grew up on liberal critique. What stands out for me in travel writing—and in travel—is the traveler's constantly lamented difficulty in maintaining a familiar social position in the midst of a forest of alien objects and symbols. Whatever bits of gender or national identity these travelers display, their sharpest displacement is that of class. Are those they encounter "gentlemanly" or "ladylike," and thus trustworthy—or at least predictable? And would they seem too "low" to keep a reader's interest?

As one commentator on this genre notes, "the most pervasive fiction constructed by the nineteenth-century travel writer was that of the gentility of the writer and reader. . . . Any writer who did not choose to write up . . . and adopt the tones and the values of gentlemanly society would find book publishers unwilling to publish, book sellers unwilling to sell, and bookbuyers unwilling to buy. It was a hard combination to beat."[5] The very intent to publish encourages a writer to flatter both reader and self by using the alien setting to test our joint social mettle. By writing and reading of trying journeys, we give evidence of our sterling qualities, untarnishable by the worst that aliens, inferiors, and (for women) sexual threats might oblige us to suffer. Those good qualities are occasionally characterized as nation- or gender-specific, but far more frequently they are those of a putative superiority of breeding and / or education—of class.

In Mary Wollstonecraft's account of a summer spent in Scandinavia in 1795, she illustrates this confusion of categories:

> Travellers who require that every nation should resemble their native country, had better stay at home. It is, for example, absurd to blame a people for not having that degree of personal cleanliness and elegance of manners which only refinement of taste produces, and will produce every where in proportion as society attains a general polish.[6]

[5] Ibid.
[6] Mary Wollstonecraft, *Letters Written During a Short Residence in Sweden, Norway, and Denmark,* ed. Carol H. Poston (Lincoln: University of Nebraska Press, 1976 [1796]), 49.

Wollstonecraft, a wise, well-traveled, radical-minded supporter of the French Revolution and the rights of all, here ignores completely the vast majority of her own compatriots, who, she knew well, could never meet her class standards of "personal cleanliness and elegance of manners." For "home" to be superior to Scandinavia, she must represent England as a nation composed solely of cleaned and polished ladies and gentlemen, while the lands in which she travels are muddles of many and ill-distinguished classes. Wollstonecraft would have been truer to her own meaning had she written that "Travellers who require that every nation should resemble the British bourgeoisie, should stay at home." When she—or Bishop, or virtually any of their peers—encountered gentlefolk, she felt, for the moment, "at home." Even an impoverished attempt at gentility is praised by class-conscious Hester McClung, traveling in darkest Colorado in 1873.

> [T]he literary aspect given by the large round table in the center of the room furnished with writing materials and late papers and magazines, and the fine collection of handsome specimens of jasper, quartz and gold, silver, copper and iron ore together with curious specimens of petrifaction and fossils, and last but not least the refinement and culture of the inmates—all these served to cast a kind of halo over the little plain cabin and its rude furniture.[7]

When we travel somewhere for the first time, we inevitably miss most of the nice distinctions that, for the local folk, bound and organize the social landscape. But the most necessary evidence of class status is written in universal code. The powerful do not carry their own baggage, have rough, work-worn hands, eat sparse and coarse foods, wear ragged clothing. While I am easily puzzled by unfamiliar cultural etiquettes, I can read directly the differential power conveyed by a calloused handshake or a groaning table. Like Bishop, my current self can tell a lady when I meet one. I will have more in common with the mistress, whether she is Chinese or Swedish, than I will with her drudge who scrubs the floor.

Unlike Mrs. Bishop, however, I have also scrubbed floors, waited tables, worked in factories (pickle, hat, and push button), helped run a

---

[7] Susan Armitage, "Another Lady's Life in the Rocky Mountains," in *Women and the Journey. The Female Travel Experience*, ed. Bonnie Frederick and Susan H. McLeod (Pullman: Washington State University Press, 1993), 31.

small business. Even the soft-handed segment of my life has been spent in learning to connect the assembly line with the long currents of culture. The smudgy boundary where Mary Wollstonecraft and Isabella Bird Bishop drew in their skirts marks my passage to useful knowledge.

While I delight in travelers' tales, the meta-amusement of writing or reading *about* them quickly wears thin. Analyzers of these texts are particularly fond of dichotomies that ring false to me, notably those of "travel / home," "other / self," "foreign / domestic." But travel is part of home, home is full of the traces of travel. My very body (the overstressed immune system, the biochemical instabilities, the weak right ankle that I repetitively sprain on bad roads) incarnates the interdigitation, the symbiosis, of both. "Other / self"??? My boundaries are far less sharp than this—I know what it feels like to be tired, love-blissed, anxious unto death for a child I cannot save from her difficulties. Doesn't everyone? And seriously entertaining the thought that "foreign and domestic" are separable—in *this* post-Columbian global economy!—should qualify the thinker for the Presidential Medal in Mindless Patriotism. These are dichotomies only from the perspective of an amazingly sheltered and class-homogeneous life. A whitebread curriculum vitae is invaluable to meeting the gentility requirements for successful publishing, but such innocents abroad all too easily mistake class disorientation for more abstract themes.

West Yunnan's towns are concrete, its hamlets are mud, women are up early. The shrubby growth that should be persistently preventing hillside erosion is bundled and stacked beside every house, fuel for cooking. In the small towns, where shrubs and roots are long gone, mounds of coal dust wait for housewives to cut them with wet mud into a gloppy paste. Pushed through an outsized pasta maker, the muck pops out as ventilated briquettes that precisely fit their small ceramic stoves. The housewives and their stoves—given minor fashion adjustments—form squatting tableaux identical to those outside Taibei kitchens before the 1970s government cracked down on soft coal. To fire up the stove and cook fresh rice gets a woman up a good hour before breakfast. Those not cooking are scrubbing clothes in pans, on stone tables that serve as washboards, or in the slowly drying ponds where the ponies water.

I long to pace off these village streets, to inventory what is sold, to ask where it comes from. Planned economy struggles visibly with human error and human ingenuity in the little collective shops on every main street. Whoever distributes the flower-stenciled enamel washbasins, spittoons, and mugs does a terrific job; they are identical everywhere in China. The folks responsible for seeing that every town gets a few badminton sets and guitars do their job well, too. But broad plastic sheeting—a gift from God to farmers in wet seasons—is so rare that when I see any, I want to jump off and buy some, just in case.

Always, I watch for the visible stuff of religion. Ancestral tablets in living rooms? Earth God temples in the fields? Incense sticks and spirit money in shops? Rural Yunnanese display none of these. Rugged hillsides nearly useless for agriculture are so abundant that graves are allowed, as they are often not in more densely populated regions. But the tombs are plain, undecorated. Is this austerity tradition, choice, or compulsion? In Taiwan, folk religion not only expresses people's belief in supraindividual forces. It pours out a cornucopia of lively arts, creates an elders' club where women can seize public equality with men, offers judiciously spaced occasions to get seriously drunk with friends, and—not least important—performs as subversive street theater in which communities thumb their collective nose at those in authority. This last exercise must be carried out cleverly enough to be funny, yet ambiguously enough to be safe from reprisals. In Taiwan, sacrificial pigs have long been frilled with garlands of Nationalist flags. Everyone knows this visually links the piggishness of the ruling party with that of the offering. Should any party loyalist object, however, the flags are smirkingly reinterpreted as signs of community patriotism. The Confucian moral of an outdoor opera performance is larded with extempore political satire; the timing and supernatural personnel of a traditional "god's birthday" are distorted to accommodate Sun Yat-sen's official celebration. Rather than being punished for worshipping the local trinity, Samgai Gong, my Taibei neighbors receive grudging and insincere praise from ward politicians for adding to the jollity for Father-of-the-Country Sun's national holiday. Without folk religion to fool with, how do the Yunnanese get a bit of their political own back? Has it all mouldered away, all but the dandruff of notes and coins that litter images in official temples?

Lijiang town suddenly appears around a curve in the fractal road. It is impossibly beautiful, a wooden city where the founders foresightedly combed a skein of clear canals through the neighborhoods so every woman can wash her onions directly out her back door. Bridges, willows, grayed cedar siding and grayer tiles, happy ducks, rosy children, the geomancy of the valley responsible for all this blessedness funneled from the farther hills by a wedding-cake temple and its dragon pool: Lijiang is a dream of hippie happiness.

Lijiang belongs to the Naxi people, and Naxi-ness everywhere greets the ear in speech, the eye in dress. While men and women both mostly

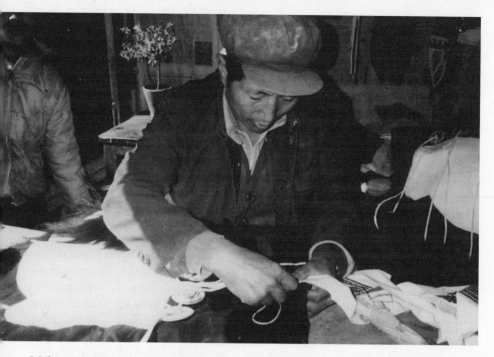

Making Naxi Dowry Capes, 1987

wear classic blue twill suits and workers' caps, women add an entrancing touch: goatskin dowry capes, black fur-side inside, white-sueded skin-side outside, bound between the breasts with black-and-white cross-stitch ties, and finished across the shoulder blades with seven beaded, be-streamered stars. Babies snuggle warmly beneath this weatherproof cover, but women wear their capes lifelong even when they carry no baby. When the bus sets us down among them, I feel seriously underdressed.

I sent word to Toby weeks ago that I would arrive today. He wrote to agree, and to give me the name of the guesthouse that will give us rooms. Inquiring about it, I am pointed to an official-looking gate where I all but trip over my friend. Our meeting is a perfect accident, for he had received my message almost too late to trek out of his fieldsite. In luck, he caught an unexpected official car and has just arrived in town. He looks as though he badly needs a vacation from the rigorous life in the distant tribal village where men his age lubricate their uneasy social relations with too much liquor and tobacco. Getting enough clean food and water takes more fieldwork time than he had imagined, and hiking the miles that separate the region's hamlets exhaust his strength as well as his time. Nights are bitterly cold. And, like all anthropologists, he gets very lonely. Seeing his delight in having company, I realize I too have grown tired of solitude. We check in, then go out to paint Lijiang red.

JANUARY 1, 1988. LIJIANG

Toby's providential jeep carried a second hitchhiker: a Naxi scholar home from the Minorities Institute to do further research into Naxi history. Padded with cotton and breakfast, we three climb a hillside to welcome the new year. Our companion has brought pocketsful of local piñon nuts from the piney slopes on which we wander. We sprawl on the fragrant duff, flavoring ourselves inside and out with the essence of holy trees. We visit the grave of the greatest Naxi scholar of the last generation, inscribed in both Chinese and Naxi writing; I am too enchanted by sun and sociability to puzzle out much of what I hear about his complex resume. The beauty of the town's roofs and watercourses, of its timber houses and house decorations, almost closes my ears. Snow peaks glisten beyond this valley, the sharp, clear border of the Tibetan plateau, where Toby's villages perch. Why did humanity walk away from lives in flowing valleys, from pulling and washing one's own vegetables, from time to carve flowers on the houseposts? I ignore the answers I know to be true about ecological intensification, social stratification, and cultural immiseration; I eat more pine nuts, and open my Kunming coat to the warmth of the cosmos. We are three scholars together, reading nature, each other, and the odd line of poetry: Daoist in our grand retreat and simple refreshment.

Yet it is nature itself that saves us from fossilizing on the hillside and growing a moss of permanent pleasure. We are out of pine nuts, and it is noon. Lunch and other urban distractions are in order.

On this pragmatic plane, our scholar loses his confidence in my adaptability.

"There's nowhere to serve you Western food in Lijiang, I'm afraid. What would you like to eat? Chinese-style or Naxi-style?"

Even this question may be simply a form of courtesy. As we thread our way over the cobbled paths to the town's central market, I see nothing that resembles a Han-style restaurant. A woman is making take-out pancakes on a slate hibachi, and around the market's edges other women roll them around local specialties. We will eat Naxi food.

I am simultaneously delighted—I love to eat new things—and appalled—everything in use by a stallkeeper is washed in a bucket of water by her side, water that obviously does sanitary service all day. I know this lunch is a bad idea. Curiosity, companionship, and overconfidence override my doubts—I generally have a very reliable digestive system—and we wolf a series of Naxi burritos washed down with strange, regional soda pop. They are delicious. The women purveying them cheer us on.

If the lunch is good, the ambience is incredible. This is one of Yunnan's classic periodic markets where local produce is swapped for local convenience, and a few important products are bulked and wholesaled for serious profit. The kaleidoscope highlights haystacks of both uncut and shaved golden tobacco, which everyone smokes as home-mades stuck into short pipes. Artisans selling "spotted copper" pots and pans and tin tea containers would be delighted to furnish my distant kitchen with their wares, but refuse, guffawing, to deliver them to Hong Kong for me. The pots are so unbearably handsome (and I am so atavistically house-proud) that I actually consider hauling my weight in yuppie extravagance back to the Kunming airport. Only memories of the tiny bus seats and Toby's visible incredulity bring me to heel.

Once released, shopping hormones create powerful behavioral cascades. In a permanent shop on the market's edge, a middle-aged man is cutting leather, making starry women's capes. Still surging with unappeased acquisitiveness, I fulsomely admire a finished cape hanging on the wall.

"Well, I made it for a particular girl's dowry. She'll be along to get it soon," he says mildly. This is as blunt a refusal as one is likely to get in China. The man peers through thick and thick-rimmed glasses at my transparently disappointed face, at my well-spoken companions, one obviously a local man of considerable clout, and sighs. "I can make her another one. I suppose you want a souvenir of our Naxi culture." He wraps the bundle in newspaper, and I shamelessly steal the unknown maiden's dowry with some meaningless banknotes.

By teatime, I sense I have unintentionally acquired another souvenir of Naxi culture. I dine lightly, retire early, and hope my premonitions prove exaggerated. But no, the burritos have done me in with the most dramatic case of bad gut I have ever experienced.

January 4, 1988. Lijiang

I am too weak to go out for two days, during which Toby and the Naxi scholar are profuse with unnecessary apologies and herbal remedies. Toby rents a bike to tour the valley while I recuperate in the guesthouse's sunny courtyard, wash my hair, and swear off various forms of greed. On this, our last day in Lijiang, we walk to the hillside temple that is now a museum, with Naxi archaeological finds and examples of Naxi script. The ideological corset that informs the displays obscures how, if at all, Naxi folk religion may have differed from local Han tradition. Toby, so much closer to it, and so much more expert, sees differences that seem only superficial to me. Lacking common assumptions we can reach no conclusions, and drop the subject sourly. My own sourness persists on the long bus ride to Dali. I almost insist on a quarrel over interpretation of Chinese intrafamily emotions about which I know nothing. We are both glad of the solitude of our hotel rooms, and gingerly of each other's sensibilities over dinner.

January 6, 1988. Dali

Dali is a status-enhancing notch on the backpack traveler's gun. There are many determinedly distinctive young Europeans on its streets, and one prominent roadside restaurant offers burgers and cokes. The town is old, walled, with stone city gates and timber architecture, and it commands views of the largest body of water for many, many miles: Ear Lake. Toby and I, readjusted to a slightly forced camaraderie, have enjoyed its beauty spots for two days. Perhaps from my sudden crash into vulnerability, I have lost my fine traveler's equilibrium, and begin to obsess silently about my meeting in Chengdu. We see spectacular things: a larger-than-life copper and cloisonne elephant; a national butterfly park; a perfectly scaled temple on a miniature island in foggy Ear Lake, where I draw a magnificent fortune ("You will always have people to love you"), and Toby gets a depressing one he rates at about C-minus. At a hotspring bath, I am neurotically nervous about sharing my pool-sized tub with small colonies of no doubt harmless algae, wash only in running water, and envy Toby's rosy relaxation when he emerges from his hot soak. Getting back to Kunming takes an eternity, though we travel in a faster, more comfortable "breadloaf" van rather than a grotty public bus. Toby's mother has made delicious Yunnan specialties for this homecoming dinner toward which I appear insufficiently grateful, and my gifts to her and Toby's baby son seem paltry beside their expansive hospitality. I even manage a substantial bout of insomnia from guilt because I am flying to Chengdu in the morning, rather than taking the spectacular rail route the construction of which, in the 1950s, killed close to two thousand workers.

These bad vibes resonate insistently with the bass beat of anxiety that metronomes my months. Will depression set my brain stem oscillating, pouring out feelings out of all proportion to the real world outside my biochemistry? I have my pills, and thus far they have done well at damping the waves. But I am still not over jet lag, my disequilibrating menses roar like a Taiwan typhoon, and my body has been universally resentful at having its electrolyte balance perturbed by days of diarrhea. Leaving the dysentery I contracted on my first fieldwork untended for two years had been a really serious error, perhaps the one that first set me up for these excessive biochemical reverberations. When I set out on *this* journey, memories of terrifying downward spirals made strong arguments for staying home, or at least for finding a traveling companion. Having been well at home for so long made clear how much of my life I had already spent afraid to act, for fear of falling. I hoped for a due dose of biological luck, and now will it to continue. A single concatenation of two dipping curves must not doom this enterprise.

JANUARY 9, 1988. CHENGDU

Luck is with me. Grouchiness has not been the slippery slope to the abyss. The pilot finds Chengdu, and my host finds me. Professor Qin Xuesheng is so kind, solid, sane, and comforting that when he tells me to rest, that we will not begin our program of meetings, sightseeing, and planning sessions until tomorrow, I acquiesce instantly. He gives me a printed itinerary of these events, which he courteously asks me to vet. It seems both perfect and terrifying. Perhaps by the end of this day, I will feel up to even a part of it.

In the hotel's massive, empty dining room, I absorb fresh greens, wonton soup, the sound of an ornamental waterfall. The Sichuanese call wontons *chaoshao*, love them inordinately, and claim them as aboriginally and ineffably Sichuanese. An unlikely figure enters. She looks like my aunt, graying, heavily dressed, with an English-language book in her hand. She too orders *chaoshao* with greens on the side, and settles luxuriously into her padded chair. We eye each other cautiously. In China as in

Taiwan, Western travelers often make a point of ignoring other Westerners, and I am slowly learning that women my age must accustom themselves to snubs. I break first, go over, introduce myself. She is from Cornwall, has been here for three months, is teaching English in order to get away from her husband and sons for a season of privacy and new thoughts. She comes to this costly restaurant on her day off for a simple lunch, "To get a bit of clean." She would love to show me around.

We spend a tranquil afternoon telling one another things we would tell no one else, and she passes on her hard-won knowledge of Chengdu. Who would have imagined that the best silk bargains in town are in the exhibition hall behind Mao Zedong's statue? Or that the best places to change money discreetly are in small restaurants run by angel-faced women?

JANUARY 13, 1988. CHENGDU

Anxiety had so corroded my enthusiasm for initiating research here that only the kindly scholarliness of Professor Qin has saved it. My Chinese is in stutters, I laugh in all the wrong places, I am embarrassed at a welcome that seems wildly disproportionate to my academic and personal standing, and most of the time, I can't understand a word of Sichuan's version of southern Mandarin. Professor Qin still speaks the English of his U.S. graduate student years and is a master of standard Mandarin, but his motherly wife and delightful daughter have few words in common with me. Luckily, three days into my Chengdu stay the graduate student Professor Qin has deputed to shepherd me about—an honored guest should have an attendant—puts me back in focus.

"Professor Gates, I am sorry to ask you, but we are embarrassed. Our Institute has never had a foreign visitor before, and we don't know if we're doing enough for you. Are the arrangements satisfactory?" she murmurs in the elevator.

The uneasiness that makes me inscrutable cracks, flakes off. I remember that I am not only a stranger come to ask a favor, but a family friend through Professor Qin's brother in Taiwan. While the Institute should not be paying for a suite in Chengdu's best hotel for me, I have gleaned that they are paying for it at traveling-official, not tourist rates. I recognize the obvious: that Professor Qin is eager to resume his former place in international scholarship and that I can be a helpful piece in his network. As we visit Chengdu's many museums, parks, and monuments, I

Professor Qin Xuesheng

relax enough for this wise old scholar to size me up, and for me to recognize my fortune in having found such a mentor.

Professor Qin's friends and associates in Chengdu's Sociological Association mobilize to brief me on their research and hear my plans for mine. They will help as much as they can. Grateful but cautious, I note that the three in a dozen who are women seem long-retired from anything very strenuous. We pass some casual academic chat, and—totally unexpectedly—the semiformal meeting metamorphoses into a birthday party.

"You spent your Christmas on a train, so we thought you needed a celebration, and we knew your birthday from your official papers," Professor Qin twinkles. Later, after killer-calorie birthday cake chased by tongue-numbing Sichuan dimsum and sorghum liquor, he looks rosy and cherubic, more Santa Claus than Saint Peter.

"Now that you've rested from your trip and had a look around Chengdu, we should talk about your research plans. You've met some of our sociologists, because I thought you might like to work with people at the Sichuan Academy of Social Sciences. Or, I have an old friend who is very high-ranking in the provincial-level Women's Federation. Which organization do you think would be best for you?" he asked.

I make many mistakes in this culture, but the Chinese have taught me one thing well. When such a person offers a choice, ignore all hyper-Anglo training in initiative taking, and gratefully request guidance. I hear myself saying, "Which do you think would be better, Professor Qin?" as a good daughter does when better-informed, mature parents offer a choice of suitors. What a relief not to have to make this critical choice alone, simply in order to prove my independence.

"The Women's Federation, I think," he replies gravely. And the Women's Federation it is.

JANUARY 16, 1988. CHENGDU

The Women's Federation, or *Fulian* ("Women United") are what is know as a "mass" or grassroots organization: a branch of the Communist Party responsible for ideological, educational, and legal work with women. They are interested in helping me interview a hundred female entrepreneurs for several reasons. Small business is attracting many women with whom the organization has no institutional links; working with me would help them survey this new territory in a friendly and scholarly atmosphere. Members of the Fulian's newly constituted research section hope to learn new academic methods. And the propaganda section can take credit for some foreign exposure of one of China's new, liberal tendencies.

From my side, too, there are many advantages to this choice of colleagues. While many academic men in China have shamed my chauvinist prejudice with their civility, it is still easier for me to work with women. Allying with a Party organization will spare me the oversight of the byzantine Ministry of Education, which supervises foreign academic projects conducted through universities. The Fulian women I have met simply radiate competence. And our agreement includes the clause that I may seek out our interview subjects in person, on a bicycle, riding the stream of traffic, and learning the city in the normal rhythms of daily life.

Vice-President Dai, a woman of staggering presence, signs for the Federation on the understanding that I will raise funds to cover our jointly arrived-at budget. I believe—and am later proven right—that her agreement insures that the Rockefeller Foundation will extend their grant supporting my upcoming project in Taiwan. Replicating this study in both Taiwan and Sichuan will add immeasurably to the interest of each, for as yet, few scholars have done systematic comparisons of any aspect of Taiwanese and Chinese life. Except for the numbers, I have understood hardly a word that the high-ranking Women's Fed cadres have said to me; they might as well have been speaking Hungarian. But Hua, the translator, has put it into manageable Mandarin, we have all smiled a lot, we have a contract.

The old Ilyushin cuts through the fog, and Sichuan disappears below. I head for Hong Kong, then Taiwan, to begin the year's fieldwork. The miracle has happened.

城都行

September–December 1988

**Chengdu, West Sichuan, Jiu Zhai Gou,
Hongyuan, Chengdu**

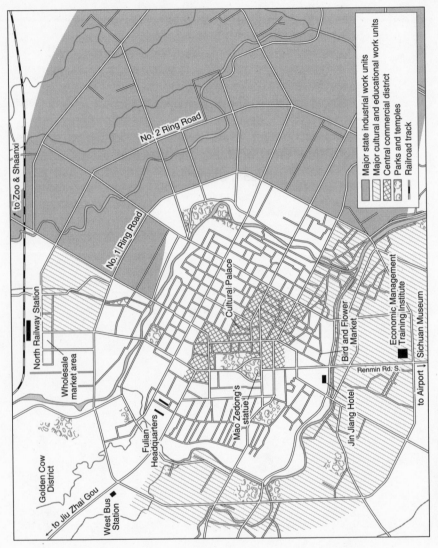

2. Chengdu City, 1988

Map legend:
- Major state industrial work units
- Major cultural and educational work units
- Central commercial district
- Parks and temples
- Railroad track

Map labels:
- to Zoo & Shaanxi
- No. 2 Ring Road
- No. 1 Ring Road
- North Railway Station
- Wholesale market area
- Golden Cow District
- to Jiu Zhai Gou
- West Bus Station
- Fujian Headquarters
- Mao Zedong's statue
- Cultural Palace
- Bird and Flower Market
- Jin Jiang Hotel
- Renmin Rd. S.
- Economic Management Training Institute
- Sichuan Museum
- to Airport

CHAPTER SIX

城都行

To Work

I return to Chengdu after a hot, tiring Taibei summer and have been holding my breath. Am I going to have to live so rough that my health will crash? Will I be ferociously lonely? Can my new laptop draw local current without harm to its absurdly expensive innards? Will the Fulian make outrageous last-minute demands and rearrangements?

No, no, no, and—so far, so good.

For starters, after a few initial days in the familiar but expensive Jin Jiang Hotel, I have been assigned a posh apartment in the Sichuan Provincial Enterprise Management Cadre Training Institute. This billeting disposes of my worries over both comfort and some culturally transparent companionship. Though there will be no heat, nightly hot water is supplied in the guesthouse, the grounds are spacious enough to allow for quiet sleep, and I will even have access to a washing machine! These suites are alive with cheerful and intelligent "foreign experts" from Canada, land of my birth and thus surely persons of character. Ten long steps away is a research institution with a faculty full of business professors! Living just across the way, with their families and their cluttered academic lives are several hundred people who teach what I need to know as context for "my" businesswomen-interviewees.

My worries over high tech have also proved unfounded. Provided with an appropriately socketed extension cord, my computer sucks with satisfaction. The effort of buying this machine, dragging it from Hong Kong, and learning its eccentricities will not have been wasted. Its blue eyes will keep me company in the evening writing-up of the day's notes.

Finally, the Fulian. Am I right to be suspicious, to wait anxiously for the revelation of a hidden agenda? Will these women play fair? Do we even define "fair" in the same way?

So far, superb. My associates are handling with cheerful efficiency the tedious and exhausting task of finding interviewees who meet my conditions. Jiang Yinghong, Hua Xinghui, and Li Jufang, who speak a Mandarin I can understand, have been deputed to form our main team. They seem calmly certain of finishing the job—interviews, coding, and some simple tabulations—before I leave to keep Christmas at home.

Their professional assumption that all will proceed as scheduled contrasts sharply with my own perpetual unease in a new fieldwork setting. The fundamental task of the anthropologist, getting the confidence of strangers, is a nerve-wracking one. In Taiwan, it ruins my sleep, digestion, and emotional stability, a rolling catastrophe of misunderstanding and collapse. There, I struggle with my own luggage, pound the pavement to secure an apartment, gamble on getting effectual field assistants, and am politely told to go away by about every third person I try to interview. Everything I accomplish stands or falls on my ability to be a healthy, energetic, optimistic, and gregarious leader of my assistants, and persuader of unwilling informants to tell a foreigner their most intimate secrets. The material for an article can cost me a year of hard time.

This Chengdu undertaking is already a smooth-running and predictably successful project, in large part, I suspect, because I am not administering it. Little as I like having to tell other people what to do, it feels extremely odd to have most of the daily decisions made by others. In Taiwan, spending my days up to my ears in the ordinary lives of ordinary people, I am absolutely "free," for whatever good that does me. Here, I am quite isolated from everyday life, so I will not learn so much in my usual way—by blundering through things on my own. Can I, really, learn anything of interest if I go about convoyed by cadres of a "mass organization"? Though the Fulian has assiduously spared me any drudgery in setting this all up, they have asked at every turn for my choices, and are following our agreement to the letter. When I suggest, in midmorning, that we change the plan, our flock of bicycles wheels round as one in the new direction. If I am actually in control—and I seem to be—why am I having such a good time?

One source of my perduring unease has nothing to do with Fulian, but rather with academic snobberies at home. No matter what superficialities I return with from Chengdu, they will count for something simply because they come from China, and not Taiwan. I am going to obtain data by what are primarily fetch-me-a-pygmy methods, yet I am already receiving invitations from real universities to lecture on this perhaps too-slick research. More fuss will doubtless be made about my four months here than has ever been over the four years of sweat, tears, and lowered serotonin levels that the Taiwan findings have cost me.

But I *am* here. Perhaps I can adapt to comfort. Surely I will learn things of interest, despite the assiduity with which I am being sheltered. The family pessimism flourishes poorly in the guesthouse atmosphere, where I have a starring role as Old China Hand and bucker-up of nice people on their first Asian sojourn.

What I will probably learn most about in these early weeks is the peculiar shape given to life when it is lived in the embrace of a state (actually, provincial) work unit. Jobs where the government is the employer (feudal overlord more like it) have been eagerly sought by aspiring Chinese for hundreds of years because they offer the ideal combination: secure tenure, adequate salaries, opportunities for infinitely expandable perks, and very little work, none of it manual. My experiences with Taiwan's government and research institutions have given me a glimpse of this life. Bureaucrats and scholars, quartered in official housing near their workmates, accept goldfish-bowl standards of privacy, political caution, and interminable red tape as the inevitable inconveniences of their highly esteemed positions. They live or die by the documents that announce appointments, allocate funds, permit research cooperation, legitimate the export of computer disks. The way local intellectuals work the system here looks similar. History and the logic of bureaucracy promise that it will be.

I am living in a "neighborhood," if that is the right term, entirely inhabited by intellectual work units. Renmin South Road, broad, handsome, tree-shaded, and pointing straight at a superannuated statue of Mao Zedong, is lined for blocks with cultural, medical, educational, and who knows what other provincial-level units, all with apartment blocks, courtyards with trees or a fishpool, basketball courts, the occasional government shop. They *look* like any ugly cluster of sketchily maintained Asian high-rises—balconies brightened with laundry, bougainvillea, people seeking a few minutes' privacy—but the people in them come and go on their unit's schedule. The Management Institute rings bells for meals and classes, as one might expect in an academy, but other nearby units also pulse chiefly with collective movement. The concrete reefs attract not only barnacles of permanent small shops to serve local needs, but a pelagic population of hawkers and delivery people set up under umbrellas to mend bicycles or slipping in quietly to distribute milk.

Renmin Road just West of Mao, Engels, and Marx, 1988

Dawn comes late in Chengdu in September, because we, like everyone else in this vast country, are on Beijing time. Often sunrise hardly comes at all. Low cloud cover is as common today as it was above the heads of nineteenth-century missionaries, some of whom it drove to neurasthenia, early retirement, or the bosom of Abraham; in World War II, it saved the city, because Japanese bombers could never find it. On gray days I depend on cocks crowing to distinguish between a foggy morning and a night with too many fluorescent bulbs still burning across the way. Perhaps whoever keeps the cock does so for the same reason, for otherwise day comes quietly here.

Though the Institute has three large canteens where many residents eat breakfast within a minute's walk of the guesthouse, there are few morning noises but the soft clink of metal bowls. People appear silently, consume huge breakfasts of buns, pickles, and rice porridge in uncompaniable haste, and glide off to class or office like ghosts in the gloom. Later, bursts of song and accordion scales drift from open windows, or a group practices the invertebrate motions of traditional exercise to shouted commands. Some nights, rowdy dancers jollify on the twenty-two-story main building's penthouse roof, perfecting their disco. But in the morning, people emerge slowly from the privacy of sleep into their crowded world.

Perhaps, too, they are focusing on breakfast, as they well might after an early dinner at about five-thirty the previous evening. Chinese breakfasts are not generally popular with foreigners, so it is sometimes difficult to find local fare in a China trying hard to cater to tourist foibles. The first morning I awakened here, I had forgotten to sign for breakfast in the guesthouse dining hall. By extraordinary and kindly dispensation, the man who keeps the gate escorted me to one of the Institute canteens, supplying me with a large, clean enamel bowl and chopsticks, and paying for my choices from his office slush fund of meal tickets. I ate two meat-filled steamed buns, some scoops of salty pickled vegetables, and a nice, hot dipper of soy milk, to which the pickles gave the flavor I prefer to the more common sugared variety. I considered breaking an egg into the soymilk, but decided that my meal contained plenty of protein. I could also have had steamed meatless buns, tea-cooked eggs, or a bowl of rice porridge flavored with meat shreds, peanuts, and pickles. A breakfast containing two kinds of grain foods, choices of meat, egg, soy, and peanut protein, along with interesting and spicy vegetable tidbits can hardly be bettered for its healthful and rib-sticking qualities. It is curious that so many non-Chinese cling to the wretched bread (smeared with industrial-grade jam), miserable coffee, and nasty eggs that pass for Western breakfasts here.

When I realized, the next morning, that I was the only resident who patronized the guesthouse dining room for breakfast (the Canadians all have kitchens and prefer to consume their instant coffee, vile jam, etc., in privacy), I tried to convince the extraordinarily handsome foreign affairs man in charge of us that I, and the cooks, would be happier if I were to be issued a supply of meal tickets to exchange for lovely buns and pickles. Eating alone was boring, I noted. At first he agreed. How splendid! I could get up, have my morning run, and go for breakfast inoffensively in the great outdoors (the canteen buildings are simply sheds) before going through the gyrations inherent in getting a good wash with the contents of a vacuum bottle (hot water 7 to 10 P.M., daily). I would also get a decent meal free of lipids, and at least the illusion of company in which to eat it.

I do not know if this arrangement would have embarrassed the cooks, the guesthouse, or somebody else in the hierarchy all the way up to

Deng Xiaoping. As I knew, and should have taken more seriously, without at least one guest to serve, the three cooks and two waitresses might be seen as redundant. The smashing Mr. Tang came by to tell me that dining room personnel would go out for my canteen order in the morning and bring it to my room. Through a series of small adjustments of a sort with which I had already become ruefully familiar in Taiwan, this has evolved into my having instant coffee, bread and jam, and plain boiled eggs, alone, in the dining hall at an hour early enough to make a morning run quite unlikely. By reading the paper firmly (sometimes the same paper for several days in succession), I have gently repulsed the command-performance companionship of the waitress, who speaks in a dialect of near total incomprehensibility. And I run just before lunch, until the daily interviewing begins.

SEPTEMBER 14, 1988. CHENGDU

Today I am to enjoy China's finest form of entertainment, the correct performance of a social ritual. I hold my first interview, which is also a social call at which I will receive presents. Forewarned, I have brought Hong Kong lipsticks along to give in return. The call will be returned when the entrepreneur in question returns from her visit to Guangzhou to check out the latest in food technology. This visit / interview (they are the same word in Chinese) begins with five of us—myself, the translator, the primary assistant, the part-time assistant, and her substitute— rolling off merrily in the Fulian's van so that we can all see how things go, and I can instruct everybody on the spot should problems arise.

I am not prepared for the holiday atmosphere as we bounce down the ring road that circles central Chengdu. My companions fall at once into the lighthearted style of schoolgirls playing hooky or prosperous matrons on a pilgrimage. They laugh, make jokes, widen their gestures as Chinese do when they relax, and pile out of the van in a rush when we arrive at Ms. Yeh's restaurant.

Yeh turns out to be very chic indeed—a far cry from the overworked and underdressed women I have been interviewing in Taiwan. None of my Taiwan "boss ladies" would have showed up in a sleek black nylon sleeveless shell and pegged pants, black heels, and simple gold jewelry, no matter how much advance notice they had. Yeh is a very attractive woman with charmingly cut short hair and absolutely flawless, warmly tanned skin. She falls in at once with the merrymaking on the short ride to her house. Her restaurant, specializing in "small eats"—*jiaozi* (boiled dumplings) and noodle dishes—is left in the capable hands of the young women she employs. I am sorry to leave, for it is cheerful and clean-looking, jammed with customers, a good place for a party.

Yeh lives in a suburb called Golden Cow, named for a now-submerged village of low brick houses laid out in typically jumbled rural fashion. Chickens, vegetables, very old women, and very young men are much in evidence. In this bucolic setting, her house is a surprise, with a large and well-furnished living room, two bedrooms upstairs, and four small cubicles behind for the country girls who work in the restaurant. As she shows us around, she points out a group pictures of herself and her husband, hanging in their bedroom. They are on their honeymoon, ludicrously costumed in fake American military uniforms rented at an amusement-park stall. For an instant, her face signals consternation. A glance at my enjoyment of the joke reassures her that she has not thrown a spanner in the works of U.S.–China relations. Throughout the afternoon, she presses food and drink on us; the sturdy translator later admits gleefully to having eaten four bananas.

As we work our way into the interview, I learn that she had been a woman's work activist, a volunteer *ganbu*—cadre—with the nominal salary of five *yuan* ($1 U.S.) a month, for several years before her marriage. This was at a time when she was learning to make noodles for her production brigade, working hard at that and at mushroom raising. An obvious natural energy would have fueled her political activism; activism is as dependable a way to better one's self in China as is getting an MBA in the United States.

That energy came into its own as the responsibility system began in 1978, earlier in Sichuan than elsewhere in China. She then contracted to make the brigade's noodles with the right to make a profit on the deal; she used her dowry sewing machine to make all her and her husband's clothes, and more to sell on the street, and encouraged him to save every *fen* for capital by smoking cheap cigarettes. In six years, they opened their restaurant. They have lent money, interest free, to friends and relations as capital for three new businesses, and they are planning a substantially larger restaurant for the future. Her husband now smokes Kents.

I might have raised a skeptical eyebrow over this Horatio Alger tale had I not spent the previous half-year hearing near-identical ones from Taiwan businesswomen, some of whom I had known long enough to see in action.

Activist Restaurateur's Cook, Kitchen, and Cat, 1988

With children and a business, she is no longer an official activist, but she still knows well how to put people at ease, how to take charge of a situation, how to expand her network of contacts both for future need and for the pleasure she gets from energetic sociability. I can see the Fulian thinking up ways to get her to take part in some of their activities, building yet another link to the women of Golden Cow.

The Fulian women with whom I work take their jobs seriously. They seem to have decided that I—or at least my research—matter, that what they do here for China and Chinese women will get an international airing in what I write. They quite naturally want positive responses from me; it is their job to get positive responses from people.

I could easily feel manipulated; some Westerners get prickly rather easily when they feel that all the cards are not on the table. But how clearly one sees the cards depends very much on one's own eyesight. I understand the Fulian's job at least as well as they understand mine, I think. Besides. Though they want to do their jobs, they are being quite straightforward about the problems we may encounter. They have found me a capable activist with an admiring husband for our first interview, a woman with the resources and charm to spend the afternoon entertaining me, and presenting me with glass-boxed fuzzy dog-dolls. But they have also told me, repeatedly, that not all our subjects will be comfortable talking to us. Some may refuse altogether, or skip the appointment, or give misleading answers. Of course, I say: it happens.

A Chinese friend warns me that a lot of what the Fulian say and show me will be propaganda, that I will get a highly skewed sample. I have read about Potemkin villages and presidential visitations. I assume the long list of potential subjects I have been given contains no battered women, no incest cases, no families so badly hurt in the Cultural Revolution that they will be surly or panic-stricken over an interview, no women who have successfully flouted the urban one-child policy. I assume most of the people who agree to talk to me will do so because a good relationship with the Fulian is worth something to them. Good businesspeople here, as in Taiwan or Mt. Pleasant, Michigan try not to alienate the authorities; contacts in offices and bureaus are a competitive resource.

Even so, in talking about sensitive subjects, I find people here *far* more straightforward than many in Taiwan, where official surveillance was, until recently, stricter than anything the Communists were able to routinize. Experts at evasion, Taiwan folks adeptly answer uncomfortable inquiries with harmless platitudes about Chinese culture, rather than with usable information about actual events. Chengdu women are more responsive, even to touchy issues, though they show skill in abruptly changing the subject—often by proffering food or beverages—when they don't want to answer a question. Anyone who has spent time with Chinese knows what a frantically recirculated candy dish means. Finding out what actually is sensitive, and what is not, is sometimes the most interesting part of a visit.

So I enjoy the ritual of this first interview, assuming that whomever we interviewed first would have been friendly, open, activist-minded. When I take people through Prosperity Settlement, *my* showcase field site in Taiwan, I take them to call on people who like me, not people who will slam the door in, and on, my face. These local stars are the women I want to know, the ones who can put the little bits of opportunity together to shape things for themselves. Anyone in this system who would not find a way to be comfortable with and active in political participation that offers such opportunity is missing a trick. And anyone who writes off the importance of politics in taking charge of one's own fate in China has misread the Chinese, not only here and now, but also those of long ago and far away.

SEPTEMBER 21, 1988. CHENGDU

We arrive on time in heavy rain at the end of a muddy lane to find that Wang, our subject, has been called to a meeting. She sometimes takes temporary jobs she gets through the meeting's leaders, so she can't miss it. But she'll be back in an hour. Will we come in and wait?

Of course we will, if only because I doubt I can get my bike back up the lane until some of the water has ebbed. Wang's mother leads us through the five-by-eight-foot grocery store her daughter runs here, and makes us comfortable in the family's main living and sleeping room. This (I later conclude) is one of the poorest living situations we will visit. An open, unroofed kitchen-cum-washing-space is behind the shop; the room in which we warm ourselves with tea and candies just holds a double bed, two cots, a few chairs and cabinets, a black-and-white TV, and an electric fan. Wang's mother, the mother's second husband, Wang's mother's mother, and Wang's little boy sleep here. A second room is used for stock, some of which, like cooking oil, liquor, and cigarettes, is quite valuable and must be kept secure. The teenage daughter of Wang's stepfather has her own room built on top of the house, with a small, pretty roof garden; the toilet is a privy in the back. I saw worse crowding last spring in Taibei, though not among shopkeepers.

Wang's mother is a lively, stagey woman wearing a gold ring and earrings whom I am not surprised to learn was once a singer in the Sichuan Provincial Opera. A reputation for vulgarity and loose living gives this occupation low status in most Chinese eyes. In Taiwan, I would have guessed at once that she had been an actress. None of us reacts with prejudice, I think, but she nonetheless immediately informs us of her educated connections: her married third daughter, who works at the Jin Jiang Hotel, has just been accepted at a Canadian university and will leave on this adventure in a few days, paying her own way. (Will *her* child too end up on one of the cots? I wonder.) A nephew works in Japan for a provincial-level propaganda [read public relations] unit. *Her* mother, quite deaf at eighty-seven, chips in cheerfully and irrelevantly to our discussion of the family. The old lady, who has no sons, has lived with her daughter since they were both widowed. As we chat, the surly stepfather brings a load of ten-liter cooking-oil bottles into the kitchen space and argues irritably with his busy daughter. She is washing the family's clothes in what must be very cold water; her hands are blue. Wang arrives.

She has her mother's former good looks and is well if cheaply dressed in black stretch pants and a bright sweater. We have already heard the outline of her story from her loquacious parent, but she, more than most, seems to want to tell us about herself.

You see how small my store is, and how busy I am, having to do temporary jobs and also keep the store. My mother can't even help me much, because she doesn't understand business. This is all because of what happened a few years ago.

We have a poor worker class background, so I was able to get a pretty good job in a state factory after I finished middle school. By 1979, I was a forewoman. I had a good position, my wages were fine, it was very secure. I really loved my work, and was enthusiastic about the Party's policies. I already had one child, so when my birth control failed and I got pregnant again, I was quite willing to have an abortion, even though the one-child policy was not law yet. I wanted to show my loyalty. But for one reason after another, I didn't get around to it until I was seven months along.

Well, the doctors made a terrible mess of the abortion. My periods were awful after that—I really suffered. Finally, my mother-in-law—we lived with her then—told me, "The only way to get your system working right again is to have another baby." I couldn't stand being sick all the time, so I did it. When the factory birth control workers found out I was pregnant, they told me I had to have an abortion: we had the one-child policy now. But I refused. It was for my health. So I lost my job.

Wang was crying by this time, her face tight.

I really liked my work, and it was such a good job! I would have got a worker's pension and everything, but I lost it all. And there was a lot of trouble because I refused. I was ashamed to be the center of all that fuss. To go from being a regular worker in a state company to just a temporary worker is embarrassing.

My husband is a driver for the same foodstuffs unit. While I still had my job, we saved enough to buy the house that was here before—it was just mud and thatch—and to build these rooms. The original house cost us only 400 yuan, which was very cheap, because my work unit had influence here. We built all of what you see except the shop—that came later. We had to borrow from relatives to build, but we had it all paid back before I lost my job.

After I lost my job, I tried to run stores at a couple of other places, but there weren't enough customers. Finally we realized that this place was becoming a better business location because of the big factory that moved so many people into the area. But it's too far for my husband to travel to work. So we moved to mother-in-law's again, moved my mother's family and one of our kids in here, and added the shop. I thought Mother could keep an eye on it while I do other work, but . . . she's not much of a businesswoman. [Throughout the interview, the mother interrupted to have her daughter handle transactions; it appeared that the mother was not to handle money.] Anyway, Stepfather moves stock for me (my husband does too, after work, when he can use the truck), Mother can at least keep people from walking away with things, and she takes care of my older child. Mother-in-law has the younger one. For about twelve hours a day, I just run around, trying to manage things.

We started the grocery with 700 yuan of our own savings and 400 borrowed from Mother, a few hundred more from Mother-in-law. Altogether we had 1,400 in initial capital.

We spend 100 to 200 yuan a month to live, and save my husband's salary. He has put about 4000 into expanding our stock, and I increase the value of stock at least 40 yuan on each turnover. The shop profit is about 300 a month, so I can save 100 to 200 a month. We pay about 20 yuan a month to the small business association representative, who turns it in to the tax office. That's mostly a tax on profits, but there are some small fees

Mom-and-Pop Shop, 1988

thrown in—for administration. One of our biggest expenses is for snacks for the kids. I guess I spend 30 to 40 a month on myself—clothes, cosmetics, and so on. The house is mine, so there's no rent, and I don't charge Mother anything to live there, since she keeps our stock safe.

It's crowded here, but we're used to that. Dad and Mother were singers in the Sichuan Provincial Opera. Before I married, we lived in the Opera's housing—five of us in one small room.

From 1969 to 1971, I went to the countryside near Chengdu. My background was fine, so I was sent back to the city after only two years, and assigned work in a food factory. I was soon earning 20 a month, then 30. Food was cheap then, so that was good money. I was in the factory eleven years, and became a forewoman, managing the business end of things. My best salary was 100, including bonus. I'm still mad at having lost that job.

I ask Wang one of our standard questions: "Does having her own capital raise a woman's status?" She is of two minds: "If you're capable at your work, you will have status whatever you do. If you're not, it will be low. Of course if you do business, money gives you power." Then she adds, expressing a characteristic contemporary Chinese attitude that a woman's various contributions to the family are more or less interchangeable: "For example, I know someone whose husband said if you have a child you don't have to work, but if you don't have a child, you have to work."

A quarrel, now too loud to ignore, has broken out between Stepfather and his daughter over her missing tape recorder. Wang groans quietly about the man's bad temper, looking more harassed than ever. To distract us from her family's bad behavior, she begins to pop soda-can tops under our noses, urging us to drink and enjoy ourselves. In the kitchen, the fat is in the fire, or the vegetables in the fat, so lunch is imminent. They invite, we decline; they insist; we refuse. The rain has stopped, the lane is passable. As we go, the quarrel over the tape recorder becomes more general, and louder. Nobody staged *this* interview.

CHAPTER SEVEN

城都行

Ambient Atmospheres

SEPTEMBER 25, 1988. CHENGDU

My initial fears of loneliness in the field were thoroughly off the mark. By day, the comradely productivity of work sessions is interspersed with giggly lunches and political economic discussions over tea. By night, the Canadians enliven dinner with their intelligent silliness and whole city blocks with their loud parties.

Canadian comings and goings stir up a playful, faintly sexual atmosphere in the stuffy Institute guesthouse. There are no other unattached women in residence and only four married women. All are shy, except for a honeymooning Edmonton bride who has overcome severe culture shock to become a skillful expatriate in record time. Sixteen men live here in bachelor splendor, several of them very attractive. One is especially so, but his frequent references to his wife advertise that he is absolutely married. Although I like to think he fancies me, and I entertain occasional lascivious thoughts of him, we called a truce in the first week, help each other with shopping for our significant others, and complain delicately about our celibacy. Another, in his twenties, appears in need of tea and sympathy. He is a delicious child. I have considered taking him under my wing, but decided against it on the grounds of general human decency toward the young, who often take such matters more seriously than one intends.

This companionable masculine crew responds to my slightly flirtatious but basically unambiguous signals (and to the notorious photograph of What's-His-Name at the head of my bed; the plug in for my laptop is only in the bedroom, and people want to play with it) with teasing and gallantry. One former hockey jock heroically bodychecks open the flimsily locked door to my kitchen when weeks of official

81

requests fail to produce a key. They hug me when (I suspect) they need hugs, bring me fruit and flowers, drop in for no apparent reason, and say charming things. Some occasionally mention, shyly, their sweethearts and wives. We ride all over the city at night, a shoal of singing rowdies seeking out night markets and restaurants that my interviewees had suggested would be worth sampling. We make communal meals and dance everything from Viennese waltzes to an embarrassing icebreaker (that the Chinese love) called the Chicken Dance. They are dears, even if playing with them does beguile me away from finishing my book.

My days so full of the flavor of women are thus balanced by evenings seasoned with the imperceptible odor of men. This atmosphere is nothing like love, or even desire, though desire rises often enough over these long months. It is more like my morning vitamin B, or the songs the Tibetan men who live nearby sing at night to give them some needed sense of home. It is better to feel occasional sexual heat, even if generalized, a small stove that promiscuously warms whomever is near it, than to be constantly chilly. It is strange, it is not quite the right thing, but it is not entirely the wrong thing either.

Perhaps in some other place I would not feel this need for a sexual subtext on the day's events as strongly as I do among the Chinese. An Austrian woman traveling through talked about her responses to Tibetans. As sexist under pressure as myself, she described them as "real men" in contrast to the podgy, stodgy Han. Fieldwork in China means being immersed in the sexual equivalent of bleach, taking the brighter colors out of life. One hungers for a sense that sexual love is present in the world, even if I am separated from my lover and cannot enjoy it myself. The Chinese are so self-controlled that it is easy to imagine that no one delights in a lover's body. There are no sights and sounds and smells to recall memory, to sharpen anticipation. China is like a time of my life when all my sexuality died to the roots, and I thought it was gone for good. Perhaps, indeed, China is not like that at all, but only seems so to me because my sad, unseasonable winter came among the Chinese. But the Austrian woman—and others—says the same.

The Canadians rescue me from this cold, and I them. Not as my lover would do. But more than books can, or keeping busy, or being determinedly cheerful. They are real. They are—perhaps—as subcutaneously lustful as myself. And so I make washtubs of salad for them because they believe sinology reveals the secret of safely preparing raw vegetables. We sit in my apartment, listening to one another's stories of the week's adventures and to my Julie Brown tape. We drink bad wine, eat idiosyncratic Chinese cookies, and they all go off to bed. I sit alone, writing, listening to the Tibetans sing in sorrow and desire. An odd collectivity, an odd collection of people; all longing for intimacy, or even simple touch, all alone in our single Chinese beds, thinking of our lovers far away. Peculiar primates, too clever by half.

SEPTEMBER 28, 1988. CHENGDU

Because Chengdu is Sichuan's capital, it is home to a very large proportion of people whose living depends on extended education. Many medical facilities, universities, and training institutes are concentrated around my guesthouse. Students are easy to meet, not only because they want to practice English, but because they are eager to feel out for themselves the contours of Westernness. They want to know what I think about women's and human rights, but they want a sense of the concrete, of "foreign life," too. On being quizzed at length by a young English teacher about American food habits, I incautiously reveal that we usually buy fish cut up, with the heads off.

"You people eat *dead fish?*" she gasped in disgust.

She'll probably never respect Hemingway again, but I taught her to say "Eeeeeuuuww, gross!" like a Valley Girl.

Extensive grapevines broadcast information about resident foreigners, so strangers sometimes show up at the gate with enough facts about me to get past the gatekeepers. One desperate-sounding young woman, a stranger, brings me a letter in English from a male American teacher who has written her in friendly fashion after his return home. A few minutes' conversation with her makes the reason for her visit clear: Is this a love letter? Is he serious? She really needs to know. As gently as I can, I tell her the letter means friendship, not love, and try to find out if she is pregnant. Her indignation convinces me that *that* is not the problem, only heartbreak. She is twenty-two, she says, and still not married.

"Doesn't the government encourage late marriage now?" I wonder.

"Oh yes, but nobody pays attention to that. *Everyone*—us girls—is married at twenty. If you're not, you have no future. All the boys want young women who aren't too sure of themselves, and everyone laughs at us old maids."

With due allowances for differences of style, conversations with students in Chengdu generally sound a lot like those with my undergraduates at Central Michigan University.

Focused on late adolescent terror at the burden of approaching adult decisions, such students make poor informants about their wider world. The Economic Management Training Institute's older students and young faculty, indeed intellectuals of all ages, however, have much to tell me about things they can not, or need not, tell their Chinese acquaintances. A middle-aged faculty woman, introduced casually at a Canadian party, announces in my living room:

"I have done nothing worthwhile in my life; I have traveled nowhere; my marriage is a disaster; my life is simply without value. Do your studies of women's lives have anything to teach me to improve myself?"

Thank goodness for the flimsy techniques ("Oh, really? What makes you feel that way?") learned in a few weekends of rape crisis counseling! Several women unbosom themselves to me about the hopeless difficulty of marriages in which there is no longer any feeling, but which they do not dare to abandon. Disgrace, shame for their children, poverty, inability to find alternative housing—some or all of these consequences of divorce would be too heavy to bear. Unable to help, I cry and comfort, reminding them that all of us must make our own peace within ourselves, that many Chinese women have survived divorce, that life alone can be serene, even joyful.

Younger intellectuals, especially men, speak of the cramped quality of their work lives. Maybe they will move ahead, find a comfortable position with enough autonomy and intellectual interest to make life worthwhile, and enough power to keep them safe from shifts in the political wind. But they greatly fear they will fail, will be trapped in mindless work under the bureaucratic thumb of equally mindless authority. Those who speak of such things are usually people with a family political history, some counterrevolutionary albatross hanging invisibly about their necks. Their stories are like those of the entrepreneurial women I interview, many of whom have concluded that their lingering class or political stigmata outweigh any achieved or possible educational attainments. With the road of learning closed to them, they bravely find something else to do with their lives: they make money, they become perfect, omniscient mothers, they dream of passports. But the intellectuals who sit edgily on my red plush chairs at the guesthouse want to hang on, at almost any cost, to their membership in a class that keeps its hands clean and channels a chosen few into positions of real power. They are not simply being elitist, although there is plenty of elitism to go round. When I suggest to one would-be administrator that he abandon this byzantine scholar-bureaucrat game and go into business for himself, he literally writhes.

"But we don't know what will happen to these reforms! Maybe everything entrepreneurs can do now will be criticized again! What would happen to my family—things would be even worse! Besides. I'd be ashamed. We Chinese have never respected merchants."

People who have already made their choice to do business are more stoical:

"No one can foresee the future. All we can do is use our abilities as best we can now, take care of our families, and hope that nothing goes wrong."

The shame of being declassed bothers men more than women, I would guess. One brilliant female acquaintance is trying tactfully to free herself from her school-teaching obligation in order to freelance as a translator or publisher's assistant.

"I feel strange about changing my class position. Even though translating is still intellectual work, I would have to go out and hustle to survive in it. But my work now is so narrow! I can't make any decisions, and the students in that working-class school don't really want to learn from me. I want more out of life than this!"

Should I tell her that in the United States most schoolteachers, office workers, managers, even politicians feel as she does, that their work is cramped and valueless, often boring and sometimes humiliating? That even a lucky teacher like myself subsists on an occasional student shooting star, a few good friends, and whatever inner resources I can muster? Better not. She needs hope that more humane work-lives can exist, somewhere. She probably would not find the fulfilling job she dreams of in the United States—I've heard too many rueful Chinese immigrant tales of how much they've lost for so little gained. The pep talk I pass back and forth with my colleagues, and pass on to my students—that we must invent and demand a genuinely socialist future—is useless here. The concepts, the language that might shape a vision of a better society, have been hopelessly devalued, like a chisel used to open paint cans, a screw stripped of its thread by a clumsy carpenter. I listen, and say little.

Now and then I hear of people who solve their job problems by upping stakes and moving to a more open part of the country—Hainan Island, or the export-processing zones of the southeast coast. But the pioneers I learn of all have powerful relatives to give them a start in their new workplaces. The spoils of development go disproportionately to the "sons and younger brothers" of high officials.

"Is this corruption?" I ask.

"No!" is the usual, startled response. "Who should look after you if not your own people! We Chinese really believe in family ties. People all try to pass opportunities on to their children, their kin. Corruption is much worse than that."

What do Chengdu people mean by corruption? They do not simply mean bribes for licenses, or high officials' children grabbing off all the best import-export opportunities. They mean the after-hours use of a company truck (and maybe some of the company's goods) to help in a wife's store; they mean that only families with members in local government win contracts for formerly collectively owned inns or clothing factories; they mean that medicines leak from hospitals for sale, cheap, to travelers who are then reimbursed back home for falsified receipts; they mean that illegal currency exchange funds an enormous trade in smuggled American cigarettes, sold openly everywhere; they mean that hookers now work in government hotels, and their tough managers hang out in all-night hot-pot joints; they mean businesswomen can afford one-thousand-yuan sweaters from Shanghai; they mean private cars, luxury houses, extravagant banquets at state expense. Where do people draw the lines between crime proper, an oxymoronic "ethical capitalism," and common or garden vulgarity? Educated, sometimes harshly, in an earlier version of socialism, many Chinese expect these boundaries to be well policed. But under "economic reform" which in large part equates to the appropriation of public goods by private persons with good connections, corruption is the essence of the system.

Every day I pass the huge image of Mao that no one dares tear down "because there are still many people in Chengdu who believe in what he taught us." Mao is still watching.

SEPTEMBER 30, 1988. CHENGDU

Pride goeth before embarrassment, if not destruction. Mine has just taken a considerable tumble. I was asked by the Canadians, and unhesitatingly agreed, to act as interpreter and go-between for the purchase of some paintings by two well-known local painters, a married couple. I know little enough about Chinese painting, although more than my Canadian friends, but art criticism is not the issue here. I am to be the negotiator over price. Well, I can do a little of that, and I speak well enough to mediate. With real artists—and these people are—one does not haggle. No problem.

We bike, on a glowing Sunday, to the Children's Cultural Palace where the painters teach gifted kiddies on the weekends. We meet, introduce ourselves, I express our pleasure in the examples of the artists' work we have previously seen, translate the words of praise for those we now see, chat about our presence in Chengdu, are delighted to learn of their recent exhibition, with other Sichuanese artists, in Gaoxiong City, Taiwan, arranged by the Sichuan Fellow Provincial Association of that town. The conversation is heavy going in spots, for while I have a fairly standard north-China accent, I have the vocabulary of an uneducated shopkeeper's daughter. This is perfectly natural; I talk mostly with shopkeepers. The artists, however, speak of tone values, of schools of Chinese painting, of levels of artistic production within a national hierarchy, and they do it in full-blooded Chengdu southern Mandarin. They speak no more in my (and their national) dialect than my entrepreneurial informants do. They are eloquent, allusive, literary (I think).

Incomprehension does not, after all, matter very much. I do not have to interpret most of this, for my Canadian clients are touring the paintings and divvying up the spoils. Eventually, however, the truly difficult moment arrives. How much does each of these objects of desire cost? the Canadians ask me. I am going to have to talk price to Chinese intellectuals; it is *not* going to be easy.

It is, in the event, far worse than I had imagined. I phrase my inquiry in the most general, the most genteel, the most periphrastic fashion I can. They understand me perfectly, they hide their amusement courteously, likely feeling some of their own. But neither wife nor husband can be brought to name a price. For anything.

"Bu hao shuo"—"It's hard to say" is their only answer. I back off, we talk about other things, we drink more fruit juice, I attempt to express my delight in the subtlety of his colors, the delicacy of her line. We agree that oil painting, which my mother does, is quite another matter, and cannot easily be compared with Chinese painting. The Canadians are looking puzzled. I edge toward the topic again.

"Bu hao shuo."

A Chinese idiom tells us that "The good is not sold, and the sold is no good." Might the artists be telling me, in the nicest possible way, that they do not want to sell their things? No, for each of them has offered to produce multiple copies within two weeks of pictures admired by multiple potential purchasers. I tell them about the Institute and the Canadians' role therein. These men are teachers, people with advanced degrees, lawyers, intellectuals, I point out. They collect paintings, and value them. They recognize the fine quality of what they are seeing, but do not know how much such paintings are worth in mere money terms. I myself, though I know a little about Chinese culture, am absolutely ignorant of such matters, and have come merely to try and translate for my friends. We would not dare to suggest a sum ourselves, for fear of unintentionally insulting their talent.

"Bu hao shuo."

There seems nothing for it but to ask if we might delay this difficult decision and return in a week when things might, perhaps, be clearer. How delightful, they say, with genuine enthusiasm. Come back next Sunday.

We do.

"Bu hao shuo."

By this time, I have taken the precaution of recounting the scene to several educated Chinese friends to be sure that selling the pictures was at least a possibility.

"Oh, of course they want to sell them. But they're embarrassed to quote a price."

"Why?"

"Well, they're artists, you see, not merchants."

I understand that well enough, of course. I am writing a book about the difference in economic outlook and practices of merchants versus scholars in traditional China.

"But how do you get them to tell us how much?" I ask.

"You can't. You offer them money, and they give you the pictures."

"How do I know how much to offer?"

"If it's not enough, it'll be embarrassing."

Right.

The end of the story is as uncomfortable as its beginning. On the second visit, I have assembled enough information to hazard a guess at the price of an extremely elaborate bird-and-flower painting. Their faces fall. The only way to save the situation—by now I am fully under the spell of Chinese politesse and fast losing any concern for my friends' pocketbooks—is to offer considerably more for the next one. That seems about right. Suddenly, the deal is done. I figure out about how much I'd lost the woman painter on the first guess and buy a landscape for myself at a price that, I hope, will even things out. With exquisite, two-edged kindness, the injured artist makes me a present of a sketch of fine-leaved narcissus for my role in this fiasco, which I will receive at our next meeting. They will invite us all to a dinner to celebrate the initiation of our friendship.

I attempt to escape having coals of fire thus heaped upon my head by scheduling an important meeting for the feast day, but it is no use. The Canadians bring me my gift, along with a lovely stone name-seal, carved by the artists' talented son, and the couple's warmest regards. The painting is unsaleably flawed by an ill-painted leaf. I imagine them rolling their eyes, wondering in mutual amusement whether I'll even notice, and if I do, if I'll recognize the insult.

"She probably meant well," I imagine the husband saying.

"Bu hao shuo," his wife replies.

OCTOBER 3, 1988. CHENGDU

The Fulian's cast of thousands has been reduced, for my purposes, to a manageable team of four: Hua Xinghui, Li Jufang, Jiang Yinghong (whom we call Teacher Jiang), and Lu Xiaocui, grandly addressed as Lu Fubuzhang: the vice (fu) head (zhang) of the propaganda unit (bu), to which we are all attached. Lu and Jiang spell each other when other duties call. Hua falls ill for a couple of weeks early in the work and is replaced by a wonderfully giddy daughter of someone important. Her English is better than Hua's, but then I don't need English translation particularly, only the reformulation of some Chengdu patois into more standard Chinese. When Hua returns to work, our work group settles into efficacious routine.

Each weekday morning, I bike out to the day's subjects with Hua or Li; the other team meets us for lunch to discuss that morning's and the previous afternoon's interviews. Frequently the second team suggests, or I request, that I meet some of the women I have not formally interviewed, so we vary the daily routine of about six hours of hard listening with a few more casual visits. Sometimes, I go out with Li, but rarely with Jiang or Lu, who will not bicycle in Chengdu's dangerous traffic.

Hua intimidates me at first. Stocky and direct, her stint in the People's Liberation Army and her research trips to the United States and Colombia have given her considerable fluency in English and the confidence of a tugboat. She is funny, relaxed, a woman who plainly loves her husband and adores her son. The Cultural Revolution enabled her to move from village life to Sichuan University and then into a prestigious place in the military. Transfer to the Women's Federation has made it possible for her small family to stay together in the city where her husband works and where she can best educate her son. By comparison with this much younger woman, I feel like a dithering airhead.

This anxiety too, she smooths away. She is too down-to-earth, too lacking in pretentiousness in any form, too ready to laugh at all of our misadventures to be genuinely threatening. I am invited for a delicious dinner in her tony beige apartment picked out in black, treasured stereo equipment:

"It's all take-out; we don't have time to cook in this house. But I made the pickles," she confides.

Li and Teacher Jiang are invited, too, though not their husbands or children. From differences in temperament and age, these are good comrades rather than intimate friends, and Chinese do not invite spouses to what are essentially business dinners. Hua's husband is there, but mostly in capacity of waiter. The tall, teenaged son appears to eat, to offer polite greetings and good-byes to the various aunties, and to retreat to his books under the radiant maternal gaze.

It takes me much longer to like Teacher Jiang. Initially, I assume that she is trouble, that she will report my improprieties, that she will block me whenever I stray from the mission of the propaganda section, that I will want to kneecap her before we are done. Looking back, this was a reasonable assumption. It simply happened to be wrong.

Jiang is fluent with the party line on every conceivable subject, taking her job of instructing me with great seriousness. I begin to see the sly humor that motivates her colleagues' continued use of her pedagogue's title. A Southeast Asian Chinese by birth, her family sent her "home" to the Fujian coast and thence to prestigious Beijing Normal University, sparing her the dangers of mid-1960s Indonesian massacres of ethnic Chinese. She arrived at Beijing Normal just in time for the Cultural Revolution to explode around her: at its worst, the campus was an armed camp. In those years, commitment to Maoism was all. Jiang became an activist, eventually graduated in Russian, and was posted to Sichuan. Here, she taught for some years, as did her husband, until she was transferred into the Women's Federation when Russian-teaching became a dead letter.

Such a career develops one's talents for political correctness. But not Suharto, or homesickness, or the Cultural Revolution, or being condemned to a lifetime of spicy food seem really to have altered Jiang's fundamental good sense, decency, and love of scholarship. She has plunged into our project, worked assiduously to find interesting interview subjects and cajole them into revelations I could never have elicited, writes and publishes essays from our materials, and tells me when to shape up for the good of the group. Only she, in the face of my moments of hypochondria, has ever had the wisdom to tell me crossly to get a grip.

Jiang lives in an apartment belonging to her husband's work unit, a long and gruesome bus commute from either the Fulian or my guesthouse. We go there for dinner now and then, enjoying her witty husband's amiable commentary on our "boss ladies," seeing photos of her grown and absent son and daughter, watching TV, chatting with friends who drop by. The apartment is large, comfortable, well-furnished, but Jiang does not have a decorator's eye. In her sunroom-breakfast nook, she grows a jungle of flowers, and she promises me cuttings from her night-blooming cereus to smuggle back into the States.

It is a long time before Li Jufang invites us to her installment of this rotating dinner club.

"My apartment is so small, so dark, so ugly. I'm ashamed to have you there; we know Americans have beautiful houses. It's on the first floor, not a good location at all. You will laugh at my furniture, but it's so expensive with two children, we can't afford to buy a lot of things!"

This first-floor flat in the Women's Federation is small and dark and crowded, but I find it homey to have to move the sports equipment out of the way in the narrow hall by the toilet, to see these two shy, attractive children—girl and boy—weave in and out of the adult goings-on. Li's husband is almost exactly the same medium height and chunky weight as she. From behind, with their short hair, sports jackets, and trousers, they are hard to tell apart, salt and pepper shakers. Touchingly, they are similarly shy, given to blushing, to down-turned eyes, to modest disclaimers of any competence extreme even by Chinese standards. They went to the same high school, but never spoke until they attended Xinan Normal University together and were ready for marriage. Husband became a professor, probably the sort of absent soul who eats his frog and dissects his sandwich.

"We could get a flat at the university, but they are not very big, and Jufang would have to commute a long way every day," he offers to the conversation, which continues to revolve around real estate. "You know how afraid she is of riding a bicycle."

Oh dear.

Li Jufang, with whom I often ride to interviews, has occasionally mentioned how dangerous bike riding is, and how I must be careful. In my usual perverse, egocentric fashion, I have assumed she is worried about me. To show how unnecessary such concern is, I have generally responded by pedaling faster, taking more chances. Poor Jufang, getting a foreigner who emulates the Hell's Angels.

Li Jufang has come the furthest distance up China's social ladder of any of our group. Born in a distant village that was extremely hard-hit during the "Three Bad Years" of the Great Leap Forward in the late 1950s, the Cultural Revolution—and her unselfish meticulousness—brought her, too, to university in a way that must have seemed like magic to her friends. Teaching Russian, marriage to a fellow-student, transfer to the Women's Fed: Jufang has never left Sichuan, and has to be reminded to speak to me in Putonghua instead of her native Sichuanese. Though almost overly deferential to my quirks, she is transformed when we interview. Her shyness vanishes, and she pursues an ambiguity with terrier tenacity.

After a round of these familial dinners, I make the effort to cook for Hua, Jiang, and Li in my newly opened kitchen. It is a disaster in respect to food, if not to fun. The guesthouse kitchens are equipped with two gas rings and a sink jutting out of the wall; there is no counter space, and the pots, pans, and dishes have been scrounged from what the earlier-settled Canadians did not want. Excuses aside, the meal was bad enough to prompt me to vindicate Western cuisine by inviting them to the elaborate set lunch of Chengdu's premier French restaurant.

Two of our three had never eaten foreign food and were curious. Hua, who had, was tolerant. A salad of barefacedly raw vegetables, onion soup with stringy, unmanageable cheese, bland and strangely sauced fish, roasted half-chickens that vigorously resisted the unaccustomed fork, bread instead of rice, and a sugary / creamy dessert that could have induced lactose-intolerance in a Norwegian left them hungry, puzzled, and unimpressed. As I was paying the check, I heard the whisper,

"Western food is supposed to be full of nutrition, but you'd think they'd learn to make it taste like something, too."

CHAPTER EIGHT

城都行

Paying Calls

OCTOBER 5, 1988. CHENGDU

Leaving our luncheon restaurant (bad Princess Chicken, good eels, not enough vegetables) at two, we set off to find Mother-in-law Zhu (Fulian workers habitually address older women by this respectful title). Widowed early, she had run a small brewing business before Liberation, when women entrepreneurs were less common than they have now become.

Her house is hard to find, for the streets in this old part of town change their names every block. The address we want—Gold Fish Street—is homonymous, except for tone, with Gold Jade Street, which everyone keeps sending us to when we ask directions. I thought only foreigners made such mistakes. Li and Hua remind me that they are provincial-level workers; the city is not their beat. Finally, at four, we find the tiny alley into which the Zhu front door opens. We are hot and bothered, but Mother-in-law Zhu, at sixty, having made her own way during hard times before Liberation and after, handles inconvenience with aplomb. Her gray bob, her blue tunic and pants, her soft, cloth shoes in the old style mark her as the generation of women who "came out" to work only after the revolution. In fact, she ran her own business before Liberation, though from need more than from choice.

Two people can hardly pass in the alley she shares with a dozen households, but inside, the house is comfortably spacious: a living room with bamboo chairs and sofa, and three bedrooms for herself, her son and daughter-in-law, and her two grandsons. An unenclosed kitchen lean-to and outhouse toilet stand in a small courtyard. The living room is skylighted, an aquarium with goldfish balances the TV. Zhu has lived here for twenty-five years, since she bought the place for 500 yuan in 1963. Her son, daughter-in-law, and two grandsons are at work, her housework is done, she has enjoyed just sitting, thinking of what she would tell us.

She grew up in a rural household with a family business: making and selling *cao xi*—woven reed bed mats. Her family was a large one, with seven elder and one younger brothers, one elder sister, three sisters-in-law, her mother, and two of her father's brother's sons all living together at the time of her marriage. She married at nineteen; her husband died when she was twenty-two.

After my father died, when I was only a few years old, my first six brothers stopped studying to became apprentices in brocade making, paint manufacture, and automobile driving and repair. There was enough money for me to study. For a while, I learned from a tutor who taught several neighboring girls together, and then attended home economics classes at a girls' school.

My classmates and I studied very diligently, leaving no time to play like other children. My studies continued until I graduated from middle school at eighteen, when I began to help at home with the cooking and washing. At that age, too, my mother began to expect me to learn formal etiquette. When I performed these duties well, my oldest brother or his wife gave me new clothes; otherwise, I got nothing new to wear.

Forms of etiquette existed for every part of life. When guests came, we young girls just served them, waiting till later to eat ourselves. We were taught not to open our mouths while laughing enough to show our teeth, and so on. This training was useful later while doing business; my manners showed that I was from a respectable family. Even though I had to work outside and rub shoulders with all kinds of people, people respected me because of my mother's training.

Young women were expected to keep close to home in those days. Even after I was married, I was not allowed to go out, even to a nearby shop. If I needed money, I asked my parents-in-law, or they gave me some at festivals so I could amuse myself a little. My in-laws used to go to temples and festivals, but I didn't like to spend money, and always saved as much as I could. Then, if I wanted a pretty dress and the family wouldn't buy it for me, I could use my own. On my New Year return visits to my mother's house, my parents gave me money. My parents-in-law were really good to their daughters-in-law. They were very capable, too, which was just as well. Because my husband was no good at business. He depended on his mother for business sense—he didn't like to haggle and negotiate. He would rather have done electrical work.

When my husband died, I had two little ones to support, and I needed to work. I could only get work as a maid. I said, "I'm a cultured person! I can't do that!" So I started to work in my husband's business. He had begun in reed bed mats, but switched to liquor. He'd left ninety *jin* of liquor. From four relatives I borrowed twenty more *jin* from each, making eighty more as new capital. Every month, when I bought new supplies, I paid for half of it first, then paid the other half after it was sold. It was very hard at first, since I still had to borrow from relatives for a long time. When I dealt with people who weren't relatives, I had to pay the whole cost of things until I'd established my creditworthiness with the seller. Then he'd trust me once, then twice, until I had a solid reputation. Finally I could afford to hire a girl to help with the children. I gave her one yuan each month, and she ate with us.

To get into the market, I had to buy goods by the standard shoulder-pole load—200 *jin!* I went around to other businesses to learn things, especially to Old Boss Wang, who had a good business. I would help *them* by picking good-sounding characters for their signs. Old Wang told me to ask the carriers for the prices, because they knew the market every day, and how to avoid middlemen. By the time I was thirty, I had learned all the tricks. I learned to detect whether the liquor was watered, and how to determine its alcohol content by how a chopstick floats in it. And to *smell* it! Everyone treated me well, never cheated me, because I was pretty good at it. People came to trust me in business; local people all supported me when people were being classed as capitalists after Liberation. They said I was an honest producer, not an exploiter.

At first I knew how to make only two kinds of liquor, but later learned the methods for more than ten kinds. I could earn a decent living, more than our daily needs, putting some into increasing my capital.

After 1956, when the cooperatives were organized, my shop was merged with ten other sellers of salt, cigarettes, and other things. In that cooperative, men generally sold the liquor, but I was in the liquor section. It was right over there on Ningxia Street. I earned 25 yuan a month at the beginning; specialty cooks in the co-op got 30; ordinary workers 18. People didn't necessarily get work in their own old business, but I did. I became accountant in the co-op.

By then, my parents-in-law had died, so I managed alone. (That was when I got the babysitter in to take care of the children.) I was so busy I gave all the money over to the babysitter to take care of!

When I entered the cooperative, my house, with the shop and brewery, was worth 400 [yuan]. My total capital amounted to 785.25 yuan, including equipment, stock, everything. The co-op gave me 30 yuan in interest every year on the 785. I put the interest in the bank.

Why had I wanted to run my own business? For one thing, I could stay at home and take care of kids while earning my living that way. Also—if you work for others, things get complicated, there can be trouble for a woman. Some people have no culture. And I didn't want to put up with other people's tempers. I had *good* relations with everyone around. I behaved very strictly, never used makeup, but was always clean and neat. Proper behavior and etiquette are really important. Women have to watch out for themselves and insist on good behavior.

My oldest sister also lost her husband. She had four small children, and was worse off than I was. To our way of thinking, you couldn't remarry—it wasn't decent. I helped my sister with money—I basically supported her for many years.

After collectivization, I worked in our branch of the City Grain Company for twenty-two years until I retired in 1980 at 75 percent of my former pay. That had been 70 yuan, so I now get 62.8 each month. I cook breakfast and dinner—my children and grandchildren are all workers in state industry, so they have good canteens for lunch—and I do the food shopping and manage the household's money. Everyone in the house washes their own clothes; the housework is not heavy. In 1983 I was a group leader for women's work in the local Street-and-Lane Committee. We reminded women about birth control and so forth. But I don't have the energy to do that anymore, so I stay quietly at home and enjoy my retirement.

I've told you about my work; let me tell you about some of our Chengdu customs for women. Marriage is just as important as work for women. Under socialism, women's work has changed a lot, and marriage has changed too.

In my time, people were starting to marry for love, but families still didn't agree to such independence. Girls met boys at school, but didn't dare tell their parents. They kept it secret. My future husband was a very good student who got very upset if he wasn't at least third in his class. I didn't know him to speak to—I wouldn't have dared have a boyfriend—but he was well known because lots of girls were chasing him.

I figured out that my mother's elder sister's relative knew his family. He only had a mother, and not much money. But my family got our relative to act as go-between so we would have been properly introduced, and negotiations started. Our relatives arranged for my husband and me to meet in a formal way. We didn't dare look at each other—that was not permitted. Only when my brother was talking to his mother did I sneak a look at my future mother-in-law. When I got into the rickshaw to leave, his whole family and all the neighbors clustered around the door staring at me and whispering that I was to be the bride. It was all awfully awkward.

On her return call, if a prospective mother-in-law didn't like the look of a girl (and she looked her all over), then things would not go forward. She'd just politely leave without eating the prepared meal, and that would be the end of it. If she stayed and ate, the go-between passed information back and forth until both families knew enough about each other. We were very enlightened. In the countryside, young people didn't meet at all. The fathers met at a teahouse and made the initial contract.

Once an engagement contract had been signed by both sets of parents, a girl had to embroider a pair of handkerchiefs for the husband's family to show her embroidery skills. She also had to make embroidered garters for them, everything in pairs, and a little apron with pockets—very pretty. Her husband would wear it on holidays to show off his fiancée's skill and love for him. The embroidery on both sides of the handkerchiefs was different; both sides were "face" pictures—there was no backside. It was very fine embroidery. I gave my mother-in-law-to-be two pairs of socks, a pair of shoe tops embroidered with cranes and other symbols like cicadas. These images referred to the blood shed by mothers in childbirth and menstruation. They expressed a girl's wish that her mother-in-law would be spared punishment in the afterlife for her "crime" of polluting the world with this blood. It showed she was a filial daughter-in-law.

Our family also sent his some packages of rice cakes that represented long life. On a carrying chair, my husband's family sent ours four kinds of delicacies, several kinds of silk and cotton cloth in four colors, cosmetics for me, and a pair of gold rings. My family sent back the rings with our two personal names engraved on them. They sent us no brideprice at my engagement, although my elder sister's in-laws sent some for her. Only the go-between accompanied these gifts that formalized our engagement—my husband and his family didn't come in person.

While we were engaged, we didn't see each other, but they sent people to visit Mother when she was very ill. A lot of his relatives came. We entertained them a few days, so I was able to see him in this group. We were a very enlightened family. In less progressive families, this wouldn't have been allowed. These meetings were embarrassing, but they put my mind at ease. In the old arranged marriages where the couple never saw each other, if the husband didn't like the wife's looks when she came as a bride, terrible things could happen. He might spend the wedding night reading, or go out with the wedding guests. Then she'd have to go home. Or he might agree to keep her, but very soon set her aside and take another wife, leaving the unwanted one to do all the housework.

Before the engagement, our names had been sent out to see if our horoscopes matched, and they really didn't! So my mother-in-law opposed our marriage. But my fiancé really liked me, and told his mother that if she got him a different wife, he'd *still* love me. So Mother-in-law gave in. We really fell in love. Our parents finally let us write letters to each other. I made slippers for him, and he gave me a necklace with his picture in it. [She still smiles when she talks of him.]

He started the letter-writing—I wouldn't have. His first letter asked only about my family's welfare, with nothing personal in it. My Father opened it, and everyone read it. The second I was allowed to open myself—it even had my name on it. We corresponded for nearly two years before we married. He wrote very warmly, I was more reserved. For a while, we wrote every two or three days. But his sisters got jealous, so I told him to burn my letters and not write so often.

This felt lonely, so I asked my parents to hurry up and start the marriage. Ten days later, we were married. I was nineteen. For my marriage, my family sent a dowry of a bed, four clothes chests, bedding (including quilts and a fine hemp mosquito net), and a set of clothing for me for each season. On the day before the wedding, my husband's family sent over a set of five pieces of wedding clothing to be worn at the ceremony. The five pieces showed that they hoped I would have five children.

There were so many marriage customs in those days!

If you set the marriage date, you shouldn't back out; if you've ridden in the bridal chair, then you *really* can't.

Both sides invite guests to the wedding feast at the groom's home—in some parts of China, only the husband's family invites guests.

At *bao qiu* [when the marriage date is set], the husband's family sends the woman's side gifts: four each of chickens, ducks, fish, pig heads or pig legs, and one *dan* of liquor. The woman's family has to pay the bearers for these, although the husband's family pays men hired to carry the dowry on the wedding day. At *bao qiu,* the bride's family sends the groom cloth and a hat. The man's side sends food; the woman's side sends clothes. Both sides separately invite and pay for their own guests at *bao qiu.*

Before the wedding, a bride goes to each elder in her household to cry and sing bridal laments because she is leaving them. Then they give her money—this was especially the custom in the countryside. I didn't do this—it was sort of old-fashioned—but it was still required that I at least pretend to cry. Only women in their 70s and 80s would remember any of the laments now. The songs reminded the family of how much they would miss the daughter when she was gone, and thanked elders for their care in bringing her up. Some girls used to complain that their dowries weren't big enough, and try to get gifts by singing pathetic songs.

A girl can keep these little red envelopes of gift money as her private hoard, hiding it in a box of her own, but I gave the wedding money that friends gave me to my elder brother. Some rural girls traditionally got forty silver dollars. Rich families gave their daughters silver jewelry as well, but poor girls might get almost no dowry, especially if the husband's family sent only food. City girls in my day thought all this was a bit crude, though.

I was carried to my husband's house in a *very* fine sedan chair, the newest and best. I was all made up, wearing a red veil, just like on television. Clothes were like official clothes with dragons on. A bride was like a female heavenly official—like the Minister of Foreign Affairs. Even officials would give way to her. She was like an official returning to the Central Government—to her husband. She had one day of outranking everyone. Everyone must respect her—that's why the chair is so important.

Not all women married in this dignified way. In our area, families sometimes brought their daughters-in-law into the family when they were eight or nine years old. They'd be older than the boy, who might be between three and five. They were just like slave girls, and came to their new home riding in a small chair, not a big red one. When the boy became eighteen, his family invited guests, the bride made up her face and wore red clothes. Sometimes she went home to her mother for three days beforehand, and was sent back to her marriage with some style, but she got no dowry.

If a bride was not a virgin, the man's family might decide to send her home. The husband's parents went to the bride's and, kneeling formally, asked them to take her back. The husband's family could write a document freeing the girl to marry again. The girl put her footprints and handprints on it. Or—if the bride's family were to find she was ill treated by her husband, they could try to get her back legally.

A daughter-in-law arrives with vegetables that need washing. Our hostess shepherds us through the maze of alleys to the street once more and firmly closes the huge door in the anonymous brick wall behind us. We giggle again over our earlier errors in orienteering and rush off to our own dinners.

When we made up our initial list of interviewees, I specified that I wanted to see "women in a wide range of small, family-based businesses." Over the past few days, the Fulian has been overdoing the "wide range" part to the serious detriment of the "family-based" part. We have seen half a dozen women recently who turn out to have been accountants in city or state enterprises, sometimes with no family business background at all.

My commitment to real social science orthodoxy is shallow in spots; rather than fussing about contaminating my sample, I have been fascinated by these visits. Though they detour from my main path, getting into the blocks of workers' flats that huddle around Chengdu's many large state factories clarifies for me what my businesswomen are *not* as I learn more about what state workers are: not prospering, not insecure, not displaying vivid individualism in new houses with new decor, not interstitial and cautious. To my eye, these urban socialist villagers are more like rural dwellers than like the producer households I mostly study. The entrepreneurial families, after all, have cash, tools, and valuable stock lying around; they do best when they and their workers are closemouthed before strangers, who might, after all, be tax assessors or sanitary inspectors; they are set up to deal with a constant stream of customer–strangers using a superficial hospitality and a fundamental defensiveness.

The inhabitants of an apartment block that is shared only by workmates relate differently to their homes and their neighbors. Their lives, to each other, are comparatively open books. So-and-so is a grade eight machine operator? Then she makes so much, lives in an apartment with so many square meters, has the same problem as everyone else in the block with low water and gas pressure, knows she will retire at fifty-five with 80 percent of her salary. She has never had a lot of money to spend—though she always has had enough to eat, and no worries about buying housing or where her children will be schooled. She will not have spent any money fixing up her flat because that is the company's responsibility. She has nothing much to steal. Neighbor children tear in and out of each other's houses, and women visitors follow the old country custom of calling out as they come up the stairs, then walking right in. These workers do not have to make a place for themselves, or to justify their existence. They are what the decades of revolution have been

Opera-costume Wigmaker, 1988

about. Like peasants on the land, they live here because the factory needs them, and the factory exists because of, and through, their labor.

Hopeless bourgeois that I am, much of this comes to me from a starting point of housewifely dismay. These dwellings are perhaps the ugliest arrangements for living on this earth. While the housing of "intellectual" work units near my guesthouse is softened with trees and open spaces, worker housing is often devoid of any greenery but what people grow in pots. The constant rain of pollution from nearby smokestacks makes maintaining basic cleanliness a hard task, and no one wastes energy on frills like sweeping the public stairs and landings. The oldest and poorest industrial complexes were built with no private toilets, and the common-use ones—usually on the landings—are noisome. Walls, floors, and ceilings are unfaced concrete, lightened, sometimes, with whitewash. Door and window frames are clumsily carpentered, letting in storms and mosquitoes in their season. The rows and ranks of gray and crumbly seven-story buildings around dank airshafts and malodorous alleys are truly grim.

Like rural folk who consider a house with a tight roof, a dining table, and a few wooden stools well furnished, these families in their concrete cells often view their housing as fully adequate, homey, and unpretentious. In such homes, I hear a lot about the value of work connections that reliably provide things much more substantial than wallpaper and Formica.

"The Fulian woman who told us when to be home for your visit said you were interviewing a lot of those new-rich businesswomen. Well, we're workers in this family. You wouldn't catch us doing anything sleazy like that!" said Old Liang, a gap-toothed retiree.

We reminded him that we were here to meet his daughter, who was starting to do well in her one-woman glass-cutting business. She has a mobile, folding stall, and has closed up early today to be at home with her husband and fat little boy for our interview.

"But that's different. My daughter is doing something with her hands, something people need. It's just like being a worker. She'd have been a worker, too, but the factories don't hire girls much anymore. I retired so my son could take my job here at the bicycle corporation, but we couldn't find a way to get her in, so she's doing this glass business. It's not her fault."

"Your daughter and her family live with you I see," I tossed out.

"Our family got very lucky with this apartment twenty years ago, when we were assigned. We got an extra room, and we managed to keep it all those years. So when she married this young fellow—his unit is too small to provide housing—they just stayed on here. Makes it a nice big family."

He smiled his innocent, almost dopey smile. I realized I was in the presence of proletarian genius.

"And the glass she sells? Isn't that hard to buy?"

"Yes, it is. But her old Dad puts in a word with the factory buyer, and they give us a bit of a break. After all, we're an old worker family: me, my wife, my son, my daughter-in-law. It's a good work unit." He looked smug.

When the daughter and her family arrive, we ask our usual questions of "Little" Liang, who, like all Chinese women now, keeps her maiden name. She answers with enthusiasm, assuming full credit for her slow, handsome husband, her fine boy, her business independence. The world is her hotpot.

People who want to know how Chinese women choose occupations in this ever-more-fluid economy often urge me to include more in my interviews about their self-expression, their identity, how these women find their career paths. I ask Liang one of these confectionery questions.

"Well, you see, my father knows the man who orders the sheet glass for the factory. . . . " Kin ties, pragmatism, timely opportunity, not "when I grow up, I'm going to be a ballet dancer" are what shape working-class careers in China, and probably everywhere else as well.

OCTOBER 9, 1988. CHENGDU

We have blundered into another inappropriate interview, and it is very short. Wife and husband are both well educated, in their late seventies, plainly, even poorly dressed. Their sixth-floor flat is stark and pitilessly clean. What was her work before she retired?

"I was an accountant in this factory."

And before the revolution?

"We had a building-supplies business."

She gives me short, precise answers, but never a spare word. When I am through—in this chilly atmosphere, we are done in under an hour— I put away notebook and pen.

"I don't like to talk about that business, so long ago. I really had nothing to do with it. I was a wife. I did what my husband and his parents told me to. Because of that business, we were called capitalist elements.

In the Cultural Revolution, Red Guards came and threw all our furniture—even the TV—out the window, and burned it in the courtyard. Don't include me in your writing as a businesswoman. All I ever tried to do was to work at what I knew how to do. That was accounting, because my parents sent me to high school. It's just that simple."

October 10, 1988. Chengdu

A chemist believes—with reason—that her presence in the lab has no effect on the processes in her test tubes. An anthropologist, however, is not merely an observer, or even a situation-containing Florence flask. She is, herself, one of the reagents, part of the chemistry. The people anthropologists meet present a different face to us—apparently irrationally snoopy outsiders—than the ones they turn toward their mothers, a police officer, or their boss. As anthropologists, we are not usually very interested in the impression they wish to make on us except as something to factor out. We hope rather to see past the odd products of an unnatural interchange to the ways in which they engage with each other.

Like everyone else, most Chinese would like us to see them as good to their mothers, law-abiding before the police, and diligent at work. It is interesting, part of our job, to see how they define "being a good mother," "honesty," and "working well"; distinctions in such values are the very stuff of cultural difference. But *asking* about values, indeed about behavior in general, calls those we talk to into a relationship with *us. Our* presence, *our* anticipated response, becomes part of any answer. In extreme cases—and there seem to be many of these in China—an interview resembles a catechism. The respondent struggles to find the "right" answers to my questions, answers that will show me she knows her society's ideals and strives to approximate them. Like a catechumen, she assumes I am testing her on an important intellectual code rather than wanting to know concrete things about her none-too-perfect reality. And, like a catechumen, she fears not me—not Hill Gates, a bafflingly meaningless intrusion into her morning routine—but the Chinese authority that stands behind me, that requires she pass this test. It is necessary to acknowledge one's own presence in the paying of a call, and even more necessary to accept that that presence is virtually empty, for the respondent, of one's own, complex self.

On some subjects, straight questions and answers between strangers are possible. "What year were you born? How much schooling did you have?"—these are plain sailing. But "How many children do you have?", while simply a matter of fact for older women, becomes an edgy issue for those bearing children under the one-child policy. Admitting to two may be an embarrassment to herself and to the local cadre responsible for maintaining reproductive order in her neighborhood. "How long have you run this business?" is another hard question. Older women, talking of a family firm existing before the 1949 revolution, will want to minimize the degree to which their families might have been seen as capitalist. Younger ones, starting up since the privatizations of the late 1970s, like to stress that they got in early and are well established, but would not care to confess to jumping the gun.

One of the trickiest inquiries for these entrepreneurs is "How many workers do you hire?". A government regulation distinguishes between "individual" firms that may hire up to seven people and the larger, more heavily taxed "private" firms that hire eight or more. Our figures for numbers of employees show a sharp spike at "seven." Some bosses are cautious in their hiring so as to remain licensed at the "individual" level, a sort of amateur standing, others are simply rounding down their actual payroll to avert trouble.

We are two women, sitting on tiny stools in a doorway, representing international feminism, U.S.–China relations, state and society, and our individual likes and dislikes to each other. Whether in China or in Chad, the anthropologist's job is to wrest some useful generality from this intense, human particularism. It isn't easy.

Always, the best fieldwork tool is the eye of the beholder. Unlike anthropologists who live and die by the word, I like to watch. I trust the common humanity I share with these women to alert me through posture or tone that we have hit a nerve. The way a woman touches a grandchild or spars with her husband are surer signs of family amity and spousal trust than any questions I might frame.

Looking carefully at the things that inhabit a house along with the people is also effort well spent. The semiotic of Chinese domestic decor is not so different from my own. The rectangular rooms with locking doors have recognizable furniture and appliances, not parents' graves under the floor or sharply distinguished male versus female spaces. Family histories of accomplishment are hung on walls as photos and certificates, inherited dowry furniture shares the living room with the grandson's motor bike, and if the household has a washing machine or refrigerator, it will probably be visible from where I sit. I can read this stuff—we all shop at K-Mart today.

What matters most to fieldwork, though, I cannot have on these excursions. Only time can really peel away formality, give context to the women's words, and show me the consistency and consequences of their actions. The classical anthropologist would camp on these boss-ladies' doorsteps until they grow weary of putting up a front.

OCTOBER 12, 1988. CHENGDU

We are at the halfway point—fifty interviews complete. My assistants have gratified me by insisting so hard that *I* must be tired by our routine that I understand that *they* are growing weary too. It is time for a rest. After this refreshment, we will resume twice-daily interviews at the moderate pace of four days a week, broken by coding on Wednesdays and Saturday mornings—the schedule I had originally requested.

The gentle game of wearing me out so they could get on about the work without me has been played for weeks. Every evening, after a day in which often three hours or more were spent on bicycles in heavy traffic, they would ask kindly, hopefully,

"Are you going out again tomorrow?"

They took my cheerful affirmative like women, however, and out we went.

Their motives for trying to get me to stay out of the interviewing are mixed, I think. The political sensitivities I had so feared would complicate our interviews have so far been nearly invisible. Our subjects understand well the limits of what should be opened to me. One of these unexpectedly open topics is the Cultural Revolution. The government derives some of its current legitimacy from publicizing the very real tragedies of this period. Foreigners are easily titillated by its horror stories, and the years 1966 to 1976 are used as a lightning rod to distract attention from earlier, more disastrous moments of revolutionary history. The Cultural Revolution, last of the Maoist attempts to reshape Chinese life, though dramatic and even lethal for the educated elite, had relatively trivial effects on those who did not depend on education or "culture" to make their livings. Earlier events—the initial 1949 revolution itself, the anti-Rightist and Great Leap into communization of the 1950s—reshuffled property and jobs, and hence class status, in ways that deeply altered life for everyone. The process often hurt, and its enduring pain still cannot be discussed with foreigners.

The only moment of real anxiety about bringing political trouble on my associates here occurred some days ago, after an unusually forthright and angry woman told us—spontaneously and in detail—about her family's very raw deal in the mid-1950s. Labeled "rightists" by a spiteful neighbor, they lost all claim to their small machine shop. Her openness surprised me, but I assumed that this was one more example of the ideological thaw of which our project was the happy beneficiary.

A few days later, I was called to the gatehouse to meet a young man I did not know. Introducing himself as a fellow social scientist, he quickly made the purpose of his visit clear: our interviews had raised an alarm in no less a venue than the provincial governor's office. A short chain of gossipy coincidences had raised the specter that I was really investigating the anti-Rightist movement.

"Watch it, will you? That could really get people in trouble. I know—I tried to write an undergraduate thesis about the movement a few years ago, and nearly got thrown out of school," he said, ruefully.

The Fulian's gentle attempts to keep me from interviewing has apolitical motivations as well. Genuine concern for a foreigner's health is common among Chinese who deal with visitors, for we are mostly jet-lagged tourists and businesspeople having trouble adjusting to an alien environment. The Fulian are quite reasonably concerned for my safety on the busy streets, for my boasted bicycle commuting in Mt. Pleasant is far from sophisticated by their standards. Chengdu bikers ride eight inches apart, stop for nothing short of ten-ton trucks, and have frequent minor but dramatic collisions. Getting me off the streets would have spared my assistants considerable practical anxiety.

Also, of course, there is the matter of face. Isabella Bird Bishop shamed and infuriated the Chinese with whom she was associated because she refused to ride in a covered sedan chair; a brand-new bicycle is the best compromise I can offer, but it is not a limousine.

Chengdu people feel they have been a bit cut off from the great world, and the Fulian women are pleased to be participating in international research. How that research—and I as the principal researcher—is identified can enhance or detract from the tone of the project. High-ranking people do not doodle around on bicycles in the rain, wade down muddy streets, and sit shivering in the meanest of apartments. Underlings do these things for them. And underlings bask in the reflected glory of the personage (invisible except on formal occasions) who retain them. I owed it to my assistants, as well as to myself, to show a little class. As I refused to do so, they stepped up the frequency with which they referred to me as a professor and a Ph.D., and widened the geographical range of my researches considerably beyond what my resume claims when they introduced me.

With some of our subjects there are advantages to having me along, but on some interviews I am sure my assistants wish me gone. Women have told us some unpleasant stories—blighted educational hopes, miserable marriages, lives ruined by political campaigns. Once, our intended subject simply shooed us off her doorstep. But the assistants translate and explain everything, as far as I can tell, neither concealing nor softening what the women themselves say.

At the halfway point, it is clear that I am in this, in person, for the long haul. But one assistant has been noted to have lost weight, another to look tired often. Lu Fubuzhang, our group leader and sometime replacement interviewer, announces we are going on a trip.

CHAPTER NINE

城都行

R and R in a Van

OCTOBER 13, 1988. CHENGDU

Entertainments provided for foreigners by sponsoring work units in China are command performances. While the pleasure of the entertainee is certainly hoped for, it may well not be the primary purpose of the event. Here and in Taiwan, I have been honored with a good deal of this kind of hospitality and have learned that its postponement or refusal may destabilize some very complicated social relationships. Trips and dinners are occasions when unit personnel may legitimately invite friends and relatives to "accompany the guest" and thus to travel or dine at the expense of the unit. In this fashion, the Chinese host repays social debts (or puts others in her debt) or takes her family on vacation, efficiently making the excursion serve multiple ends. To undertake such a complex performance, however, a guest of honor is an absolute necessity. Naturally, a high-status guest enables the host to be more lavish than a lowly one. If the guest finks out—is sick, or trying to get her work done, or cannot face one more banquet this week—she is being a very bad sport indeed.

This trip to western Sichuan, I am told, will last a week. I demur, pleading a heavy work schedule. At least a week, Lu Fubuzhang says firmly. We will drive two days to a recently opened place of magnificent natural scenery in its finest autumn colors, enjoy these sights for three days, spend the night in a Tibetan home (ethnic Tibetans are numerous in western Sichuan), and drive two days home. It is not certain when exactly we go, but go we surely will. Two days before the appointed time, I am told to start packing.

I genuinely do not want to go on this trip. Seven days is too long a dose of Chinese courtesy and close supervision for me to keep my always uncertain temper. The week will coincide with my usual week of premenstrual crankiness. I have four delicately balanced outside-the-plan interviews arranged for the evenings that, once delayed, might never be recaptured. So I make the effort to discover the real agenda of the journey from a young Chinese-Canadian who will travel with us. Blandly, she repeats platitudes about Chinese hospitality. Only much later was I to learn that the timing and much else about the trip were the decision of her husband, who is compounding on my foreign presence to treat an artist friend to an outing. None of these people is in my unit, but the woman has a loose connection with the Fulian, and while the Fulian will pay the cost, the woman's unit will supply the van and driver. The driver's wife, too, will come along for the ride, and to hold the wrenches.

Early on the 13th, then, we set off under the usual Chengdu drizzle: driver, driver's wife, Ms. Gao, her husband, Teacher Zhou the artist, Lu Fubuzhang, and me. I anticipate a rotten trip, not believing for a moment that the scenery will actually be spectacular (I've heard *that* before) or that the Tibetan domestic visit will be anything other than a *China Reconstructs* dog-and-pony show. I will probably even have to watch little children do folk dances.

The hour it takes to get completely out of Chengdu's influence, the couple of hours of travel through the thickly settled Sichuan countryside are eventless. The Chengdu plain is relentlessly fertile, jammed with small villages, single houses set in bamboo privacy, and crossroads market towns where the produce of field and pigsty is exchanged for cheap industrial goods. Farmers making good money selling vegetables and pork to city buyers build new concrete houses with brilliant tile facades, as identical as need be to those raised by the rural newly prosperous in Taiwan in the 1970s. We stop for lunch at noon at a small privately run restaurant (food and service both better than at those the state manages) for a very Sichuanese meal of peppery hot eels, peppery hot Mapo bean curd, peppery hot twice-cooked pork, cabbage with peppers, bland soup, rice, and white sorghum liquor.

One of the reasons I do not like traveling in Chinese style is that I never get enough liquids to feel physically well. Such liquor as is served is doled out in tiny quantities (some is fairly strong) with much tittering and bravado about how much one can drink, or how one cannot drink at all. Interesting social things happen around the sharing of alcoholic drinks, but the drinks themselves do not constitute an addition to one's fluid intake. If liquor (or even beer or [god forbid] sweet Chinese wine) is served, rice does not arrive until the drinkers have stopped their macho imbibing. Eating rice mops up too much of the alcohol, so if one is drinking to get a buzz on, the custom makes superb sense. Abiding by that custom in Sichuan, however, means that I face the highly seasoned dishes without a cooling mouthful of anything. Soup comes last, and is no help at all to a palate conditioned to a glass or two of water during a meal. It is often possible to get a cup of boiling water to drink, but asking for it generates fuss and confusion. Chinese do not drink water with meals, and sometimes simply refuse to supply it. They find you a soft drink instead. I drink soft drinks only *in extremis*, for sugar shocks my biochemistry almost as much as dehydration.

I have been bullied into coming on this trip, but am determined to have enough water to drink. Specters of past, horrific journeys collapsing into physical illness and mental unravelment warn me that I must insist on my hydraulic idiosyncrasy. I am not asking for a rare delicacy. Potable water is everywhere: in kettles, in thermoses, in large hotel drinking-water tanks, for the convenience of Chinese travelers who constantly make and drink tea on their boats, buses, trains, and planes. I request only the omission of tea leaves, and a modification of the usual timing for beverage consumption—just to have the stuff at meals rather than between them. And I am prepared to carry supplies en route. I have bought a one-liter plastic bottle with a screw-on cup top, an inner spout, and a carrying strap for 3.6 yuan. It is not a thermos; the initially boiling water will get cool enough, by mealtimes, to offset the scalding food; my innards will be tranquil. That water carried in it tastes like liquid polyethylene and will eventually give me liver cancer seem trivial in context. I am bringing water and will drink it when I want to.

I have reckoned without my hostess.

At every meal, the scene is replayed: "Are you drinking *water* again? That water's not hot; you can't drink that. Let me get you some Coke or some hot tea." Nobody drinks cold water, and most especially, *guests* do not drink such an inferior thing. They must consider the hostess' face, her embarrassment if people think she will not supply her guest with the appropriate consumables. In addition, Chinese people have as many, if not more, weird and unscientific ideas about what foods are good and bad for you as I do. They, however, are united in their claims. Everyone jumps on my water bottle every meal, in chorus: "It's winter! You can't drink cold things like water and beer!" One particularly cranky morning, I speak sharply to the table at large about their constant advice about my intake, and the nagging stops. Thereafter, Lu Fubuzhang gets up an extra few minutes early so she can get to my room, corral my water bottle, fill it with boiling water for breakfast, and carry it to the table for me. Nobody can say *she* doesn't know how to treat a guest.

Reader, forgive the pettiness of this preoccupation! I am trying to stay well and civil, but I dislike even well-intentioned personal surveillance more, perhaps, than most Westerners. In Taiwan I have been round this rather uninteresting track with so many different well-wishers that I have lost patience with both them and myself. In Chinese company, I usually do what everyone else is doing because it is the most comfortable and enjoyable thing to do. It is also the most polite; often there is really no other choice. But I am wearied of compromising my shifty health simply in order to fit in, at least when I am ostensibly on holiday.

Visiting the toilet after our first confrontation with my water bottle cheers me up for the next lap of this long first day. Over both women's and men's bathroom doors are bilingual signs reading in English: "Please Take Care of Pubic Health." Is this a glorious typo, or a message in a bottle from a quirky English major trapped in a sign factory?

After an hour of mountain roads, our alert driver hears the sound of bolts breaking in the rear right wheel. He rigs up a replacement and drives off to get more bolts. The artistic party and myself are left at a roadside noodle restaurant to await his return. This remote eatery offers its minimal cheer to travelers who have come there in order to walk two hours almost straight up the mountain to a reputedly spiritually potent cave. I am a sucker for caves, and prefer walking in unfamiliar ecologies to almost anything. Had I known the van would not return for three hours, I would have had the climb. Instead, the four of us head for a hanging bridge that leads to a cluster of farmhouses. Sitting on the supporting cables, we chat with a leprechaun of a man, a young father of two, and the plump cheerful woman who has borne them for him. He is delighted to be talking to an obvious foreigner, quizzing me on my travels in China and on American rural economy. We soon began to talk of the birth limitation policy.

"Two's the limit for us farmers," he says. "They come round and check up—there's nothing you can do about it. If you have a third, they fine you 3,000 yuan"—easily several years' cash income.

"What happens if you don't have 3,000 yuan?" I ask.

"They raze your house," he replies succinctly.

His wife chimes in: "How many children do *you* have?"

I can fib that I have one or two, and pass on to other subjects, or, by revealing that I am fruitless, precipitate a well-worn discussion. The van is still not in sight, and perhaps this clever, lively twenty-something woman will have something new to add. I tell the truth.

"I never had any."

"What's the matter with you? Or is it your husband? Men are sometimes at fault, you know." She glances slyly at the father of her children, both of whom bear the unmistakable genetic imprint of his chunky face. Nothing personal, just a way to rattle his masculine cage a little.

"I decided not to have children. I travel a lot in my job, you see, and it seemed too difficult to take care of children."

"You really didn't want any?" she says, shocked. "What will you do when you're old? You'll be lonely, and there'll be no one to take care of you."

Her husband's mobile face conveys more than shock; he is outraged. He withdraws a few feet, distancing himself from this subversive conversation. She, however, is just getting started.

"If you wanted to have them, how many could you have? How many do most people have? Does America have a birth limitation program?"

"Most people have one or two, like the people in China's cities, for the same reasons: we don't need the children's labor and have to send them to school. And children take a lot of time and money to take care of. But if someone wants to have a lot, they can. The government doesn't have any regulations about it," I spell out.

"She's right about the time and money," she says to her husband. "You don't know how much work taking care of children is. City women have washing machines, too."

By now, her husband has secured both children firmly by the hand. "We don't have time to stand here gabbing; get moving."

They walk away without formality, she looking back, her mouth still full of questions, he striding in the lead, a baby on his shoulders, held high against the dangers that can overcome a man even on this quiet path.

Turning with pleasure from culture to nature, I explore the crumbling granite, identify as many wildflowers as possible, and ponder what will happen if more broken bolts trap van and Lu Fubuzhang somewhere on the road, and us at this ungenerous resting place. We sit on wooden benches at the noodle stand, eating biscuits and packaged herbal drink, trying to keep warm.

A drunken old man stumbles into my reverie and over my foot. As I try to help him up, he shouts bathetically, "She's taking care of me!" before his slovenly, noodle-pushing son shoves him back into inner darkness.

We are all looking a bit glum when the van arrives. We climb aboard apprehensively, and fifty kilometers further over increasingly bad roads, the bolts break again. This time, Lu Fubuzhang and the driver's wife, by incredible luck, find them on the road a few hundred yards back. I take this as a good omen, and chatter about how fate is on our side. This is taken far more seriously than I intend it. Educated Chinese are so busy trying to repudiate feudal superstition among the populace that casual references to good luck make them nervous and preachy.

"We don't believe in that luck stuff any more. There's no other world where our lives are accountable, you know," says Teacher Zhou, the artist, always happy to instruct me.

While the second set of bolts are installed, I rummage in the roadside vegetation. A shout from Teacher Zhou stops me an instant too late to prevent my being stung by an astonishingly well-armed Sichuan nettle. With the joy that simple scatology can elicit, the artist tells me a story about an invading general who unwittingly used the plant for toilet paper, thus either saving Sichuan from invasion or condemning it to vicious repression. His mirth and my language limitations in the strong local dialect prevent my being sure of the political outcome of this botanical error. He says that my barely-grazed finger will sting till the next day, and he proves correct.

The roads get worse, darkness falls, passing farmers refuse to answer our questions about distances, the river runs far below. Because our driver is skilled and because there is only one road, we arrive at last at a county guesthouse, dinnerless, about nine o'clock.

The guesthouse is a good example of the sort of squalid accommodation that traveling officials and the cheaper group tours(e.g., Hong Kong students) put up with in China. It has cleanish bedding and boiling water for thermos bottles and sponge baths, open unisex cold water wash troughs, stalls where one in theory can get a hot shower, but not this night. The critical feature of guesthouse toilets is their location: in the building, near the building, or a good long hike across a huge bus parking lot, for example. These particular privies are not only indoors, but on my floor, and partially lighted, through broken panes of glass, by the flashing strobe lights of the disco palace in the wing across the way.

OCTOBER 14, 1988. THE ROAD TO JIU ZHAI GOU

Last night, Lu Fubuzhang told us to rise at six thirty, be at breakfast at seven, and on the road at seven thirty. My personal preference to opt for biscuits and fruit in the van and a wake-up time of seven fifteen, oddly enough, was accepted. While the others breakfast, I wash in thermos water, fill my precious bottle, pack my kit, tie my wet towel to the strap of my traveling bag where it will dry. And we are off.

This day passes pleasantly amid increasingly lovely mountain scenery. Our adventures are few. At midmorning, I think I smell an over-heating engine and ask the driver to check. He finds instead a rear door that has popped open and is admitting the fumes. We have lost one of the five large (and gaggingly smelly) gas cans we carry and all the lug-gage of two of the passengers. At first, everyone jumps to the conclusion that they have been stolen. After a moment's thought, however, the driver recollects a particularly bumpy stretch of road and a peculiar sound. He leaps into the van and tears off, leaving us in a pretty valley. It is cold, and one of our group has not snatched his jacket, as I have, from the hightailing van. I set out to stretch my legs and see if the river wrack will supply us with bonfire fodder. Because I delay to look about me at the pretty things nature keeps inventing, the fire is never lit. The van returns amazingly quickly, the lost found. A little boy had rescued the can and bags and was sitting by them awaiting their owners' return. He was warmly congratulated and given a whole package of biscuits by Lu Fubuzhang.

This countryside is panda land, though the creatures themselves do not make an appearance. Bamboos dominate absolutely, and the pyra-canthas and barberries that Euro-Americans take for granted in home gardens grow wild, scarlet with fruit in this season. Wild asters, espe-cially a brilliant sulphur yellow variety that I have never seen in North America, glitter among the rocks. Where the valley widens, we see vil-lages or solitary farmhouses surrounded by fields of beans, maize, pota-toes, and amaranth. What did these people eat before the last three of these—all plants domesticated in the New World and reaching Sichuan only well after 1600—came to make the valleys populous? I look with nostalgic interest too at the handsome, seed-laden marijuana plants, grown for rope and stomach-soothers, standing eight feet tall, like bushy young pines.

Han farmers here live intermixed with a regional variant of the Qiang minority. I am forced, in such rapid travel, to fall back on the most embarrassingly primitive characterizations of ethnic difference. I know the Qiang of this valley only by their funny hats: women wear ruffle-rimmed goathide boaters perched on the very tops of their heads. Upright in the middle of these odd chapeaux stand single, long, white rooster feathers. My companions try to photograph these colorful folk from the van windows, and are angrily shouted at. I think of the mixed reactions to "summer people" in New England resorts and to the "fudgies" who bring their ambivalently grasped tourist dollars to Michigan's Mackinac Island. Is a dislike for being treated as part of the local scenery another human universal?

A few miles farther and the villagers are all Qiang, their garden patches running up the steepest mountain sides. Ethnic Han appear only in the hard, gray, square, concrete towns depending for their existence on public offices and sawmills.

As we slowly climb, the colorful deciduous trees are replaced by larches, turning golden against tall firs. Soon we come to birches and rhododendrons—again, an indigenous Sichuan shrub. A plant which in flower, leaf, and seedpod is simply a buttercup blooms (in October!) five times its normal size—and bright pink. Cerulean clusters of the prize flower of the trip explode on the sandy soils—a short, needle-leafed, gregarious gentian, which I was never able to photograph but will recognize ecstatically, in another life, in a Cambridge botanical garden. As we near a divide, the trees are hung with pale-lime streamers of a Spanish moss very far from home.

In the van, we ride in pleasant sociability, everyone gay with the good fortune of having found our lost luggage. I insist on my nonfeudal, serendipitous interpretation of luck, and everyone laughs at the odd concept. We eat fruit, peanuts, biscuits, offering each other bits of this and that. The rubbish goes into a red plastic washbowl; when we stop, the driver's wife neatly dumps it in the road. People enjoy the autumn leaves vociferously, then settle in for naps. Although I am not tired—indeed, cannot take my eyes from the passing botanical show—I envy the Chinese ability to sleep even in this rattling, shockless van.

With our arrival in fir forest, the houses we pass begin to catch the eye with their handsome carpentry. The facade of the second story is finished in fine, straight-grained, unpainted wood. Either the natural color lasts a long time or many of these houses are new. A graceful valley cradles an elegant village of such houses, surrounded by fields of corn, cabbages, and beans, and protected by straw scarecrows in patched-to-shreds Mao suits. My companions are horrified at my fantasy of living for a year in such a place, seeing no beauty in it, and probably more accurately aware than I of its unseen physical discomforts. But the distinguished carpentry speaks of resources and skill better than those that have housed most Chengdu people. In town, older timber-and-stucco dwellings are framed in crooked softwoods twisted by the early theft of their lower limbs. Accustomed as I am to Taiwan's summer typhoons, Sichuan houses often look dangerously flimsy, bedecked with loose tiles and other oddments that would become lethal missiles in the hundred-mile-an-hour winds of coastal China. It is one of the paradoxes of Chinese life that the farther people are from the centers of power and wealth that everyone wants to move to, the better and more commodious is the housing. Many of the hills we now drive through are logged off, stripped and eroding. It will be costly, in the future, to build new houses with these welcoming wooden faces.

A broader valley harbors a population of Han farmers specializing in fruit. Gamboge persimmons hang, disproportionately large, like a child's drawing of magical apples, in every courtyard. I learn that the Sichuanese do not wait for frost to touch and sweeten them, but pick them while still firm. They soak them a week in some gray mixture to ripen. When I am given a dozen later as a gift, choking two down for politeness' sake is all I can manage. They lack the astringency of unripe persimmons, but taste foul and will never attain the custardy, slippery texture for which the true devotee eats the messy, oversweet things.

We stop for dinner in Nanping, consume the usual emphatic Sichuanese dishes all seasoned alike, with too few vegetables. While we wait for the food, I case the market. The narrow main street is full of yet another minority people and of small private stalls selling acrylic-brilliant ready-made clothing, yarn, and yard goods. A hardware peddler on the restaurant steps has a clever tool for splitting kindling; a heavy, short machete tipped with a hook that hits the ground, sparing the tool's cutting edge from contact with the earth. The old man tells me I have no use for such a thing. He is wrong. I buy the splitter for my father—dead now for twenty years—who loved camping and bonfires and travel. Like a Chinese ancestor consuming the essence of a favorite dish offered to celebrate his death day, Daddy will enjoy a dematerialized version of this novel tool. Later, pragmatically, I will present it to my lover's father, who splits lots of kindling against the northern California chill. The peddler reiterates that I am wasting my money, but he takes the four yuan anyway.

A fast-talking ten-year-old has no such scruples in selling me a handful of "wild bananas." These are clusters of four-inch-long locust pods, thick as my thumb, and colored an unnatural ultraviolet. They split open easily along the seam, revealing two neat rows of black, shiny, oval seeds, each encased in a thin coat of transparent flesh. This yielding jelly scoops out easily with the tongue, and tastes like Emperor grapes. I save a couple of pods' worth of seed to grow at home. Teacher Zhou tells me that monkeys are especially fond of these odd fruit; none of the others will touch them. "I don't dare," says the driver's wife.

As usual, we eat fast, shoveling it down. As always, before I am expecting it, the cry goes up to get moving, so I leave the restaurant struggling with the fast disaggregating parts of my water bottle. We will make it to Jiu Zhai Gou, Nine Villages Canyon, the famous scenic spot, tonight, but the next fifty kilometers of road are ominously allowed to be "rather not good."

I am astonished that this ordinary Japanese van, with a relatively low undercarriage, can make it through the rest of the road. The extreme raininess last summer has brought downslides, washed out sections, and left long patches of deep mud filled with jagged rocks the size of pumpkins. The driver is amazing: we never bog down, the tires hold. When he approaches really sticky spots, he stops, thinking it through with the face of the martial arts masters who break bricks, or a spirit medium about to go into trance. Then he guns it, and we somehow land in safety.

By seven, we are at the main gate to the park, where a local Fulian representative has made us reservations. Even in the dark, this hotel is a pleasant place. It stands by—has a tea-house being built *over*—the rushing river that cuts the valley, and the buildings are knee-deep in pink, lacy cosmos. The cold, damp air, the wooden-framed buildings scattered under tall pines remind me of childhood camps in Canada's Algonquin Park.

I have just been seen to my room when the lights go off for the night. Everyone squeals and rushes about, though I learn the next day that it is turned off regularly at this time. Hot water here depends on electrical heating coils, so there will be no bath tonight. But the toilet is clean, indoors, and near my room; I am given a candle; the sheets smell of mountain air rather than of old hair oil. Two quilts will keep me warm if I leave on two pair of long underwear and a couple of sweatshirts. River-song soothes me into sleep.

October 15, 1988. Jiu Zhai Gou

Morning is like the first day on earth. The mountains are towering and lovely, the sky shows the first blue I have seen in weeks. I am going to play in the woods! Wash in the basin, put on more layers, be cautious with the dribbling water bottle, find the dining room. For once I, too, want to gobble and run.

I add another eccentricity to my mealtime repertory by eating a tangerine with my steamed bun, boiled egg, and hot water. I pick at superb fresh pickles, made from scarlet radishes as big as pineapples, though I worry about their saltiness; too much salt at meals, and my cerebral arteries clamp down with agonizing headaches. Pickles are a necessity with the main dish, *xifan*, however. This gruel of rice boiled to a soupy porridge is mother's milk to southern Chinese, a breakfast staple seen as soup seasoned by exotic relishes: pickles of all imaginable vegetables, eggs (boiled, salted, tea, thousand-year-old), peanuts, and delicious, winy, leaf-wrapped packets of fermented bean curd. I eat xifan when there is nothing better, but it reminds me of lumpy library paste. Nor do I care for hot sugared powdered milk, the other liquid choice. My preference for water is discussed again with amazement, amusement, some alarm. Still slurping from my bottle, I follow my companions to the van.

"How far is it to the next guesthouse?" I inquire.

"Seventeen kilometers."

"It's a beautiful day—why don't we walk it?"

"Much too far, and for a long way you won't see anything interesting," says the driver. "We'll stop at all the good places."

Drivers are persons of note in Chinese units, people with technical skills that give them status and good incomes. Their decisions stand. I get in. Speeding through the lovely morning in a smelly van where I can hear nothing but engine noise and my companions' rhapsodies on leaf color is beginning to make me grumpy. The grumpiness increases at each stop.

We leap from the van at marked points where unusual landscape features have been given the usual trite Chinese names: Two Dragons Pool (a One, Two, Three . . . to Nine Dragon label is stuck on every other body of water in China), Mirror Lake, Pearl Beach Waterfall. As they have done with cloudy mountain peaks and striking geological formations throughout the trip, the artistic party appropriates the landscape by comparing it to (Chinese) paintings. Having thus reduced it to manageability, they complete the transformation of nature on a grand scale to the simplicity of graphic art by photographing it as background to portraits of themselves. Lu Fubuzhang, a dab hand with a camera, quietly experiments with the scene, putting herself in the picture only as the unseen, discerning eye of the beholder. She was not wrong, back in Chengdu, about the beauty that surrounds us.

On these ten-minute stops, I am increasingly torn between micro- and macrovisions. I want to feel the flowers and smell the earth, but also to sit and watch the light move mountains. I want to *hear* this landscape of earth, air, fire, and water. I even want to take a picture or two, waiting, if necessary, for the right light. A side valley channels a single shaft of sunlight across a Tibetan family's house, fields, meadow full of peaceful horses. By the time I sprint to the place where the shot must be taken, the sun is gone. There is no label on the horses, so no one wants to wait the fifteen minutes it might take for the sun to gild Eden again.

I walk wide of the van to escape its exhaust fumes, to try to find enough silence to hear the wind. When, at the third or fourth stop, my companions are descanting on how clusters of trees growing on ridges in water "are just like dish gardens," I wave good-bye and head on up the road. Even seeing becomes impossible in the midst of these slightly hysterical attempts to miniaturize, domesticate, simplify this grand, wild, endless complexity.

By Chinese standards for middle-aged people, I walk very fast. I want to see, to stop and touch, but I can hear and smell at any speed. If I move briskly enough, I will lose them for a while. Luck is with me; I have an hour to admire passing yaks (not very shaggy down here), to take the temperature of the bluest waters I have ever seen, to hear the river drive a prayer wheel the size of a gasoline drum, centrifuging blessings to the four quarters. I remember this hour as I remember lovemaking. There is little point in reciting a sequence of events, or of trying to describe sensations. It was lovely; it came to me through my whole body, not just the linear and analytical eyes. If you want to know what it was like, go there, do that.

And then they catch up with me. It is still several kilometers to the mid-valley guesthouse, our goal for lunch and the night. I must be tired; I must get into the van. There is more here than meets the eye, for the ever-bland Lu Fubuzhang and Teacher Zhou are discernibly in a fuss over something. I politely worm my way into the hydrocarbonated van to be carried off to Falling Water Water Fall or whatever comes next.

The mid-valley guesthouse is short on plumbing but long on goats, a satisfactory arrangement. It is tremendously ugly, all concrete boxes and weedpatches where gardens had been intended, but it is graciously staffed by young Tibetan women knitting gaudy woolen long johns in sunny corners. There is lots of yak beef for lunch, and I buy the most expensive bottle of white liquor the shop sells to accompany it, and to repay Teacher Zhou for guzzling a good deal of his. (The fifty-five-yuan stuff tastes no better and no worse than his fourteen-yuan version. It tastes terrible, as do all indigenous Chinese drinks except tea.) My room has an indoor bathroom with a Western-style toilet that swallows only liquids and a pink tub that promises a long, warm bath before bed. Happily, I summon the wit to ask Lu Fubuzhang if *her* room has a bath. As it does not, I urge her to bunk in with me for the sake of a soak.

It is during this afternoon that my fears about the trip begin to be justified, and the cross-cultural plot to thicken. After lunch, we go for the mountaintop, fifteen kilometers along this lovely road. I want to walk it.

"By the time you get there, we'll have had to wait a long time for you," Lu says, reasonably.

"Then I'll walk until I meet you coming down. That's convenient for everybody."

"You'd miss the view from the top that way. It really would be very hard walking. Let's all go in the van," she persuades.

The whole group chimes in with a unanimity and determination that make me more stubborn yet. I get in with the others, but set off briskly at the first stop on my own. I am not twenty minutes gone when they pull up and begin the argument again. It is no use; they are going to keep at me until I acquiesce. People have been ground down into renouncing parents, terminating pregnancies, and building monster reservoirs with teaspoons through this technique of unified persistence. It has been perfected through the legendary five thousand years of Chinese culture; sweet reason and simple assertiveness are feeble defenses against it. I get in.

I have, however, a final card to play, one that Chinese people themselves occasionally use, but are bad at countering. I let my fury show. Anger frightens the Chinese, makes them begin to recalculate the costs of suppressing disagreement. When we get out for the next stop, my mentor asks if I am angry. The proper answer is, of course, "No." Instead, I allow loudly that I am very angry indeed and, if I were not an extraordinarily courteous person, I would have a great deal to say. But I do not want to talk about it now. Everyone wanders off silently to look at a spectacularly beautiful pond, which appears to have been dyed sapphire, while I sulk.

When Lu reappears, in far less time than a Westerner would have allowed for anger to abate, she tries to smooth me down again, this time with the hard truth.

"We couldn't let you go alone on *this* road especially, you see. Some of the Tibetans are not very happy about all the changes, and there have been incidents. One of them tried to throw a rock at me this morning, did you see?" I had not.

"What if something should happen to you? We aren't far from the summit now. Let's the two of us walk up there, and the van can catch up to us."

It is the last thing I wanted to do; Lu's legs are very short. But in Rome . . . . Like a good Chinese, I put on a pleasant face, say the appropriate things, and pledge vengeance in my heart. Andiamo, andiamo! E meditar vendetta!

Later, as we prepare for bed, Lu confides to me that the trip had been hastily put together to accommodate the visiting artist. He had visited the valley before the new road opened it to the public, and knew some horror stories about local Han being attacked by Tibetans resenting the intrusion of tourism. It is he who insists that I ride. They really would be terribly worried about me if I were unescorted.

I thank her and we end the day companionably enough. My inner response is still combative, though not really aimed at my travelmates, who are all decent folks. I want badly to preach to a more general audience: "Of course the Tibetans would attack you Chinese! You're the ones responsible for all this. I'm just an innocent bystander!" Only later, when my indignation cools, do I remember what my Chinese friends already know. In their loss and anger, the Tibetans are probably not concerned about fine ethnic discriminations among the tourists who besiege them. Walking alone in this penetrated paradise puts me at as much risk as it would in third-world parts of Detroit.

CHAPTER TEN

城都行

Yak Heaven

OCTOBER 16, 1988. JIU ZHAI GOU

A week or ten days of premenstrual tension each month has bedeviled my life for years; stress, including that of suppressed fury, makes it worse. I awake on the sixteenth, the day after my graceless disagreement about walking up the mountain road, with the ice-pick-through-the-eye headache that no drug I am willing to take will blunt. I take what medicine I have and go back to bed, leaving the rest of the crew plus a jolly little local Fulian woman to traipse up the other fork of the valley in a cold rain. I promise not to leave the hotel area and to keep up my end with our hostess that afternoon. We are to visit two local Tibetan households after the sightseeing.

At lunch, cultural incompatibility reduces me to tears as I struggle against the combined effects of shouted conversations, the same old discussions about my water bottle with our new hostess, and well-intentioned Chinese solicitude about my every mouthful. Telling them I have no wish to spoil the party, I explain my condition, and my need to monitor my own intake and get proper exercise. Like civilized people, they begin general dinner-table chat and leave me alone.

It is humiliating to cry in public, before strangers, for reasons one knows cannot seem persuasive to others. When I can, I time participation in events such as these for the part of the month when my emotions are a bit more connected to my brain. At the same time, however, I knew well that my tears would make it clear that some kind of line has been crossed. I sit and snivel quietly, shaking with the effort to stop. Lu later tells me that she had had terrible premenstrual depressions before her menopause, losing all interest in life and wanting to "leap into the river."

123

One day, at nadir, she overturned the entire dinner table—dishes, food, and all—onto her beleaguered family. She understood, she said. I would be better off in a few years.

After my luncheon tears, the suggestion is kindly made that those of us who want to walk down to the first guesthouse may do so; the van will wait for us below. The artists, Lu, and I begin to walk together. I almost must pause between steps to keep so slow a pace. Feeling the familiar anger growing, I decide that action will serve me better than the passive aggression of spoiling their walk along with my own. Perhaps they concur, for when I begin to walk in earnest, the conversation continues behind me, fainter, until I am alone.

Only after about a third of the distance is past do I forget anger and shame enough to hear and see and smell my surroundings fully. There are no adventures. But I see more clearly now how many small changes the stream of tourists is bringing. Here and there, people offer the opportunity for me to be photographed dressed in patently synthetic "Tibetan" clothing; families rent out small pontoon boats to shatter Mirror Lake; a small boy begs candy from me. Of this walk, I remember most the body's movement, the long stretching of leg muscles habituated to bicycling, the heart thumping pleasantly, the sweat that soaks my first layer of long underwear. My legs ache from instep to waist for the next three days.

The van checks up on me once, then again. Lu offers me a drink of water and an apple, and I am cheerful and jolly, telling them how much better the walk and the sweating were making me feel. When, two and a half hours later, I reach the park gate, Lu and the local Fulian woman are waiting with apples and applause for the bad little girl who had had to have her own way.

I feel thoroughly sorry for the young Fulian woman, who has never entertained a foreigner before and has been faced with this messy spectacle. But she manages with aplomb, and I daresay will dine out on the story for years. In the evening, she pays me a brief, formal call, just the two of us by candlelight in the cold bedroom. She repeatedly assured me of her pleasure in my visit and her hope that I and all my friends will return to Nine Villages Canyon. She will make the (troublesome) arrangements. She will do anything she can to further my enjoyment and research. I as warmly, and as repetitiously, thank her for her hospitality. Her branch of the Fulian had sprung for a very nice dinner that evening, buying a bottle of sweet China red especially for me. Alcohol is almost as bad as salt and anger for PMS, but I cannot shame her further, so I drink. I thank her, or her candlelit eyes and teeth, for helping me to see unique and lovely sights. She gives me an elegant little enameled pin bright with the colors of autumn leaves; I present her with a packet of Central Michigan University stickers. We are both sincere, and both very glad to go off to our respective beds when our duty is done.

When I return, I must look up the account of how Isabella Bird Bishop escaped, in west Sichuan, the official supervision to which most of her trip was subject. She imperiously, indeed, imperialistically, launches her tiny expedition into tribal country, pursued there by soldiers and officials bent on returning her to the beaten path. The passage proves to read that the officials "politely told many lies" before their last effort at restraint, "which they made with a vehemence which was almost piteous, entreaties being resorted to when threats failed, but all collapsed on a special clause in my passport being pointed out."[1] It is a tribute to a century of anti-imperialist struggle that Chinese officials now have such an easy time of it.

OCTOBER 17, 1988. JIU ZHAI GOU

No Tibetan houses are available to be visited on this bright morning, a matter of some uneasiness between Lu and the local Fulian. As we leave the valley, we pass a village not two hundred yards from the park entrance and find the whole area solidly Tibetan, their muslin pennons fluttering everywhere. Are the Han on such bad terms even with hotel-attendants' households? Are people busy with harvest? Or have I scared everyone spitless with my unpredictable ill nature?

Up a substantial mountain, badly logged off, through a valley with bright wood-fronted houses, up a *big* mountain, with snow enough to remind us to hurry—and we break into the grassland. Yak heaven.

By now, I had seen a few yaks and been disappointed. They looked like cows that had slept in their clothes. But here are yaks by the tens of thousands (basin population: 20,000 people, 400,000 yaks), in full cold-season dress: long-haired bodies in all cow colors, full, fluffy tails of two-foot hairs, and, on bulls, great manes at the shoulders. Hilaire Belloc was correct about the yak. "It will carry and fetch, you can ride on its back, or lead it about with a string." They are loose on the range, tethered to pegs

---

[1] Isabella Bird Bishop, *The Yangtze Valley and Beyond* (London: John Murray, 1899), 398–399.

or each other, being milked, nursing calves that romp like huge, bumbly puppies, saddled for riding, carrying timber, and loaded with the possessions of a migrating household. They fight idly, lick themselves and each other, moo in pleasant baritones, and smell delicious. The great, golden, rolling plain is sprinkled with them like the "hundreds and thousands" on childhood cupcakes.

Their owners are equally in evidence. The Cultural Revolution efforts to settle these nomads have been given up—they brought disastrous declines in production. Once again the land is open to such local users as might have need of a patch of pasture or a stretch of creek. Fifteen-foot square black tents stitched together from sixteen-inch strips of hand-woven yak-hair fabric are the peripatetic planets around which the herds slowly circle. Each tent stands alone, home to women and girls in bright headscarves and dark corduroy robes, and to barefoot boys and men in equally grubby and colorful costume, topped with high felt cowboy hats. Tibetan men, and women carrying babies, belt their padded outer coats tightly with a pink or scarlet sash, and ease one arm and shoulder out of a sleeve. This creates both a useful pouch behind, and an air of stylish insouciance that goes well with their ornate daggers and general air of being willing to spit in your eye. Both sexes ride and drive horses, as well as yaks. Glorious Tibetan women on horseback, scarlet scarves flying, match well with their tall, hawk-nosed men.

Unlike the circumspect Han, Tibetan men look one in the eye with transparent sexual assessment. According to Lu, one of the biggest "women's work" problems of the regional Fulian is the number of babies born to mothers who cannot be entirely sure just who fathered each child. This is a problem only to the puritanical and patrilineal Han, however: Tibetan women share in the family herds, so children they bear are not seen as thieves of their patriline's property, as illegitimate Chinese children are. Chinese speak of the Tibetan enthusiasm for song and especially dance with that fascinated tone they reserve for sexual activities. Is it sexuality per se that discombobulates Han observers of visible lust? Or is over-expressiveness of any emotion a kind of pornography to people who value self-control so highly?

Early on in our grassland journey, we encounter a cartload of red-cheeked girls, women, and infants being driven to town through Fulian arrangement, to "play": shopping, a movie, and the sights of one of the smallish towns through which we have just driven. Are they also a carefully arranged photo opportunity for me? Quite possibly, though that hardly matters. They are resplendent in their best clothes: plenty of rich dark corduroy with bright embroidered edges, brilliant scarves and sashes, and broad red headbands—looking rather Ukrainian—surmounted by seven or nine lumps of butterscotch-colored amber as big as babies' fists. The amber in turn is topped with finger-sized chunks of pink coral, worn to smoothness by the years and hands that had brought them from some Indian sea.

The women, in gleeful holiday mood, wave gaily at us, and we at them. They stop; we stop. We ask if we might photograph their lovely costumes; they ask us please to do so, and to send them copies. It is delightful. I dandle babies, admire their hairdos of long, twine-thick plaits, have my own sun-bleached curls fingered, and my scholar's hands exclaimed over. Like ourselves, these two dozen fellow females are out on a spree, looking for the new, the unusual, the exotic. By pointing to pretty eyes and cheeks, to fine embroidery or elaborate silver earrings, or just with smiles and handshakes, I greet them all, the perfect guest, hoping that our stop will give them, too, something to tell over the teacups.

Not quite ready for lunch—it is only ten thirty—we come to a town that our driver says is the last place where lunch can be got for many hours. Piling out, we find a sawmill, a mill for the local staple, *qingkou* (barley), grown lower down by farming Tibetans, and a small inn. There are no privies; we are motioned out to a spot behind a pigpen. From there I have a fine view of a simple automatic plank-sawing machine and several young women sewing fresh cotton covers on the inn's quilts, linen expected to last till spring washing, I guess. This rear yard holds a small flower garden—settled Tibetans grow lots of flowers, notably cosmos and dahlias—from which I take, with permission, seed from a pretty, primitive-looking hollyhock. Luscious pink and white opium poppies, too few for any use but beauty, fill out the bed.

While we wait for our early meal, I watch women leading laden horses to the mill next door. One old lady, passing the time till her *qingkou* should be ground, asks me to take her picture. I snap her, horse and mill and woolen hand-woven sacks and all, getting the best address I can from another waiting woman who speaks a bit more Chinese than my amber-decked new acquaintance. The mill is hazy with floating flour and smells wonderful. Two strong men hoist sacks into a huller; two sturdy women, muffled in red, channel the output of the pair of millstones driven by rushing water underneath.

European languages are laced with the imagery of milling grain ("The mills of the gods grind slowly. . . . " "Don't let the bastards grind you down"). The starches I have eaten since childhood—oatmeal, bread, pasta—are products of a long tradition that grinds its grain rather than eating it whole, as the Chinese mostly eat rice or millet. But I have never stood before a mill in the sunshine, keeping an eye on the horse, hoping the weak spot in the sack will not burst, waiting for my grain to return to me as flour from the earliest of industrialists. One becomes sappily romantic in such situations, wondering about English and Ukrainian ancestors, about the taste of bread baked by my foremothers' hands.

We are halfway through lunch (a dismal Han meal, insofar as one can make a Han meal with a great deal of yak and no vegetables to speak of) when four cowboys swagger in. One, in a red shirt and high gray felt sombrero, is a dead ringer for Willie Nelson. They sit, they down a few shots, they look us over. I contemplate the consequences for international relations were I to make Willie an offer—anybody can learn to milk, right? But as usual, our meal comes to an abrupt end before I am ready and the moment passes. The innkeeper gives us a stirrup cup of *qingkou* liquor, which tastes exactly like all Chinese liquors, and we hit the trail again.

The driver was right about the emptiness of the road ahead. The road slides up a ridge to skirt a golden basin that, we later learn, is so full of quicksand that no one dares use it for pasturage. Nowhere in that great, tawny country can we spy the specks of yaks and tents; the wind brings nothing to my ears but the song of disappointed grasses. Only by late afternoon does the population thicken, and do we again see households with high-piled packyaks seeking fresh pasture.

Suddenly, by the side of the road, something new appears on the grassland. A fence had been built—not recently, not anciently—of cubes of sod. It stands about a meter high, eighteen inches thick, and runs for miles, sometimes on both sides of the road. Its uniformity tells that it was all built about the same time; frequent and deliberately made gaps show that it is no longer in use. Why would herders who normally move freely over an undivided plain build a huge stretch of fencing and then abandon it?

My guess at an answer is later confirmed by cautious questions. During the Cultural Revolution, the authorities made great efforts to settle nomads such as these Tibetans. In Sichuan, herds were to be managed in units both larger than, and different from, the traditional nuclear family households. In some regions, where huge herds had been run jointly, tribal units were split into smaller groups. Along this road, the land was divided and put under commune ownership. The Han made the

Girls from Grassland Resettlement Camp, 1988

Tibetans build walls to mark boundaries and restrict the cattle's movements.

This experiment failed. The herders hated it, not only because it was not their own choice, but because animal rearing is a highly skilled business. Changing part of the system without developing complex adjustments in many other parts throws its operations out of whack. Animals were not properly cared for, their products went to waste. Production fell and resentment grew. As soon as possible after the economic reforms began in 1978, the animals were returned to household management, the land went back to common use, and the sod fences were kicked down wherever passage was necessary. Anyone can imagine how angry these long-settled locals must have been at having been obliged to build structures they did not want and which soon proved, even to the Han, to be mistakes.

In the region of the useless walls, we pass several villages of nomads who had been forcefully settled during the Cultural Revolution. The two we visit are nothing like the well-built farming communities with their handsome houses and tidy fields seen at lower altitudes. These Tibetans are filthy squatters, growing a few young apple trees, keeping some horses, making do. Such villages are the permanent homes of the tent dwellers, I am told. People shuttle between nomadic life in the summer and settlement in the winter. The old and the very young live in the villages, the adults tend the herds, my companions tell me.

None of this squares with what we actually see. Young children and grannies are as common around traveling tents as they are around these rickety shacks, while the scruffy villages are full of poor, ill-clad, and fierce-looking young men (they elicit the nervous description "savages" from my companions) who are just of an age to be the most vigorous of cowboys. While the villages may have been set up as winter quarters only—like the walls, they are clearly the product of deliberate and rectilinear planning alien to organic Tibetan communities—I would not be surprised to learn that they now contain mostly families that, for whatever reason, were not given beasts and access to land in the reform redistribution of the eighties.

These villagers listlessly try to sell us apples and the chance to take photos of ourselves on their shaggy horses. One little maiden follows us about with the greatest of courtesy, however, charmed by novelty. On seeing my earrings, she rushes into the house to return with a pair of purple plastic roses which have separated from their clips. She asks me hopefully to mend them. How could I have come traveling without Crazy Glue? Unable to help, I consider what out of my limited kit I can give her that she might like, and settle on a Hong Kong coin. Stupid foreigner. Money that is not money is a disappointment, and brings on a rash of requests from other little boys and girls for more, and *real* money.

In their dealings with minority peoples, many Chinese, like Americans in our own imperialist moments, assume that their technological superiority indexes a higher social and political-economic wisdom. Local political economies that depend on local production processes, however, are too complex to respond well to piecemeal and partial imports from alien cultures. Raising cattle especially tempts the pastorally naive to tamper with ecologies that conquerors rarely understand. Here in west Sichuan, the tampering may well have been motivated by Chinese desire to "better" the Tibetans as well as to increase milk, meat, and wool supplies for China as a whole. Such interference in other people's lives sometimes even works: I assume that the little cream separators we see in Tibetan tents surely make women's butter-making easier; these folks seem glad enough to have trucks pick up the daily milk surplus on roads that the government maintains. Behind a stretch of useless sod wall, however, I discover evidence for a different kind of interference that *no* ruling group ought to be unwise enough to engage in.

The ghostly pinnacles rise above bright green grass that has attracted several dozen yaks and a couple of rosy herdgirls. The fragile-looking structures are hard to interpret, partially obscured by hundreds of fluttering scriptural pennons hanging from thirty-foot posts. A bit closer, and they resolve themselves into tentlike affairs made of ever larger concentric circles swathed in the printed muslin of the pennons. A half dozen of these odd pagodas gives focus to the forest of flags and to a few grave mounds scattered among them.

I ask the young women if I might look. In Taiwan, menstruating women may not approach certain kinds of temples, so stranger women are often warned away to prevent pollution of sacred sites. The herdgirls seem perfectly unconcerned; and no, they don't know what it is—or perhaps their Mandarin does not extend to the explanation of indigenous ritual. I shoo away yaks, disentangle the left-hind foot of a rusty-haired calf from low-hanging muslin, and peer under the pagodas. It is startling to find stacked there fragments of finely carved limestone, covered with Tibetan characters. A carved, painted wooden signboard, the sort of thing that might have hung over a door, is also protected within this enclosure. Along with these remnants of what had once obviously been a temple are clusters of water-worn white quartz. Wherever Tibetans live, these can be seen piled on graves or standing in cairns.

A little more time in the area, and I might be able to find the site of the original building, to hear something of the battle in which Han versus Tibetan, or Han and young (or poor?) Tibetans versus older, more powerful ones (?) destroyed a lamasery and felled the fighters who must be resting in these graves. I might learn a little of how, and who, collected the pieces, stored them until it was safe to make them public, and in a ceremony that must have involved many working hands, a good deal of money, and much prayer, deposited them on the green grass to await better times.

I rather dislike religion myself, and find attachment to its sentiments and forms of organization something I must make a conscious effort to tolerate in friends and associates in my own culture. We have, after all, a choice in these matters. But if one is an American Indian or Australian or Taiwan Aborigine, a Pole, or a Tibetan, religion is practically the only weapon available against those who, out of greed or paternalism, would take one's land, language, and lifestyle. The gauzy temple, no barrier to wind, rain, or the passage of beasts, is the finest metaphor I have ever

Yaks and Memorials, 1988

seen for the strength of the weak, for the near-materiality of belief, if belief is all one can control.

By five, we reach Hongyuan County Guesthouse. I suborn the Chinese-Canadian woman into exploring Main Street while dinner is ordered. The Han run stores, the Tibetans swagger through the streets with flashy daggers at their belts. People's Liberation Army men are much in evidence, and there is a general "high noon" atmosphere in which even my foreignness becomes only a sideshow. After looking at all the bright ready-made children's clothes, hair ornaments, canned food, and rubber boots, we ask a shopkeeper what is the local *te chan*— regional product. She looks at us sharply, suspecting a joke.

"Hongyuan dried milk powder, of course."

"Yak milk?" I press.

"What else?"

We settle for gaily packaged incense, a tourist-quality dagger, matches, candles, and toilet paper. I consider, idly, trying to send a letter home from here, but my companion is hungry and bored.

"What a dump," she says—this from a woman who lives in Alberta.

Travelers to Nine Villages Canyon often break their journey at Hongyuan. The guesthouse is swankier than I had anticipated. The dining room has one mural of people and animals frolicking on the grasslands that is painted in folk-primitive style, and another of mysterious not-quite-religious symbols that must have been done by a Han with only a comic-book notion of Tibetan iconography. A third mural shows a dancing couple displaying the faint degree of eroticism permissible in Chinese public art if the persons depicted are minority or foreign. A representation of a naked Dai or Nordic breast is a common sight in China, on magazine covers, as statuary in hotel lobbies, as lampstands; a bared Han bosom is unimaginable.[2]

Dressing up the dining hall is a collection of colored photos taken at a recent summer horse racing meet, which is *the* event of the year. It looks like wonderful fun. The crowds of lively, mounted, drinking, dancing, fornicating, and fighting Tibetans probably give the local authorities terrible headaches for months in advance of and after the festivities.

Our room—I now regularly share with Lu—is a treat. It has no plumbing (the privy is across the yard and impossible to use without getting shit on my shoes), but it has antimacassars, potted plastic palms, odd carved furniture galore, lots of quilts, and an adorable little wood stove that smells good and will keep us cozy.

Before bed, Lu, the Chinese-Canadian, and I gossip around the stove with Fulian representatives—a Tibetan and an Abba—who have made our arrangements here. The Tibetan woman does most of the talking. She is pleasant and efficient, telling me how many yaks and how many people, how property is divided, and what women are responsible for in nomadic life. But she is not about to land any of her people with a bunch of nosy visitors; nor does she care, really, to discuss the terrible personal hygiene problems for women on the plains, as some of our party wish to do.

After she goes, I am regaled with tales of how the washbasins officially dispensed for a women's health project have ended up as kitchen utensils instead of bidets—a bit of body-ritual outrageousness that only I can view with equanimity. They tell me, too, of minority-women-trainee cadres who had been so homesick living in Chengdu that they gave up good provincial-level cadre positions to go home, and of minority leaders who, after having been given all the advantages of study for several years "even in Beijing!" either refused to go home at all or, worse,

[2] Although by 1996, this reticence was fading fast.

returned to their homes as cadres and *went native,* refusing to participate in pressing their fellow-countrywomen to behave more like Han.

Tibetans around here are touchy, I am told. If insulted, they sometimes take after people with knives. In one horrific incident, a disillusioned Tibetan cadre tore up a roomful of official documents, scattering them everywhere, like snow. The sword or the pen: which hurts the Han bureaucrat worse, I wonder?

If life is hard for the Han stationed here in west Sichuan, it is worse for those sent to Tibet, where a normal tour of duty is eight years. Han women, cadres or visiting wives, have to return from Lhasa to the lowlands to bear children safely because of the high altitude. Han children are sent home for education because of the low educational standards in Tibet, and the physical and cultural dangers. Those on duty there get considerable extra pay and a leg up on the career ladder when they return, but it is still hard to get people to stay their whole tour. Tourists who visited Lhasa in the relatively quiet year of 1988 have told me that in that center of Han presence and Tibetan resistance to it, the Han go about only in clusters of five or six. Police trying to fine a Tibetan for jaywalking recently were surrounded by a local crowd who cheered and applauded as the man twisted free and dodged out of sight.

Old Chinese poetry is full of the laments of political exiles and of officials sent to govern barbarous regions. I suppose that tradition lives on in many contemporary letters home from China's wild west.

When we escort the Fulian cadres out of my room, I am accosted by six well-set-up Chinese men speaking accentless (or, rather, Beijing-accented) Mandarin. There is going to be dancing in the dining hall. Would I do them the honor? They are a China TV crew from the capital, come to film the newly opened Nine Villages Canyon in its fall beauty for national broadcast. We chat, but I decline to dance. It is an amusing conversation, the humor revolving around the repeatedly unsuccessful attempts of two of the young men to find female company in any of the provinces they had traversed. They are just like my own college students, off to Florida for spring break. Lu and I close the door on them, laughing, and go to bed between the potted palms and the softly chuckling stove.

October 18, 1988. Hongyuan

Far too early—it is about six—these lads foregather at my window and begin to bellow jeep-loading instructions to one another. I am still grouchy, and perhaps still in pedagogical mode, for I stride to the door in my long underwear and issue a firm command to take their &*#@%$@ noisy meeting elsewhere: people are trying to sleep. It is terribly rude of me—Chinese either sleep through other people's matutinal clatter or suffer it in silence—but they shut up. Better them than poor Lu, I decide.

It is cloudy when we leave Hongyuan about eight. Along the road, the yaks are tethered near tents, being milked. Women take only a pint or so from each cow before letting the urgent calf suckle. After their warm breakfast, the calves frisk goofily, playing butt-each-other and let's-tear-off-this-way-for-no-apparent-reason. Tent dwellers are more crowded in this region than in the sparsely peopled valley we crossed yesterday, so many households live near the road. The driver chooses one with two women milking outside. Lu Fubuzhang identifies herself to the elder, requesting to be allowed to look in the tent. The woman agrees easily enough. Her daughter shouts a rapid spatter of Tibetan punctuated by the Chinese word *ganbu*—cadre, official, person in authority—and the mother responds in kind. They laugh, and move to a fresh cow.

We examine the tent. I am especially interested in the strong yak-hair cordage with which it is pegged down and in the firm, even, and surely waterproof weave of the yak-hair twill from which it is constructed. It is handloomed in strips about sixteen inches wide, the costless and irreplaceable byproduct of long, gossipy winter evenings. A center opening along the ridge lets out smoke, the door has a minimal fly, the material meets the ground well pegged, but with plenty of room for air to enter. There is no floor but the grass, with a few worn sheepskins for seating around the central fire. People sleep on cots, and the place is cluttered with purchased equipment: cream separators, a treadle sewing machine, hand tools of all sorts, bedding, clothes, cooking equipment. An ecological adaptation of hundreds of years in the making has always bound these nomads to centers of production far from their own grasslands, self-sufficient as they seem to the casual traveler to be. Lu asks a man, on one of our stops to view the morning milking, where the *qingkou* they eat comes from.

"I don't know. Chengdu, I guess."

On the plain, we had been at 3,500 meters above sea level. Last night, at this altitude, the driver got a nosebleed, his wife had headaches, but Lu and I slept soundly. As we travel westward, the mountains rise before us, and soon we leave the grasslands, grinding up a thirty-degree grade toward their snowy peaks. Only the striking black-and-white magpies so common on the plain accompany us as we ride higher into the hills.

We lunch at eleven in a small town where the driver's wife spots a sign advertising good-quality leather shoes. China's system of distributing goods is haphazard, so if you see something you want—a watermelon, an auto transmission, a pair of pantyhose—you buy it on the spot, as you may never find its like again. We check the shoes out in the large, dull state store. Although short on chic, it carries lots of useful goods at what by Chengdu standards are very reasonable prices, for state planning still supplies remote places with industrial products essentially at cost. Those receiving insulin injections and rubber boots must often feel gratitude.

The valley we ascend is dotted with logging towns interspersed with Tibetan villages in which the houses are all now made of stone, fortresslike. They have curiously shaped and decorated windows, looking at last like Tibetan houses in Lhasa. Their second-story porches are stacked with orange corn; behind them on the hills stand beflagged graveyards.

Our climb to the mountain pass now begins in earnest. The little van cruises along over an astonishingly good road, the main route to Tibet, carrying timber from the interior and military convoys back. Almost everywhere, it is wide enough for trucks to pass without stopping and creeping by, and there is often something of a shoulder between the edge of the road surface and the steep slope down. Partway up, we are briefly stuck in traffic as everything slows around a huge crane endeavoring to raise a crumpled truck body from the abyss below the unprotected shoulder. I urinate discreetly behind a big boulder, pick some snow-covered blue alpine flowers, and unintentionally scare the wits out of Lu, who fears I have fallen down the mountain. We pass all the deciduous and most of the coniferous trees. Snow and cloud appear simultaneously. The road is slushy, visibility a few yards. Our driver nonchalantly passes road-hog trucks on hairpin turns, though he conscientiously blows his horn before doing so. We are over the top, and he decides to move us briskly down the other side of the pass before the force of gravity has time to act. A hair-raising hour later, I can see down into the valley clearly enough to discern the thread of water that has cut it. The last of great bunches of roadside gentians falls behind, the yaks we encounter have scrawny tails, there are power lines, villages, and, finally, both pavement and pigs.

We are still in Tibetan territory with stone houses and fluttering flags. We stop at an inn run by a Tibetan woman entrepreneur—a rare individual, and focus of some attention by the Fulian. She is lovely, hospitable, mildly amused at the slight unease we cover by fulsome admiration of her sash weaving. She ushers us into her family's large living room, bare as a tent around a central hearth of two electric rings set into the floor. It is warm, as Chinese houses never are. Kettles simmer, and the room smells both very alien and deliciously homelike from a combination of woodsmoke, tea, and flour or pastry. Could I have been a Tibetan in a previous life? How can this smell be so *right?* Our hostess offers plain brick tea in bowls—no yak butter in evidence—that the Chinese consume with reluctance. I am a bit put off by *this* smell until I taste the tea, then like it very much.

The husband arrives, a man of great, slow charm, washing face and neck thoroughly and unself-consciously as he chats with us. She runs the inn, mostly, and manages the household with their three daughters, while he has just opened a dance hall. Three nights a week people come from all over the valley to sing and dance. He tried selling tickets, as in Han dance halls, but got no customers.

"With the truckers coming through, and all our local people, I thought a dance hall would be a good business. I'd been to a few in Chengdu City, and seen how the Han people run them. They sell tickets at the door, and also sell food and drinks inside. I tried that, but our Tibetan people refused to pay at the door. 'You can charge us for drinks—that's fair—but you can't charge us just to *dance!*' they said. 'Dancing is part of life, free to everyone. How can you ask money for *dancing?*' I had to agree," he said. "Dancing is part of life, not at all like a bottle of beer."

Abandoning the cover charge, he now makes a profit "even after paying the musicians." The inn caters for long-distance drivers especially.

"We get them from Gansu, from all over Sichuan, from Tibet, from Shaanxi—all over. We hear all the news here first."

Tea drunk, smiles and thanks exchanged, we take our leave.

The rest of the valley holds what must be thousands of Tibetan households, farmers all, with corn on their porches. We turn a corner and see, in golden, gauzy, late-afternoon light, the strange inversion of a trite Impressionist scene: a pretty, groundcover crop in apple-blossomy bloom beneath young, autumn-bare fruit trees. Twenty kilometers of slow downward grade brings us to graveyards marked with branches covered with puffs of cotton, and women wearing bright azure gowns and elaborate sunbonnets. They are Jiang people; Tibet is behind us.

Once, near Hongyuan, and later, in the mountains, we see historical markers memorializing the thousands of Communists who between 1935 and 1937 evaded Guomindang troops by Long Marching from

Jiangxi out beyond the borders of Han life into the Tibetan fringes, and finally to Yan'an in Shaanxi. They picked up Tibetan recruits along the way, some of whom returned after Liberation to become the new Communist leaders of their own people. Who were these leaders? Who are they now? Will some nice young scholar from Harvard salvage the memories for a dissertation before they are all gone?

We will not make it back to Chengdu tonight, though we could if we pushed hard. We will break at a county town, sleep in a boring but adequate guesthouse, reach Chengdu by noon tomorrow. One last, tiny adventure awaits us: I find a stone tablet standing irrelevantly in the guesthouse parking lot bearing an almost worn-away inscription. Into the age-dimmed surface has been roughly carved exhortations to "destroy and confiscate the Chinese imperialist stores and banks." Another memento of the Cultural Revolution. Was the carver a revolutionary young Han, or an angry minority youth? Later, I learn from a native to the region that the entire area was out of government control during the late sixties, and that the choice of term for Chinese on the inscription—*hua*—suggests the latter. I hope the carver knows it's still standing, and, indeed, that the carver is still standing to know it.

Chengdu is *the* metropolis for prosperous Tibetans (who fly in), for poor ones (who hitch truck rides), and for those from within the province (who prosaically take the bus). The West Bus Station is a fine place for spotting them—and a gay assortment of other minority peoples—as they arrive in the city. A woman who runs a couple of small restaurants near the station says she has to train her waitresses carefully. Some minorities just aren't used to Chengdu prices or, sometimes, the very idea of giving money in exchange for food. And the Tibetans try to seduce her workers.

Tibetans tour the city, visit Buddhist temples with elaborate reverence, seek out relatives in the minority leadership training institutes and among the many Tibetan families that reside in Chengdu, and sometimes sell bears' paws or skulls and other odd *materia medica* by the side of busy streets. One of the finest sights I have seen in my whole visit here was a handsome, high-colored Tibetan woman in wine-trimmed black corduroy gown and big boots, swinging past the Jin Jiang Hotel. In her broad, bright sash she carried both a short sword and a substantial dagger. People stared, and smartly got out of her way.

CHAPTER ELEVEN

城都行

In Golden Cow

OCTOBER 23, 1988. GOLDEN COW

We have begun the set of rural interviews that the Fulian has urged me to include in this basically urban study. "Rural" is a misnomer, an administrative convenience, however, for the intensely productive suburb we have selected. The especially prosperous "Golden Cow" district is contiguous and continuous with Chengdu. Great advantages in schooling, job allocation, and other opportunities accrue to those who are registered as city rather than country folk, as "Chengdu City" versus "Golden Cow Township" residents. But to the outsider eye, and for many internal purposes, it is all just one endless city, houses and factories only slowly becoming interspersed with the garden patches on which this monstrously populous province feeds itself.

Most fields are full of vegetables at this season: red rape, tomatoes, endless variations on "Chinese cabbage," a grand spectrum of garlic and onions, cauliflower, red peppers, and rutabaga-sized radish for pickles. Even the national press has commented on the high vegetable prices in Sichuan since this summer's floods; every farmer in the area must be cashing in on the boom. Some fields are freshly ploughed for the spring rice crop, and I enjoy again the time-smoothed coordination of ploughman and water buffalo. Since the late 1970s, households sharecrop on government-allotted land under the "responsibility system," an amazing reversion to pre-1950s family farming and tiny plots. The old / new system makes mechanization purposeless, wiping out decades of experimentation but leaving a valuable residue of irrigation works, roads, and electrification to be run collectively—or not at all.

Visitors in the last century and this have often commented on the Sichuanese habit of living in single farmhouses or small clusters of houses surrounded by gracious bamboo rather than in villages. Such a settlement pattern testifies to the peace and safety of the vast Chengdu basin, where local elders and government officials maintain a well-oiled social order. Still, Sichuan farmyard dogs are vicious, and farmhouses are built like forts against thieves. The new ones now being built everywhere maintain the tradition of small and heavily defended windows and walled courtyards closed in with massive gates.

Markets spring to life every three days at rural crossroads, tying the economy together today as they did before the socialist experiments in managed distribution. On our way to Golden Cow, we pass from jammed townlets full of haggling farmers to open fields around secluded dwellings and back again with dizzying speed. Local folk architecture runs to timber framing showing through whitewashed wattle-and-daub, topped with silvery straw roofs. Many houses were reroofed with tile after 1980, when the policy change toward a more market-oriented economy enabled people to improve their homes. The past few years has seen a rush of building of the two-and three-story poured concrete houses decorated with colorful tiles that seem to be a Chinese farmer's universal response to prosperity. Highly visible along roads, these flamboyant new dwellings thin out rapidly when out of reach of motor vehicles.

Though electric lines run everywhere, there are no roads to many of the houses we visit here. While I carry only a notebook over the narrow tracks, our entrepreneurial hostesses have had to find ways of maneuvering bales of knitted garments or crates of eyeglasses a quarter of a mile or more along foot-wide paddy-field dykes to a road that motor vehicles can traverse. Here, as in Chengdu's traffic, the bicycle is the best answer. This slow transport offers a valuable side-benefit in the form of free information-transmission. Family celebrations, the progress of house building, the appearance of new crops or new faces can be cataloged by quiet cyclists. The whiz of yarn reeling and the buzzing clack of frame knitting murmurs from all directions. A neighbor's success or failure, the ups and downs of the market are messages whispered to every passerby.

Country smells are a treat after Chengdu: fresh turned earth, the funny green odor of sweet potato vines cut for pig feed, manure from many species fermenting in pathside pits, roses and osmanthus in pots in courtyards. Even in the crowded housing and the busy small factories I have come to inspect, the air is far better than that of the city.

Mushroom Grower, 1988

The week's worth of full days we have already spent here has been too full. The women and their households run together now in memory, though my thickening sheaf of notes preserves the detail for later consideration. We have visited women who, alone or with kin, run frame-knitting shops (young women reeling skeins of brilliant acrylic yarn onto bobbins seem to toil in every courtyard); subcontract clothing assembly from larger factories; raise pigs, dairy cattle, or battery hens; grow indecently delicious mushrooms and grapes (these latter out of season, alas); wholesale or retail Chinese herbal medicines; and run a Dickensian print shop and a roadside teahouse full of strikingly handsome bamboo furniture. On the side, I have interviewed the loan officer from an agricultural bank, half-a-dozen hardworking local Fulian women, and the entire membership of a small old-folks' home.

In Golden Cow, as in town, we divide into two teams. Hua has been going off with a ward-level Fulian guide to her interviews morning and afternoon while I do mine with Li and the obligatory local woman. When the other team finishes an interview, they fetch me to meet our subject, be photographed with her, and to take at least a quick look around her business. Every house provides tea, fruit, candy, and the watermelon seeds that amount to a national tic among the Chinese (and to which I too am addicted). The dialect is harder to follow here than in the city, so I listen intently, coming out of each encounter feeling wrung out.

At midday, we return to the township headquarters for the lavish lunch that all Sichuanese like, and cadres insist on. We never eat more than half of it. My quirk about liquids has echoed down the corridors of power; the first day in Golden Cow, I was given as much hot water as I wanted. The second day, I asked for it, but there was none, so I drank beer. Thereafter, I gave up and drank beer. Eating lightly is out of the question; there is too much concern on the part of the local women that I might not like country food, might not dare eat it. I rudely eat most of the vegetables out of all the dishes—nobody seems to want them anyway, the better-quality meat and fish they are serving me being much preferred. I also work on perfecting my method of taking food constantly, but eating only very tiny bits each time. Even so, with a liter of beer and half a kilo of very fat meat inside me, I can barely stagger through some of the afternoons.

With one exception, the local Fulian cadres are wonderful. They know their communities, they are pleasant company, they enjoy the break in routine. The exception, who is simply overzealous, yips like a terrier, fusses like a hen, and tries to force people to give me things as gifts. There is no need for her to raise the issue: during this week, I have been given a kilo of mushrooms, two sweaters, two pair of long black knit underdrawers, a purse full of a green vegetable called (and smelling like) dog's arse, a bouquet of late roses, a pair of sunglasses, several packets of herbal medicine to cure ailments I don't have, and a perfectly lovely pair of handspun, handknit natural wool socks. The County Fulian leader also kindly found a blacksmith who would make me a second mountain-style kindling cutter to help light my lover's fires. As is proper for Chinese hospitality, I, as guest, come away laden with mementos. As is proper for good Communists, my Fulian people refuse even a share in the mushrooms, giving those I try to force on them to the driver. The Fulian has also tried hard to pay for everything we have been given, although they largely fail. In Chinese etiquette, as in any competitive sport, the advantage is always with the home team. In thanks for the interviews, we give both cadres and interviewees silk Fulian scarves in a pretty apricot and brown print.

As entrepreneurs, the women we interview in Golden Cow are doing even better than some of our urban subjects; people with land to work, houses of their own that can be used as rent-free work premises, and a nearby city market to sell to are much envied by many city business-people and the salaried, despite all the limitations of rural life. These women are among the most efficient, confident, and well organized I have talked to, directly responsible for the building of many houses and small factories, and for bringing new skills, like frame knitting, to the area. They are also a little more likely to cooperate directly with their hus-bands than the urban interviewees, a few even falling into the old daugh-ter-in-law's role of family helpmeet rather than "new businesswoman."

Chen Xiulian, Factory Owner

A plain-faced, tiny, forty-seven-year-old, Chen Xiulian greets us in cot-ton shoes, everyday clothes, black cloth work sleeves pulled over her sweater, and a modest gold ring. She makes hash of the sophistries of the one-child policy as she details the table of organization of her machine embroidery factory. With three of her four daughters as forewoman, accountant, and cook, and a resident son-in-law to hump the bales of cloth and finished clothing down the tiny paddy-paths, she has achieved the goal of every Chinese entrepreneur: a management team entirely under her control. Some of the Golden Cow producers of frame-knit tex-tiles and clothing capitalize complex putting-out systems among their neighbors, but Chen keeps all the work under her own roof, and (I would guess) the workers under her thumb.

Dragon-phoenix pillowcases and duck-and-kitten kiddie rompers have nearly taken over the handsome two-story house the profits have allowed her to build. My companions urge her to show us around the house, which she has not only paid for, but designed. Six large rooms downstairs are used to greater or lesser degree in the business—some are workrooms pure and simple, filled with local women at clattering sewing machines or cutting tables. Others are family bedrooms stuffed to capacity with bales of fabric or completed clothing. Only the living room is clear of work, decorated with a plain concrete floor, new uphol-stered sofa and chairs, and a table of knick-knacks. Upstairs, three bed-

Frame-knitting Magnate, 1988

rooms (with bales) cover part of the lower story; the rest of the roof forms an attractive patio. Upstairs there are also a bathing room and separate toilet, crisply tiled, for which all water must be carried.

Chen tells us:

I was born right here. My mother still lives next door in our family home. I have a lot of brothers and sisters, but they are scattered. Around here, couples always move out into their own house when they marry. My husband is a Chengdu man, whose family lived near where the Jin Jiang Hotel stands now. But when the hotel was built in the fifties, the government moved all those people into a little village where nobody had land, so I guess he didn't mind marrying a village girl with a place to build a house! We lived with his family a while—it looks better if you do that— and then moved out here into a small place of our own.

I was in a factory after elementary school until 1960—one of the Three Bad Years. I was sent back to the farm because the government thought they didn't need women in industry then. In 1963 I married and just took care of the children for some time.

When the policy toward private production changed in 1980, I started an embroidery factory, contracting for the work and machines from the former collective village factory. This was all encouraged by the new policy [she said, nervously]. I guarantee the village 7,000 yuan every year for tax and contract, and can keep whatever I make beyond that. I've put 15,000 into it so far, some borrowed, and a few thousand I lost at first, until I learned how to manage better. I started embroidering pillowcases. In 1985, I expanded into making embroidered children's clothing.

This year, I took early retirement from the production brigade—we call it the village now—so I no longer have any connection with local agricultural production organizations. I've entered into a contract to subassemble clothes from another private factory near here. They give me the material, I make the clothes, and they take it back, paying piecework for what we make. We hire fourteen women workers.

Our schedule is very tight because the factory will cut our earnings if we are slow, so I have to hire a lot of girls and keep them on. I get 3.56 yuan for each piece; the workers get about half. It's not risky—you get paid if you do it. Most of my workers earn between 100 and 200 yuan a month, depending on their skill. They're all locals, so they go home to eat and sleep. We don't have to provide dormitory space, but we do give them lunch. My daughters also get paid piecework when they do sewing, and a regular salary for their other work. My oldest daughter earns about 80 a month sewing part time. My son-in-law is a worker outside [and, I learned, uses his company's truck at night to haul Mother-in-law's goods to the wholesale market].

Chen has not yet obtained a license from the township industrial and commercial authorities, so she still pays no tax. Nor is she included in industrial statistics: "I've applied, but it takes a long time to get all the paperwork passed."

When I was young, I managed my own earnings. My parents didn't need me to contribute to the family. I'd give small sums to my sisters for treats, but never saved any. Before I married, I could earn 200-plus a year, raising pigs. That was pretty good money for those days, when everything was cheap to buy. Now I can bring in about 300 a month.

Her 300-a-month figure is such a bare-faced fib that no one addresses it; that would be rude.

Reeling Acrylic for Frame-knitting, 1988

"Three thousand after expenses is more like," Li later estimates. "And I don't believe she didn't save money before she married, either! In my part of Sichuan, whole families hardly earned 200 a year in those days, and even then, they saved some. What could she have spent it on, anyway? There was nothing to buy!"

Our suspicions are confirmed as Chen discusses family expenditures. She manages all the household's money, including her husband's, and laughs at the notion of her men handling cash.

"They spend two or three hundred each month just as pocket money. The family spends another two or three hundred on living expenses— not very much, because I grow some of our food. I myself don't spend more than a hundred, because I don't smoke and play cards, and I entertain only women—who don't smoke and drink."

She is as aware as we are that 300 a month profit would be insufficient for such lavish living. Pride in her substantial managerial accomplishments visibly wars with the prudent wish to maintain a low financial profile before outsiders. Chen's arms and legs wind around each other, knotting her up in anxiously mixed motives. Not wanting to push her into a dangerous candor, I try to turn the conversation toward her children. But Chen has thrown caution to the winds:

"1980 was a big year for me. I not only started the business, but built a new timber-and-tile house to replace our old mud-brick-and-thatch. That was a lovely house—I hired a well-known carpenter, and the beams were eight inches in diameter." In timber-starved Sichuan, this was an expensive elegance.

You need a large, clean, properly lighted house to run a sewing business. I borrowed all my initial capital for the factory—seven or eight thousand—from the township small-business credit union. This was right after I had built the house! And the business is all mine. It has nothing to do with my husband; we stay out of each other's financial affairs. He wasn't earning much, and I had kids in school back in 1980, so my embroidery work paid for it all, and my loans are in my own name. As the business and the family got bigger, I needed to expand. We knocked the old house down, and rebuilt it much bigger and more comfortable this year. I spent 30,000 building this house. It was unexpectedly expensive because costs went up so much in the spring. The credit union gave me a 15,000 mortgage at 0.00712 per cent.

In the full rush of her loquacity, I dare to hope she will tell us anything I ask and push to discover how her four daughters manage their and their husbands' money. This is going too far. Chen's pride pushes her into risky boasts about herself, but she is not going to expose her daughters to criticism. She uncoils herself, relaxes into the familiar stonewalling stance, and deftly dangles an irresistible alternative topic.

My husband is completely feudal about women, and refused to help me educate my daughters. We fought terribly over that. I was right, because with a high-school education, my second was able to pass the tests for a driver's license and my husband wangled her a job in his organization. She's trying to find a way to get a city residence permit now, and education helps with that, too.

We ask her to compare the situations of this state-employed daughter with those of the daughters who work in her firm.

Is it better to work for a family firm? You have fewer limits in some ways. You set your own hours, work as hard as you want, plan for how much to spend and if you want to expand. But it's not like being educated. I had only primary education, and my husband looks down on me for that even though I make a lot of money. Look what he's done for Number Two just because of his worker status. My work doesn't count for much with him. I give money to my mother—once several thousand when Father was sick. I gave my brother a big sum once, just to help him, not for business. But workers never think well of individual entrepreneurship. For one thing, the work's too hard.

I work every day most of the day from 6:30 until after dinner, then watch TV or read the paper. We rarely run into overtime here. All my helpers are married; they have to get home and make dinner.

In 1963, when I was twenty-five, I met my husband—a city boy who had been assigned to work in the countryside. His family was badly off then—his mother was a widow. These were the years just after the Great Leap, and things were bad for everyone, so we weren't fussy about the gifts each side was supposed to send at weddings. His family sent us some meat and candy, we gave them nothing. My dowry was only a pair of socks—Mother was so poor! I bought quilts and bedding and kitchen equipment with 200 yuan that my husband and I had saved. Everyone was poor then.

I just kept having children to give him a boy, but finally I said enough was enough. I've never had an abortion. We use a loop, but I don't bother with that sort of thing any more. We have too many kids, but they're all good daughters. I'd rather have had just one—I was working myself to death when they were small. I was really pressured by my husband and by neighbors to try for a boy. And four isn't too many if you can take care of them—look at how they all help me now. I can work with my own people, and daughters are more obedient than sons. But if I were only going to have one, the way things are for young people—well, I'd want to have a boy for the family to keep the name going. I know, that's old-society thinking, but you have to have someone to give the property to, and a son-in-law isn't your own child. Our son-in-law is only a worker, so he could never afford to buy the property we have now. I thought it would be good to bring another man in and keep my daughter at home. It's turned out well, having them here. I'll try to get local boys for the others, too, boys who will not want my daughters to move away. Not all girls want to marry near their mothers, even these days—but mine are obedient, good girls.

From the woman who gave me socks, and from several even older ones—up to eighty-seven years—in the old folks' home, I have pieced together a little of the history of women's work in textiles in this region. Machine-woven cloth only came into common use in the Chengdu basin after 1954, when the railroad reached the city. Before that, many women spun and wove a variety of fabrics from regionally grown fibers—cotton, silk, hemp, ramie, and wool—for family use and for sale.

The flat, irrigated basin fields produced rice, vegetables, and other foodstuffs; fibers were grown on hilly land around the perimeter, especially to the north and south. People always referred to these as poor areas because the land was relatively unproductive and because, in the past, women there worked so constantly at making cloth to support their families.

I was especially interested in learning whether women could keep themselves by this work: whether spinning and weaving were in part responsible for the stereotypical strength and independence of Sichuanese women. The sixty-seven-year-old sock maker, demonstrating how she spun woolen yarn as she spoke, had been the only child of a widow. She and her mother were given a home by her mother's brother—her father had smoked away his farm before he died—but were expected to earn their keep, which they did. She claimed that a woman could support herself, but no more than that. She began at seven to spin, and twelve to weave, and was able to maintain herself by her midteens. After she became skilled, she could weave ten *chiang* (100 feet) of fourteen-inch-wide cloth in "a day and a night." She and her mother spun and wove cotton for the household's clothing and wove fine, lustrous hemp cloth for sale as summer clothing and mosquito nets. Her mother's brother kept the cloth they made, selling the hemp fabric and surplus cotton cloth. They got no money for it, although in families rich enough to spare the income, the cash a daughter earned was saved to purchase her dowry.

In hilly counties, women and girls spun and wove until machine textile production in Chengdu and the transportation system were able to supply industrial yard goods even to remote areas. The last remnants of homespun cotton and hemp production disappeared as, under the Great Leap Forward in 1958, women began to work in the fields. Fieldwork for women earned them workpoints worth only one *fen* each. I guessed, and the old spinner confirmed, that this was considerably less than they had

Cutters and Stitchers, 1988

earned as textile makers before the machine-made product made their work obsolete. It seems fair to attribute at least part of the local success in bringing women into the outdoor workforce during the commune period to this sudden disappearance of the spinning and weaving in which so many Sichuan girls and women had long been employed.

I asked if any customs of marriage resistance or delay had emerged similar to those that appeared in the Canton delta when silk reeling for late-nineteenth-century export gave many women good incomes. No, she thought. Women did not earn enough for that kind of independence, and they didn't get the money directly themselves—it went to parents or husbands or whoever took care of them. But she told me of a young woman she had known whose mother, a widow, refused to let her daughter marry, the two of them keeping themselves by spinning and weaving. The widow feared that any change in her family status might cause her dead husband's family to withdraw the limited support they gave her based on her and her child's claim to the husband's share of land. Mother and daughter lived together till the older woman died, the daughter remaining a spinster throughout life.

In a Golden Cow old folks' home, four women had made textiles to sell as girls, and three had earned their dowries thereby. Villages specialized in different fabrics depending on what fibers were grown locally, they said. In their home regions, down in the basin, homespun and handwoven cotton cloth disappeared just after the Japanese war.

I quizzed these elders as well about opium growing, which in their youth was common and depended on intensive hand labor by young women and men. Travelers in Sichuan's hilly areas early in this century often remarked on the beauty and ubiquity of pink-and-white poppy fields. A ninety-four-year-old from a mountain county told me how she had cut the poppy seed capsules with a five-pointed knife in the evenings, returning in the mornings to scrape the dried sap into balls for sale. Raw opium earned more than grain as a crop—much more. Everyone grew it, if they had land and the family labor to harvest it. Hiring labor to collect opium was rare; it was grown on family land, with family labor, as far as any of the old people knew. The tiny balls of drying gum were too precious to put in the hands of untrustworthy outsiders. Opium production was prohibited after the 1911 revolution in the area around Chengdu. If I wanted to learn more about it, they told me, I should go to the mountain areas "where the minorities live."

Despite their contributions as the spinners and weavers who clothed their countryfolk and put a little cash in their parents' pockets, my informants insisted that both rich and poor families disliked girls, killing many of them at birth. The uncle of one woman had had four of his five daughters drowned. Girl babies were sometimes left where cattle would tread on them. Some girls were sold at seven or so as maidservants—one of the old women had been sold in this way. The dislike for girls was, they thought, a consequence of the dowry a girl was expected to bring with her at marriage. An old man who had earned his living carrying sedan chairs said that a large dowry might require eighty men to carry all the chests and containers. Families asked a bride-price for their girls so that the grooms' families contributed at least a part of the cost of the dowry. But the poor, all agreed, gave neither bride-price nor dowry. And really poor men, because of the shortage of girls, never married at all.

These elderly women talked too of footbinding, which all had experienced as little girls. At the urging of the staff members, and with far less awkwardness than I myself was feeling at this unexpected revelation, one old woman unwrapped her foot to show me. I looked at the four small toes, whose upper surfaces have become part of the foot's sole, at the knobby clump of broken bones that had been an arch, at the neat, quarter-inch slot (where you might fit a quarter) between what was once the bottom of the heel and the lowest toe joints, and I did not faint. But for a light-headed moment, I saw the four little girls—seven, five, three, and newborn—who had lived in the room next to mine in Taibei. Xiaoping, clattering up the stairs after school; Xiaocui, climbing on the furniture again; Xiaozhen, tippy-toeing to my bedroom to peek and giggle at the foreign auntie; Xiaozhu, a fourth and unintended daughter, announcing by the vigor of her baby squalls that she too would be a holy terror for her overburdened young mother. I saw Chengdu's streets, suddenly full, after school, of girls and bookbags and pigtails, all running, bouncing, flying. I remembered going on point in ballet classes, and learning about the blisters and the blood necessary to the dancer's grace. Those who deplore revolutions because of the violence that accompanies them should look at a bound foot, and try to total the cost of customary aggressions before condemning more limited reigns of terror.

On this, the last day of our rural sortie, the Fulian and I fall again into a giggly holiday spirit, laughing all the way home at our various initial errors and misperceptions, and at some of the more outrageous financial fabrications we have been offered. We give a lift to one particularly lovely local cadre whose face we had seen drawn with anxiety over her daughter-in-law's ordeal of childbirth, and over the unknown health of the soon-to-appear grandchild. Now she, and we, can rejoice at the successful arrival of a fat little girl. We learn the truth of the nasty rumor that a local girl had been conned into traveling to Hebei for work and then sold as a bride. But she has been rescued by the Hebei Fulian, put on the train, and escorted back home by the Golden Cow Fulian, with little harm done. We agree to take the following day off, giving ourselves a long weekend to catch up with all the women's tasks we have put off these last tired evenings. We have reached interview number eighty-four.

CHAPTER TWELVE

城都行

Getting It Wholesale

NOVEMBER 5 OR SO, 1988. CHENGDU

It is time to crawl out of being bedbound and face life. I have been a little bit sick, but mostly in hiding for four days, sleeping a lot and having meals on a tray. My ailment is a perfect example of what the Chinese call "an excess of *qi*"—a bodily meltdown caused by unmanageable anger.

A week ago, one of my Chinese visitors appeared at my room with a slip of paper that I must sign before she could leave. The men at the gate-house had been badgering visitors to register in writing and leave their identification papers at the door since a new gatekeeper arrived the previous week. A new policy about limiting Chinese access to foreigners has been filtering down from Beijing, he said. I had spoken to him a couple of times about this; no Chinese wants a permanent record of casual visits to foreigners. Some people had very bad times over even trivial contacts during the Cultural Revolution. The gatekeeper said that orders were orders. The policy was designed to protect our valuables from thieves and ourselves from importunate petitioners. I was firm, but didn't really expect to get anywhere with my insistence that *my* guests at least should not have to register.

The business with the slip of paper happened again the next night. The following day, I tracked down the functionary known in Chinese as a *waiban*—an official whose job it is to manage foreigners—and told him my views. He, unsurprisingly, told me that orders were orders and that the policy was designed to protect us. In my best hyperdemocratic American style, I told him that none of us had requested such protection, or agreed to it.

My brashness was based on the knowledge that the man had been the subject of a good deal of unpleasant gossip among the foreigners in residence. *Waiban* are by definition unpopular, but this one seemed to be playing fast and loose with currency exchanges.[1] I therefore assumed his bad conscience would make him cautious. Not so; his responses were as snide and unhelpful as ever.

I turned up the volume. Soon we were both yelling at each other (my Chinese was amazingly fluent and effective, I thought, with detached pleasure). When it seemed time to bring the discussion to a close, I informed him that his attitudes were those of the never-to-be-sufficiently-repudiated Gang of Four period, and stalked off to continue carving a Halloween pumpkin. An interested audience of Institute students—who were putting up orange-streamer-and-black-witch decor for a Canadian-organized dance that evening—cast appraising looks in my direction. Only then did I realize that the audience included the *waiban*'s perfectly nice teenage daughter.

The Halloween party will probably go down in Economic Management Training Institute lore as the gala of the century. A hundred expats and their slightly confused Chinese guests danced loudly and drank foolishly, trying with great goodwill to break cultural boundaries that have baffled both sides since Marco Polo's time. The Fulian came, good sports all. I made them dance with me, costumed idiotically as a little Chinese maiden with an outsized papier-mâché head and traditional apron updated with the legend "Girls Just Want to Have Fun." Somewhere amid the heaps of photographs that commemorated the party is one of me and Jiang Yinghong looking faintly pained (I am a terrible dancer) but game, and another of Li Jufang gazing with undisguised wonder at two Canadians in outrageous and (fortunately) undecipherable drag queen getups. A Canadian with a wide range of unpredictable talents led us all in the by-then-notorious Chicken Dance—a round dance in which we pretend to be chickens laying eggs. So our Fulian contingent all danced together, Hua and Jiang and Li and Li's little boy, who looks so much like his mother, and the pretty temporary translator and her young doctor husband, and Lu Fubuzhang, and me, before they made transparent excuses and escaped the noise and chaos and incipient drunkenness that never quite materialized. I left soon after, listening to the rest of the party—perforce—through my bedroom window. It

[1] The *waiban* was later officially charged with this, so my reference here presumably can do him no harm.

wound up to a roar and was cut off with the electricity at eleven by the uneasy security people.

The next day I felt dreadful: too much *qi* for the bureaucratic *waiban*, or simply too much punch? I went to bed, and felt worse; and the following day, worse yet. Having called off work for that morning, I was still abed at ten when my door thundered ominously. Bedraggled and befuddled, I opened it to see the *waiban*. He was backed up by an Institute employee who, it was rumored, had recently broken a woman accountant's jaw in a fit of pique. Starchily, the *waiban* handed me an envelope and began to babble about people, or a person, whom I did not remember. The effort to concentrate was too much for my low blood pressure and empty stomach; like a caricature of a fragile foreign woman, I fainted dead away.

Even as I fell, I realized that nothing could have been a more suitable move. A *waiban* who loses a foreign guest is in deep shit.

The faces hovering above me when I came round were as white as mine felt. They bore me up, they phoned for a doctor, they had me sent breakfast in bed, they robbed one of the Canadians of his electric heater to warm the room, and they even conveyed their original message with perfect clarity: the artist from the scenic trip had sent me a painting, with his compliments.

For a few days, people fussed over me in a thoroughly satisfactory way. The Fulian arrived en masse with kilos of oranges, Mongolian oatmeal, and instant coffee. Dear Jufang brought an electrical gadget like a little flying saucer to warm me in bed. The thing provided the only entertainment of this dull, unhappy time-out by defying the laws of thermodynamics: it continues to heat up after you disconnect it, and melted a round flat patch in my bedroom carpet when I left it plugged in for more than the statutory three minutes. It must run on nuclear fusion; the Chinese are holding out on us. The young woman who cleans the rooms came round to sit with me, knit, and speculate about the broken jaw. And the *waiban* visited punctiliously for the first three days.

At last I grow ashamed of this somatic drama (one of the staff tells me that the poor *waiban* is hanging on to his mental equilibrium with his eyebrows). I thank everyone for taking care of me, and return to duty.

My anger has done no one any good. Outside visitors must still submit to the gate-check. As my latest emission of hostility against all things Chinese dissipates, memory returns me to the long lines I waited in every two weeks, decades ago, in the old Taibei railway station. To go south, as I urgently wanted to do, you had, in 1974, to buy your ticket the day before. Most tickets, however, were sold out the back door to scalpers and hotels with contacts. Some were kept unsold in case an official demanded seats at the last minute. A few were actually sold to fools like me, to ordinary working people with no pull, to runners who bought for small hotels and travel agencies. The ticket windows opened at seven in the morning, but to be assured of getting a seat on a train that would arrive in four or five hours instead of eight or nine, I had to line up by six, or even five-thirty.

Already in the grip of my first, and soon-to-be-incapacitating depression, I waited the hour in gut-clenching anxiety lest the untouchable clerk behind the grille greet me with a mendacious *"Mai wanle"*—"Sold out." Now, here, older, more determined, a foreign lady in an earlier phase of semi-colonialism, I can always get tickets on *something;* but I still cannot get a general passport for my guests at the Economic Management Training Institute.

How many generations of Chinese have left official doors with gnashing teeth and compromised immune systems after a failed effort to loosen the rusted immobility of the Chinese power system? How many millions have ruefully learned that even in tiny, daily, personal matters the *gong* sphere of life—hopelessly mistranslated as "public"—will set the limits? How often do I have to sicken from the suppression of my extravagant, North American taste for autonomy before I learn to somehow grease the skids to my goal?

NOVEMBER 10, 1988. CHENGDU CITY WHOLESALE MARKET

We are concluding our work by interviewing sixteen women who wholesale goods in one of three large markets near Chengdu's railway station. It is the entry and transshipment point for half of this enormous province, and the distribution point to all of southwest China for goods from Shanghai, Chongqing, Xian, Kunming, Tibet, and beyond. In earlier interviews, we have already met entrepreneurs big enough in business scope to use this network directly. Talking to a few more should illuminate the wider marketing system into which all our subjects must somehow fit their trade.

The Fulian has already contacted the market administrators. One group seems especially welcoming. The managers of the daily goods market will allow us to use their offices (we offer, and they accept, a small fee for this convenience). Their market, specializing in clothing, tea, peanuts, sunflower seeds, and seasonings, is well run by leaders familiar with the concessionaires. This venue is better suited to our purposes than two others I have visited, where state and collective units wholesale factory textiles and mountains of fresh fruit. I later infer that my sober daily commodities traders are associated with less lunatic wheelings and dealings than the nearby wholesalers of rare and precious herbal medicines and industrial chemicals. We tour *their* turf with hasty ceremony one slow day, but interview only among the peanut candy and corduroy romper venders. Getting into the Chinese medicine market might be exotic, but the very large capitals necessary to this trade will make people secretive, and generally exclude women. The Number Three North Railway Station Wholesale Market it is, then.

The Fulian and I are tired. None of us will admit it, but it's true. These wholesalers and the market administrators—mostly men—are interesting and can teach me a lot about how business works in Chengdu. But I have to haul enthusiasm for each one up from deep reserves. The traders come to the office, two by two, to tell one or the other of us the familiar outlines of their lives, three or four a day, for a last, busy week. They are busy too, for their tiny stalls must be overseen constantly so as not to miss sales in the sometimes frantic commerce. They answer us briskly, and turn with relief to the end-of-interview ceremony of inspecting their goods and apprentices and being photographed with me in front of them.

Unexpected details distinguish individuals through my growing fog. One wholesaler is the estranged wife of a market administrator. He has pushed her out of the business they built jointly over a long marriage to take up with a younger woman. Li, who has already sat with her over the questionnaire, warns me in advance against tactless questioning of her or her husband, who will explain the market itself to us.

One interviewee recounts with uneasy awe how, a year ago, she died and was left in a morgue for two or three days, coming back to consciousness just in time to escape cremation. She is a very devout Buddhist now, she says, as the result of her miraculous escape. She and her woman partner have a tiny religious image tacked to their stall, the only trace I see here of the age-old connection between markets and the gods.

Another tells us something I ought to have known weeks ago—that price controls for all goods are fixed at the wholesale level in an elaborate compromise between a planned and a fully *laissez-faire* market. Questioned, the administrators deny that the government fixes commodity prices. Whom to believe? An economist at the Economic Management Training Institute verifies and expands on the original state-

Partners in Plumbing, 1988

ment over Canadian spaghetti and imported Spanish red that very night. Wholesale commodity prices for Chengdu and the rest of the province are set every quarter by the Bureau of Commerce and Industry. Whether it makes a difference—whether people *ever* trade at these prices—would require another study, perhaps another lifetime.

The Bureau of Commerce and Industry, I already know, issues licenses for all small businesses. Bribes speed up the lengthy process of getting these licenses that, puzzlingly, lots of my informants don't bother to obtain.

"People who work there always have three gold watches and ten gold rings," a matter-of-fact seller of kaleidoscopic socks tells me. The bribes are only really substantial, though, for businesses bigger than the ones I am studying, for those that consume unusual amounts of electricity or other scarce resources, or for those illegally using public assets as if they were their own.

Number Three Wholesale Market is a pleasant place to work both for us and, apparently, for its daily denizens. Roofs keep off summer rain and sun while the absence of walls keeps the air as fresh as it ever is in this industrial sector. One sees people here, hears the news. The kindness and helpfulness subjects have so often mentioned as they describe their experiences of learning and doing business are enacted on every hand. A baby nods off on a neighbor's sack of sunflower seeds, an old woman is helped to the well-maintained toilets, people snag wandering toddlers, and nibblers offer snacks to neighboring stallkeepers. As they work or play cards during slow times, people behave much as they might do in the half-outdoor, rarely private life of a quiet residential street.

During that last week, we encounter, by chance, four or five women whom we have interviewed elsewhere in the city or in Golden Cow, supervising their wholesale stalls or simply peddling commodities from baskets in the market's open spaces. Many of the hundreds of peddlers crowding Chengdu's evening streets with hastily spread displays of goods are agents of such women, hired to sell at retail, wherever they can find a pitch. The absence of literal and figurative overheads is good for bosses, bad for jobbers who will lose if their goods are damaged by rain or confiscated by police. For street-sellers, a stall in this market is a dream to be counted up with the night's takings.

For me, working here turns out to be specially pleasurable in many unforeseen ways. The office stands well away from the noise of traffic, so that I understand nearly everything I am told. My interpreter fills her time pouring tea, peeling apples, and refilling the trays of sunflower seeds that we all constantly consume in an unceasing tea party. By the end of the day, the floor is crunchy with a hospitable litter of shells, cores, and tea leaves. For lunch, a raucous and delicious break in the tight-focused concentration of steady interviewing, we treat or are treated by the market managers in nearby stalls. The older managers get cheerfully drunk over their official guest-honoring lunch, and I get at least a few sips of ferocious *baigar* to take off the chill. Twice, an administrator–stallkeeper who sells the crisp fungus called wood ears brings a basin of his finest to contribute to our meals.

I wish I had photos of the rough, open-fronted sheds with their characteristic woven bamboo ceilings and handsome, grubby bamboo furniture, of the overworked scullery girls and the fat, filthy cooks, of the ancient woman picking over vegetables in a patch of sunshine, of the steam and smoke and savor of frying peppers just behind our table. But, as courtesy urges, I restrain myself from using my camera on those old-fashioned, inelegant sights. To enjoy them as I do shows a laudable common touch, an absence of pretension appropriate to the occasion. To take them home in snapshots, evidence of China's "backwardness," would label me a sneaky snob.

On our last day in the market, the Fulian appears with a framed painting on glass of a colorful sunrise. We ask an administrator with experience in this medium to inscribe a poetic couplet of thanks on one side of the picture and my name and the date on the other. This is the first time this market has ever been investigated by any sort of social scientist, let alone a foreigner. The event seems worth commemorating. The sunrise is hung prominently among other framed awards and commendations; the research fee is given, discreetly, at a later time.

Number Three Wholesale Market lies as far as possible within the city limits from the Economic Management Training Institute. It is a straight shot across town on Renmin South and Renmin North roads, with Mao Zedong's benevolent statue at dead center. If I ride like hell, I can bike there in forty minutes, but coming home in traffic after one of these long days takes me nearly an hour. For once, the Fulian women are closer to their home base, also in the north half of the city.

We ride together about a third of the way home, at first sharing the more interesting bits of the day's work, later turning to the difficulties of presenting a systematically feminist point of view to a society that does not always want to see it. Although our versions of feminism differ on many points, we have much in common. And we are utterly in harmony on the frustrations of social activism.

As an amateur propagandist of women's rights to American college students, I do not have the Fulian's concern about getting my feminist "line" officially correct (though heaven knows my colleagues tell me quick enough when my ideology is adrift). Running sexual harassment programs for surly male physics and philosophy professors, steering juicy young people toward reliance on contraceptives more efficacious than beer, warning overenthusiastic wenches that competition over the notches in their bedposts is not what I mean by feminism: all these have Chinese analogs. Such interventions are usually unwelcome or simply puzzling, as when we preach to inexperienced women who believe that the battle for equality was won at Liberation or in the Sixties. At least I do not confront the Fulian dilemma of trying to compensate for gender inequities that officially are not admitted to exist.

Having spent my college years intensely aware of the absolute allomorphism of "mother" and "graduate student," I am endlessly amazed that my students perceive so dimly the tight, short link between absolutely reliable control of reproduction and female autonomy. Even my undergraduates' *parents* do not remember the bad old days before women had contraceptive options, when a night of ill-timed intimacy could permanently shatter a would-be anthropologist's future with a simple, wholesome pregnancy. A main part of Fulian work, these days, is to keep even marital pregnancies from snapping the slippery connection between population and resources. The Fulian does not have to accept the premise that a woman has a right to do anything she wants with her body; they see all too clearly the tidal wave of innocent infants that lurks in the age-sex pyramid.

Whether they are party members or not, the Fulian are part of the Chinese Communist Party apparatus. It is their job to keep abreast of policy and to promote it. On our bike rides I learn a lot about the current pressure toward returning women to domestic tasks to lessen (male) unemployment, and about how hard that policy is to swallow. These women for years have stood fast on the Marxist principle that only through work out in society can women win full social membership. Now, with "reform," they are called on to promote a market-driven ideal of women's lives. It is an ideal they cannot stomach for themselves. They have no desire to urge it on women who, by and large, very much want work for the independence and income it brings them.

We talk, too, on our bicycles, of how women who would remain at home might respond to the birth-limitation policy which thus far has limited most urban families to one baby. Will staying at home and the resulting lack of income for women put more pressure on them to contribute children to their domestic economies, as I argue it will? Or will the lower living standard of a single-income family make life so economically straitened that few couples would find a second child feasible, as the Fulian women insist? Their own families are each supported by two meager salaries from state units. The one-child mothers could hardly shoehorn a second child into their households, and the two-child mothers face with mounting anxiety the prospect of educating and then finding jobs and marriages for both. True for the cities, I allow. But *rural* families could surely maintain a few extra young ones until they reach nine or ten and can help with the chickens, after which they will pay their own way. Oh no, the Fulian rebuts. In the first place, the Sichuan countryside is overloaded with labor and very short on jobs of any kind. A mother who follows my logic pays for this ancient, pronatalist strategy by seeing her children struggle with the same—or worse—economic difficulties as she herself has endured. Many of my Fulian associates have rural relatives, cousins and nieces, whose harsh lives and truncated futures contrast achingly with the brighter prospects of their own daughters.

Theory aside, we agree, the really hard part of our activist work is to get people to pay attention to whatever it is that we want our audiences to hear. Fulian women grumbling about the difficulty of getting people to meetings, of persuading them to think in new ways, of overcoming the bland optimism of the young and inexperienced sound exactly like the complaints I hear at Women's Studies lunches at Central Michigan University. I am no fan of Leninist parties, but I had thought them a bit more efficacious than Alice, Nancy, Joyce, Martha, Ulana, and the rest of us, trying to get the Dean to spring for a broom-closet for our part-time work-study typist. It seems that they are not.

Sometimes near tears, sometimes laughing helplessly at ourselves and our sisters, the Fulian and I wave good-bye. They peel off for Ningxia Street, and I pick up speed for the home stretch. The parting of the ways leaves me in the tree-filled center of the city, behind Mao Zedong. Under the empire and early republic, this precinct housed provincial official-dom and their supernatural counterpart, the City God. His temple was razed to build Mao's statue and the vast provincial commodities exhibition hall that looms behind it. Far less visible are the well-protected home / office complexes of the provincial government, and the head-quarters of the military forces that ensure Sichuan's rule over Tibet and the entire southwest.

I am often overtaken by army convoys on this sycamore-shaded stretch of road. The enlisted men in trucks behave like enlisted men in trucks. They leer or wave or sleep as they are carried from nowhere to nevermind. Officers, however, ride in sedans or motorcycle sidecars, scarlet patches flashing, arrogance palpable. They are brothers, indeed, to "the mandarin, a good-looking young man" whom Isabella Bird Bishop watched taking his ease on a brothel-boat in 1897.

"Like all others I have seen of the higher official class, he looked immeasurably removed from the common people. The assumed pas-sionlessness of his face expressed nothing but aloofness and scorn."[2]

What a shame, what a loss, these Chengdu dandies represent. During the 1949 Revolution, China had the sense to narrow the difference between officers and men, between army and people. Since Deng, they

---

[2] Isabella Bird Bishop, *The Yangtze Valley and Beyond* (London: John Murray, 1899), 14.

have succumbed to giving high-born majors and captains reason to believe their judgment is worth more than another's. Looking like Princeton grad students at a costume party, they lounge beside their attendants, gloved hands prim, smug, and unaccustomed to civilians holding their ground in traffic. When a sidecar swipes my pedal, the occupants do not even turn to see if damage has been done. A couple of years building a nice big dam with teaspoons is what this officer corps needs.

NOVEMBER 16, 1988. CHENGDU

Finished! We have 100 interviews in hand, and are very pleased with ourselves. We are going to take a long weekend off while I entertain a guest and the Fulian holds an in-house celebration of its own (I *may* take my visitor to the *jiaozi* wrapping contest that is one of their mass-work duties) before we settle in to finish the coding.

Or rather, to be honest, before I shove the rest of the coding off on the Fulian. It is a rotten, undemocratic, indeed an unsisterly thing to do, because coding is such a loathsome job. But I am going to do it, nonetheless, and not simply because I have a grant application to write, sheaves of notes to update, courses to plan for January, and shopping to do for useful books, Christmas presents, and silk underwear. No, I am going to shove it off on them because I can. Absolute power corrupts absolutely; you really can't trust anyone over forty-five, especially when they have tenure.

NOVEMBER 18, 1988. CHENGDU

My dearest buddy has been visiting from Beijing, bringing brandy, croissants, and (gasp!) cream cheese. While ninety-nine percent of Beijingers will never have heard of these last two treats, their very availability confirms what I have long suspected: Beijing is another country. Visiting there is like visiting Venezuela or the Canary Islands. You won't learn anything much about China from it. John, knowing more about China than almost anyone from anywhere, also knows that; we don't have to argue about it. He has already seen all the visitor-friendly sights here, so we are free to prowl the shopkeeper's city that I am coming to know. He joins the Canadian bike-pack, and we all swap useful information and tall tales.

A long bus ride through heavily industrial suburbs precedes our outing to the Chengdu Zoo. We dutifully view the pandas and, with considerably more astonishment, the endangered giant salamander, displayed in a small, red, plastic washtub. We are stopped and surrounded by a dozen Iraqi airmen—very young, very homesick. They are pilots-in-training doing an interminable six months on an airfield too far from the city to allow for unchaperoned excursions. We are all fellow-Westerners, they assert. We understand each other; the Chinese are *really* strange. John quizzes them in French about Iraq-Chinese relations until their officer sails up on his large mustache and scolds them away toward the pandas.

Then, with MTV logic and timing, we find ourselves on the grounds of an immense and very down-at-heel shabby temple. Inquiring of zookeepers and old women who are plainly not here for the salamanders, we learn that the whole zoo was built on land formerly belonging to the huge temple complex, which was razed during the Cultural Revolution.

"A lot of people are still mad that some of the zoo's land was given to the Buddhist Association to rebuild this temple," a zoo worker told us. "It's all feudal superstition, anyway."

It is difficult to determine how much of Zhaojue Si—the Temple of Enlightenment—was destroyed by Cultural Revolution enthusiasts. Plenty of rubbly spaces stand unused; heaps of broken stone and timber that once were buildings and monuments are piled in corners. The structures around which the crowd now swirls are little more than sheds, erected in haste. Their cheapness is brightened by sheets of red paper on which contributors' names are listed in their thousands. More such jerry-built constructions are being hammered together, sloppily. I am saddened that Chengdu folk will have to put up with such ugliness. The old temple, judging by its fragments, was a magnificent archive of folk architecture, sculpture, and painting. Years later, I will learn that some buildings had been walled off from Cultural Revolution damage and merely need opening and refurbishment. By the time I visit these grounds in the spring of 1994, they are repaired and in use, new concrete temples and pagodas are sprouting everywhere, and the temporary sheds have vanished.

This day, I am in luck. Today is not just an ordinary first or fifteenth of the lunar month at Zhaojue Si, but a rare and special ritual occasion. The grounds are thronged with hundreds of old women, many with bound feet, arranging for red-robed lamas to chant sutras for "world peace, the great Chinese people, and the souls of those lost in the Sichuan floods of

1988." The folk religion that I have imagined was extinct in the city is reclaiming its territory, with shock troops of pious old ladies leading the charge. This is a *pudu*, a "universal salvation" ceremony giving peace to the souls of those who die unknown and unmourned.

In these Chengdu weeks, I have seen more production processes than ceremonies, more sharp young women in black stretch pants than faded old ones in soft, tiny shoes. I have listened to more people for whom *the* revolution was the Cultural Revolution of 1966 to 1975 rather than the founding Revolution of 1949, when Communist troops from Shaanxi liberated this ancient capital and erstwhile Nationalist stronghold. I have come in order to see the new and the now, but I am delighted to have wandered into the vast temple being reconstructed with the funds attracted by the poor, drowned ghosts. With field trips to Taiwan shaping my vision, the temple grounds of Zhaojue Si offer fewer surprises than the buildings of the Women's Federation. It is relaxing to get away from Communist political-economic exoticism, and back to the easy familiarity of people kowtowing to abbots and burning tinsel spirit money for the dead.

Pudu is a staple of traditional Chinese ritual. In 1974, I saw it movingly performed by Fuzhou people in a Taibei graveyard. The gathering of living and dead, the days-long holy chanting, the burning of incense, spirit money, and paper clothing were undertaken to soothe the otherworldly essences of Fuzhou compatriots who had perished in the civil war of the 1940s. Thousands of tiny paper figures, each representing a known or an anonymous spirit, and each paid for by a substantial money contribution to the event, received these offerings in temporary chapels. On the last, rainy night, the black-and-purple-clothed figures were loaded into gay paper boats. Ten-foot-tall, ghostly guides carried the fragile loads across a symbolic bridge, then returned their cargoes of souls to the world of the spirit in an explosion of bright flame. In this way, Taibei's Fuzhou immigrants salved old griefs, networked, advertised their pious uprightness to the city's other communities, and neatly circumvented government attempts to quash unofficial social organizations.

Chengdu's *pudu* was different in detail, and not so lavish. Most of the money that visiting Sichuanese were contributing in the name of the drowned would go to temple rebuilding. The combination of compassion and politically correct fundraising that governed the proceedings was the same as in Taibei, however; in the Chinese world, people must push and shove their cranky elites to gain a little cultural breathing space.

Zhaojue Si was once famous for its flower gardens, and there are still many to see. When rebuilt, it will be a pleasant place to wander, picnic, play with children, photograph the chrysanthemums that creep in graceful swags from pots, and ramble through camellia and wintersweet. These are all appropriate things to do at temples. What, besides anticipation of these pleasures, prompts the generosity of donors whose names are written on the walls? Piety? Aesthetics? Or the unimpeachably rationalized but essentially anti-government stance that Taiwanese adopt when they support folk rituals that their officials are eager to suppress? Working-class Taiwanese people like their gods, their temples, their sometimes saturnalian religious processions in large part because the rigid old government did not like them. They like them because they perform them by and for themselves, without a lot of Confucian Pecksniffery. In Chengdu, so far, folk religion remains tightly confined to a few "open" temples. I hope I will be on the scene to see the inevitable confrontation between official Buddhism and the colorful popular imagination; I will bet on the old ladies.

John and I are ejected from the zoo at dusk. It is miles back to the guesthouse, with buses few and far between. We opt for "small eats" at a roadside shelter near the zoo gates.

"Who's the boss?" I query.

"It's a boss-lady here," a broad-faced young waiter informs me.

"Wonderful! I want to interview her!" And so I do, while we enjoy her delicious, fiery *chaoshao* (wontons) and warm beer. At twenty-something, she is having the time of her life, building a new house for herself, her husband, and her little boy (who likes *chaoshao* too), and employing half-a-dozen younger fellow-villagers. I tell her I'm working with the Fulian.

"Oh," she laughs, "people will never tell you the truth with cadres around." And then she tells me just about what all the other restaurant-keepers in the sample have told me, about wages, and hours, and income, and outgo, and the endless taxes. Stuffed and pleased with our new acquaintances, we decide to pop for one of the private minibuses that pick up and drop passengers anywhere on a set route, and we go home.

CHAPTER THIRTEEN

城都行

Weighing the Harvest

DECEMBER 1, 1988. CHENGDU

Hua, Jiang, and Li have been making the trek every day to the Economic Management Training Institute guesthouse rather than my pedaling the equal distance to the Fulian headquarters, which I have offered to do. This arrangement is legitimized in terms of my status and the greater available space in my apartment for the messy business of coding. But I am being coddled. They know I hate to rise early; this way, I can be shoveling down the last of my oatmeal as they come up the stairs about nine, having had an extra hour in bed. Anyway, they say, it's more fun here than in the Fulian: "There's no one to tell us what to do." I am very glad this venue is suitable, for the weather is finally becoming wintry, often dipping near freezing at night. The Fulian headquarters is drafty and uncomfortable, with breezy semi-exposed toilets and cold wicker chairs. Nor is there anywhere much to eat nearby.

Much better to stay in the guesthouse, where the windows close, the stuffy furniture keeps one's bottom warm, and we have reliable supplies of boiling water. The Chinese call such residences, with all their comforts, "panda houses" because we, like pandas, are "cute, big eaters, and perfectly useless." An electric space heater, two sets of long underwear, sweatpants, a heavy sweater, and a shawl keep the chill off. The Fulian women bear this heat graciously, shedding jackets and sweaters; unacclimated guests burst into perspiration and open the doors to let the heat out. Thus accommodated, we set to work analyzing our informants' work versus children dilemma.

"In former times, women worked only at home, and so should have more children. Now, they also work outside, so they can have fewer," said a Chengdu matron, daughter of a pre-Liberation herbal pharmacist.

"My parents-in-law had no influence over how many babies I had because [when we married in the late 1960s] they didn't give us anything," a Taibei restaurateur explained.

As my associates painstakingly sum and correlate the figures we have accumulated in interviews, they begin to support the image of family expectations that our informants often put, very bluntly, into words. These businesswomen balance their home-and-family responsibilities as they balance their books. One has only so much time, so many resources— although one is expected to stretch them to the max. Trade-offs must be made between energy expended on care for people—elders as well as children—and that expended on earning an income and accumulating capital.

This seems obvious enough, certainly to me: I decided in my young married twenties that while I could build a career and hold up my ideal of wifeliness, I had nothing left over for the demands of motherhood. The choice was not hard, though the pragmatics of contraception were a major nuisance, and the early, big-dose "Pill" I took for years almost certainly set me up for my later depressions. All my friends made trade-offs of one sort or another. Most aimed at timing their pregnancies so they could finish their dissertations just before, or in the first months after, birth. Most, like the Chengdu women, had little choice about whether to have a child or not. The basis of a Chinese marriage is that a woman gains a new home in which she will bear children for her husband's family. Our middle-class American folk contract is only slightly more flexible: we take for granted that if one partner wants a child, the other is obliged to oblige, no matter what his or her true feelings about parenthood. To refuse to have children when your partner wants them is to court accusations that you are selfish, that you don't love enough, and that you are aiming to precipitate divorce. These disputes rapidly expand to take in all the differences of theory and practice that have ever divided the couple.

Chengdu women, faced with strong and unified expectations, are direct about their childbearing rights and duties, and largely positive toward them.

"If you didn't want to have children, why would you marry in the first place?" several said.

"If you marry into your mother-in-law's family, they support you, and you have babies. Otherwise, what's the point?" observed a shopkeeper.

And Chengdu women, like their Taibei counterparts, often insist that they themselves wanted a child or children.

"Babies are lovable, and when they grow up, your children love you and help you. It's natural to want them; all women do," a busy printer points out, plainly perceiving me as a few characters short of a full font.

"Well, what if your husband doesn't want to have children?" I persist.

"Oh, men always want children. It's not hard for them! Besides, if a man didn't, still, his mother would want to hold her grandchildren, and your mother would too. They've expected it all their lives. How could you disappoint them?" she responds.

So far, this is predictable. What surprises me in conversations about these women's double burden of family care and income earning is their plain speech, an attribute that is justly not part of the Chinese stereotype. When I told *my* mother and mother-in-law (over and over again!) that I was not going to have children, I had to bubble-wrap the spiky truth—that I disliked the messy double dependency that mothering required—and descant, sometimes fairly insincerely, on my commitment to anthropology, to travel, to political engagement. Both Taibei and Chengdu women, in speaking of their childbearing choices, slap their cards on the table.

"A mother can't have lots of children; she's got to make money for the children she has," says a thirtyish Taibei fishmonger.

"I'd have had more for them if my mother-in-law could have taken care of them for me while I worked. We could have as many as we wanted back then. But since she couldn't spare the time to do the day-care, she couldn't ask me to do more than I did. I've always brought in a really good income to this family," a fortyish Chengdu shop assistant and bookkeeper tells me.

But whether to have children or not has never been seen as a decision to be made by a woman alone, or even a married woman and her husband. Much of Chinese tradition and law as they bear on marriage amounts to endless variations on pronatalist propaganda, combined with full legitimation of social controls on sexuality. Conception has been strictly regulated in Chinese life for as far back as history illuminates the subject. Husbands, parents, parents-in-law, lineage elders, the state, the old woman down the street—everybody had a say in a woman's reproductive life. Parents carefully secluded pubescent but as yet unmarried daughters; parents-in-law of a new bride sometimes forced her and their unwilling son into consummating an uninviting union; mothers-in-law protected fetuses and nurslings against ill-timed sexual relations between their progenitors; orthodox philosophers taught even the most unlettered that of all sins against filial piety, childlessness was the worst; magistrates enforced legal codes with horrific punishments for adultery. To the best of my knowledge, they still do. What a woman gives to carry and birth, to nurse and rear a child, does not entitle her to full dominion over it. Chinese recognize more easily than Americans that family, community, and state have claims and commitments to each new person who comes among us. The 1970s switch to a one-child policy for urban women reverses the ancient philoprogenitive mandate, narrows the options, but it is hardly a sociological novelty.

The youngest of our Chengdu women—those under thirty-five—have built their families within the constraints of the "one-child policy;" in the city, its limits are hard to evade. Yet over and over, we hear them remark that their hands are full with one child. Their single child, precious as he is, is "very expensive," needing milk, pretty clothes, toys, and, looming in the distance, ever-larger sums for school expenses.

"I travel to get yarn and other supplies, I check everything that's produced by the workwomen, I keep the books so no one will cheat us, people quarrel over work division, girls get tired of the job and leave without notice, somebody's old mother moves in with her and she can't work outside any more—it's always something. With another child, I'd go crazy," my favorite knitwear manufacturer sighed. Again, comparisons with Taibei informants are illuminating—these women, like my overburdened career-women colleagues in Michigan, cannot imagine how they could manage another child. Again, they are blunt about the sheer monetary costs of rearing a child, computing exact monthly totals for the price of milk, and daycare, and shoes, sounding like "intergenerational wealth flow" demographers over our teacups.

The Fulian and I count up and code the facts of fertility expressed in children, and of money and labor turned into productive capital, trying to see if another observer would emphasize the same anecdotes as I do, find the same women illustrative of typical choices. Pleasingly, the figures line up with our hypothesis. Women who contribute a majority share of the founding capital in these small businesses have fewer children, whether in Taibei or in Chengdu, whether the women are old or young.

We divide our women into four categories: older and younger Taibei, and older and younger Chengdu. "Older" and "younger" are different not only in their actual ages, but in their place in the changing economies of their countries. Taibei people in ordinary walks of life began to recover economically from the devastation of World War II and the early Nationalist regime only in the late 1960s. When I did my doctoral field-work there, women entrepreneurs were few and far between. The shops, beauty parlors, and seamstress establishments they ran were rudimentary and barely profitable. By the late 1970s, times were much better for everyone, and many energetic women founded small businesses. Wealth circulated and accumulated faster, but attitudes toward women extending the housewife role were changing too. It was okay to have a mother running a successful business; a working wife no longer shamed her husband.

Chengdu, with the rest of China, experienced various experiments in socialism after the Revolution of 1949. Distribution of society's wealth was dramatically equalized, and a slow building of infrastructure and new skills took place. Women got educations and paid work, and it was not always the worst work. China's most recent political-economic experiment began in Sichuan in 1978, when Deng Xiaoping, who, after all, is a Sichuanese himself, permitted the reprivatization of many aspects of farming and encouraged the establishment of small family businesses in other sectors as well. Service and consumer-oriented light industry systems had worked badly under socialism. As a result, a huge market for clothing, processed foods, and a myriad of daily goods and services offered a stunning opportunity to people like our informants. Women, most with substantial education, many with work experience in the socialist sector, and all bored to the bone by the cultural stagnation of the 70s, threw themselves into newly available niches.

It is one of the odder coincidences of history that, at essentially the same moment, women from working-class families in both Taiwan's and China's cities began to limit their fertility and plunge into petty capitalism. In both, they had earlier role models to draw on. Taibei had always had a few businesswomen; pre-revolution Chengdu had accepted that widows, divorcees, and supercompetent daughters-in-law might, behind a screen of cautious modesty, feed their families and create jobs for their children. It is therefore not surprising that Chengdu and Taibei women sound so much alike as they discuss their childbearing and income-earning trade-offs with us.

Another striking similarity between these two sets of women is that each sorts well into what might be called "accumulators" and "housewives." *Accumulators* look to expand their businesses into distant territory, are willing to risk hiring wage-workers from outside the near circle of kin and friends, and are interested in technical improvements—like the producer of hot rabbit cubes who wanted a vacuum-sealer so she could export to Hong Kong, or the herbal medicine wholesaler seeking an outlet on the coast.

Housewives focus on full use of the family's current assets—a good commercial location, a couple of underemployed kids, a spousal tap into state enterprise resources that might safely be made to "fall off the truck." They talk about generating current income and about the patient amassing of a small base of capital, skill, and contacts to create an autonomous career for a son or daughter. They do not plan marketing networks or set up dormitories or training programs. Many accumulators began as housewives; but many housewives have been treading water for years, either incapable of, or uninterested in, an expanding business. Some act out of political caution, unwilling to draw public attention by too obvious a success. A few are simply lazy. One owner of a cluttered corner store says:

> I could build this shop up, my mother says, but I don't want to be that busy all the time. I like to sleep. This way, I help my husband bring in a little extra, I have money if I want to buy things for the children, and I still have time to see my friends. These *nuchiangren* [aggressive women] who want to make money—what kind of wives and mothers are they?

Little middle ground separates accumulators and housewives; few of our interviewees seem intermediate. We check to see if this career-track bipolarity correlates with age, with education, with amount of initial capital, and we come up dry. We cannot explain why a woman becomes one or the other, but we assure ourselves that they really do cluster into two types, each with its own internal logic.

A key part of the internal logic of full-blown capitalism is that profits, instead of being consumed, are reinvested into yet larger productive resources. If all goes as the capitalist intends, the next profit is bigger, and so is the next reinvestment. Capital has snowballed during the 1980s in Chengdu, and all around me I see the rapid, private development that has would-be China investors breathing heavily. Now that China has "opened," Westerners are saying, it is only a matter of time—and not much time—before China becomes marketized, democratized, and a full member of the single, worldwide system of global capitalism. Sources more intimate with Chinese economic activities—the *Far East-*

ern Economic Review and people like me, to take two fairly disparate examples—see persistent reasons to doubt these claims.

My "accumulators" accumulate, true enough. But they, to a woman, keep a sharp eye on their government's tendencies to keep an eye on them. One of the main games of "reform" China is still the channeling of privately generated wealth into government coffers. Officials require a cut in the form of taxes, and sometimes in "voluntary contributions" to extraordinary government undertakings or perfectly ordinary corruption. I remember the tales of Taiwanese who were badgered as schoolchildren to meet official "requests" that so many schools fund a fighter plane. I do not expect to hear the equivalent stories from Chengdu for years, perhaps decades, until whatever is going on now has been superseded by more sophisticated forms of state extraction, but I do expect, eventually, to hear them.

In the meantime, Chengdu's businesswomen are often candid about a business glass ceiling. Beyond this ceiling, entrepreneurs become conspicuous and are singled out for conspicuous contributions; if they hire more than eight wage-workers, segments of society consider them to be exploiters; if they flaunt their wealth, low-paid state employees will experience, and express, "the red-eye disease" of envious status-outrage. Beyond this ceiling, if history's wheel turns back against anything that smells of capitalism, the obvious accumulator will be political-economic dead meat. Small, household-based, family-supporting businesses are safer. Stay petty, unambitious; aim to provide food and jobs for your children; divide the firm into a network of trustworthy intimates rather than pyramid up to the point where, isolated by success, you become vulnerable. Stay petty bourgeois in word and appearance, if not always in thought and deed.

I will have to push our numbers around in the computer before I can present figures that my academic colleagues cannot trash. Indeed, this 100-woman sample will be brushed off by many as too insubstantial to support any statistical conclusions. Weighing up what we have garnered in their terms shows our presentable harvest as a modest one. When I return to the United States, I will write the necessary articles about comparative fertility and capital accumulation. But I can also plan a book about these women and their world in which those hard-shelled findings play a different part.

Miles of biking, dozens of bowls of *chaoshao* in roadside restaurants, chats with shopclerks and post-office workers, and funny old women trying to sell me fruit have produced another harvest. It is not one to be despised, though impossible to quantify. When I pass a shop, I can estimate in ways that transcend numbers the flows of goods, and money, and human energy that it momentarily stabilizes. Knowledge amplifies knowledge as I watch the way bank personnel pass my documents from hand to hand, chop to chop, through a dozen checks and balances before I finally extract a few thousand RMB from their richly featherbedded and thus almost embezzlement-proof system. As we loosen up over meals, I hear entrepreneurial informants condescend to cadres, and cadres riposte with a flash of their educational credentials. I learn when female body contact conveys affection, and when it is simply common courtesy. Parents tell me how they feel about their children by the lavishness of the kids' bedrooms. It all adds up.

Yes, but what does it add up *to*? I must find a way to synthesize these packrat perceptions, to convey them to a reader who has never seen an authentic dish of "husband-and-wife-fatty-slices" or "ants-climbing-a-tree." For, in the end, without the food and the underwear and the hard knocks, the numbers can be made to mean anything.

One summation is clear, though it will meet with derision among anthropological sophisticates. An imp of culture does not dangle its legs from a spandrel in each Chinese cerebellum, guiding them toward Mysterious Eastern goals. Chengdu women entrepreneurs and cadres (like their men) make choices that anyone would make, given their constraints. These days, the constraints are strongest in the areas of childbearing and of capital accumulation. Exceed certain loosely defined limits that pertain to everyone, and you pay for the privilege: in money, in political duties, in the renunciation of certain freedoms freely available to folk who make only household-sized claims on the social structure. If you can't stand the heat, get back in the kitchen.

DECEMBER 5, 1988. CHENGDU

In Margaret Drabble's novel *The Radiant Way* (1987) Alix is musing over her world. It stretches from the grand Harley Street house of her friend Liz, whose recent party Alix is still digesting, through her own modest, semi-socialist home, to the Garfield Centre, a women's prison where she teaches poetry.

Mile after mile, ribbons of roads. What was going on, behind those closed curtains? Were people peacefully frying up potatoes, or were they hitting one another on the head with their frying pans? Alix likes to let her mind wander over the map of Britain, asking herself which interiors she could visualize, which not. She aspired to a more comprehensive vision. She aspired to make connections. She and Liz, over supper together, often spoke of such things. Their own stories had strangely interlocked, and sometimes she had a sense that such interlockings were part of a vaster network, that there was a pattern, if only one could discern it, a pattern that linked these semi-detached houses of Wanley with those in Leeds and Northam, a pattern that linked Liz's vast house in Harley Street with the Garfield Centre towards which she herself now drove. The social structure greatly interested Alix. She had once thought of herself as unique, had been encouraged (in theory at least) by her education and by her reading to believe in the individual self, the individual soul, but as she grew older she increasingly questioned these concepts—seeing people perhaps more as flickering impermanent points of light irradiating stretches, intersections, threads, of a vast web, a vast network, which was humanity itself; a web of which much remained dark, apparently but not necessarily unpeopled; peopled by the dark, the unlit, the dim spirits, as yet unknown, the past, the future, the dead, the unborn. And herself, and Brian, and Liz, and Charles, and Esther, and Teddy Lazenby, and Otto and Caroline Werner, and all the rest of them in that bright party, and in these discreet anonymous dark curtained avenues and crescents were but chance and fitful illuminations, chance meetings, chance and unchosen representatives of the thing itself.[1]

Alix—who shares my political paralysis and whom I like very much—is precisely the sort of 1980s Western intellectual whom Drabble alternately satirizes and sympathizes with. She wants to understand, and thus to help, but she keeps driving, still believing that what she needs to know will be found inside her own head.

Alix knows about social research. She does not stay in the car because she is lazy, or unwilling to connect with the downtrodden. She thinks social research is a search for problems, problems that right-thinking intellectuals are then charged with solving. Britain in the 1980s is stuffed with information about existing problems, and Alix probably knows that those problems are, more or less, the same as those that Friedrich Engels documented with such heart-breaking precision on his walks through

---

[1] Margaret Drabble, *The Radiant Way* (London: George Weidenfeld and Nicolson, 1987), 68–69.

industrial slums in the 1840s. *The Condition of the Working-Class in England* is subtitled *From Personal Observation and Authentic Sources*. Published first in 1845, it counts as a great precursor to twentieth-century ethnography. Class, ethnicity, gender, that essential tripod of 1980s social analysis—they are all in CWCE. Alix knows England, with its mountains of excellent studies that tell us that the poor and wretched are so, and why. Fieldwork is not necessary for her. Problem and cause are plain—but not solution.

Isabella Bird Bishop traveled in a different, a more confident spirit, in a moment of high modernism and certainty that darkened windows could be peered through, and up-to-date gaslights installed in gloomy rooms. Isabella made amazing efforts to accomplish these goals—though we should remember she was also escaping heartbreak and boredom by her travels. Unwilling simply to muse and speculate on the commuter's world, Isabella got out and walked. Isabella, standing firm on scientific knowledge of "the social structure" that, like Alix, I must sometimes take on faith.

Isabella then and I, now, however, inherit no such superabundance of evidence as brings Alix to despair. If we want to know about China, we must do the spade-work of observation ourselves. We need to know the problems before we can hypothesize causes and to develop strong estimates of causality before we can hope to entertain solutions.

When Isabella traveled, anthropologists had not yet discovered the essential technique of fieldwork. It took the World War I internment— four years!—of Bronislaw Malinowski in the Trobriand Islands to persuade us that an intelligent, educated Westerner could work so long, so diligently as Malinowski did and still not exhaust the cultural mysteries and riches of a few thousand "savages." In book after book, despite their now-unfashionable titles, he piled up the evidence that there are no simple human beings and that even a small community could take a lifetime to know well. I owe Malinowski a great debt for his buggy, boring, and often loony Melanesian days and nights; Isabella Bird had never heard of him. I think—I think, for I know nothing of her but what her published writings tell—that she believed that an intelligent, educated Westerner, if she made an effort, could get the main issues straight and report them clearly. To do this, she needed to travel properly, close to daily life, observing and asking diligently of Chinese she encountered along the way, of her escort-interpreter, of foreign merchants and missionaries, and of the written sources available to someone not literate in Chinese. By pre-Malinowskian lights, Isabella was extraordinarily successful at "getting the data" despite her prejudices and assumptions. From her I have learned far more about the daily life, work, products, and independent carriage of Sichuan women than I could extract from a boxcar-load of indigenous sources.

Especially in *The Yangtze Valley and Beyond* (1899), she energetically pursued gender-relevant themes, including the humble textile crafts, which few others bothered to record. Consider her observations on Shashi, then a famous center of indigenous cotton cloth production. Local fiber was

> woven at Sha-shih into a strong, durable white cloth, fifteen and twelve inches wide, which I saw all over SZE CHUAN, and of which at least 20,000,000 pounds are annually exported [i.e., beyond Shashi, but within China]. Samples of this make and of English cottons were frequently shown to me by the women in SZE CHUAN villages, with a scornful laugh at the expense of the latter.[2]

In a none-too-fertile basin near Baoning, she journeyed for nearly two weeks without seeing foreign cottons. Local women were content with China homespun, and explained their reasons to her: foreign cottons were the wrong width to cut parsimoniously for Chinese clothing; they came wrapped in unlucky-colored papers; they were ugly, short-weight, insufficiently durable, and too thin for winter comfort.

> It is not that our cottons are too dear, but that the great majority of people do not want them at any price. . . . the strong, heavy native cottons woven by hand, wear four times as long, and, even when they are reduced to rags, serve several useful purposes. . . . Later, in Sin-tu Hsien . . . I saw some Japanese cotton goods, fifteen inches wide . . . an equally heavy make with the Sha-shih goods, and scarcely to be distinguished from homespun cloth. The shopkeeper highly approved of these goods.[3]

Here, and on many other of Isabella's pages, is clear evidence for how the competition between handicraft and industry was playing out in village China, and a record of what Chinese women thought of the rival product. Thrown in free is the important point that their consumption decisions had nothing to do with nationalism, with "Buying Chinese."

[2] Isabella Bird Bishop, *The Yangtze Valley and Beyond* (London: John Murray, 1899), 91.
[3] Bishop, *The Yangtze Valley and Beyond*, 307–311.

Chinese shopkeepers and their female customers purchased pragmatically, quite uninfluenced by the wholly new patriotism that was then being invented by elites in distant cities.

Yet Isabella Bird is the sort of witness of Chinese life that today draws sneers and snickers from most anthropologists. Living when she did, she must have had a colonialist mentality. If she had a colonialist mentality—and, trust me, she did—she must have imposed herself and her categories on China, and must thus have got everything wrong.

This is tricky, because it is partly true. She certainly tried to conduct herself in imperialist fashion, and she sometimes succeeded. She wanted to travel unencumbered in a China whose rulers did not want the trouble of having her there at all. She used a ladylike version of gunboat diplomacy to force her way onto, and at one point, beyond, the system of transport routes that Chinese officials thought of as existing for their own convenience. A *bourgeoise* to her toenails, she thought she had a right to go anywhere if she could pay her own way. They thought that the bureaucrat heading each of China's administrative divisions had the right to invite or exclude any traveler—and they certainly had not invited her. She faced down small-town magistrates, she persisted in the face of mass rock-throwing forays and an attempt to burn down the inn in which she lodged, she put herself into danger, and she gave fits to those deputed to protect her. She traded on the support she knew the British Crown would mobilize on her behalf, and she contributed, in her small way, to the fury of Chinese rulers and commoners that would soon be unleashed on foreigners in the Boxer Rebellion. In the end, she struggled (with a serious concussion from a thrown brick) to the end of her intended journey. But she did not make Sichuan safe for lady travelers, open to foreign whim, unconstrained by "the country's regulations." A hundred years later, I follow in her footsteps with rather less success.

Like Isabella, I believe we still need to know more about China, and that China is knowable—in large part through encounters with its bureaucracy. Like Alix I believe that knowledge of persisting structures holds the clue to solutions of social injustices. Unlike Isabella or Alix, I do not believe that paid intellectuals like me can invent solutions to the problems that torment the powerless. I can only trust, as one of the humbler sort of Marxists, that people like me are useful because we look for the solutions that are put forward by those pinched and crushed in ill-fitting social structures.

Can I justify the efforts the Women's Federation and I have made here, efforts aimed almost solely at data gathering and interpretation, at tweaking theory to suit today's Chinese? Not really, no. I hope without belief, but, in middle age, it's what I do. Hua and Jiang and Li were assigned to social research, I wandered into it for adventure, economic independence, and really challenging head games. I stay because it's a wonderful job. I am lucky; I lose nothing by gambling that what I transmit will weight the heap of accumulated knowledge in the direction of women and workers rather than men and cadres. Alix and I have lost faith that an intellectual-driven short, sharp shock will produce a better world in the West. We have concluded that we must beaver away at learning what our natures truly need, so future solutions will be less flawed than those of this century.

CHAPTER FOURTEEN

城都行

Finishing Touches

DECEMBER 7, 1988. CHENGDU

I have been a true grub since it started to get cold. The guesthouse has a slow, European-style washer and dryer for thirty-odd meticulous Canadians, so my hand-washed long-johns, turtlenecks, and unmentionables must sag in the fog on my balcony, drying and molding at non-too-competitive rates. As we wind up our work, I try to raise my sartorial level a notch so that I can appear at farewell functions looking and smelling like a lady.

Hair care is especially hard, compounded by the bike riding that makes my mane a strainer for Chengdu's abundant air pollutants. Blow-dryers are inventions of the devil, intended to ruin a woman's crowning glory and force her into dependence on dangerous chemicals. I cannot wash my hair at night, leaving it wet and risking pneumonia and icicle formation. Ditto for washing it in cold water during the day. When gritty enough, I submit myself to local beauty parlors. It is best to draw a veil over the indignities and sufferings I undergo in this process: hair overshampooed to a consistency at once limp and strawlike by people whose hair, generally, is made of sterner stuff; peculiar trims by people who have never cut naturally curly hair before, but would rather like to try; styles more suitable for a princess bride than a middle-aged academic; and, of course, blow-dryers.

In Taibei at least one can count on these pleasures being supplied at virtually any hour of any night or day. In Chengdu, I sometimes have to go greasy to a grand dinner because the electricity is off in the neighborhood of the beauty parlor. To be fair, the works never costs more than thirty-five cents, and the great majority of Chinese women live with these difficulties without complaint.

Hair is a good female subject, worth contemplating, if not sorrowing over. It is even a commercially valuable object, I learn sometime, somewhere, in an airport, from a nice young man. He travels through China, arranging for haircut sweepings to be collected, baled, and shipped to Germany. His company extracts lysine "and other important proteins" from fashion's unsavory flotsam. Why does this bother me?

Last week, we visited a hairdresser couple, the woman suffering from serious hip dysplasia, whom Jiang had interviewed earlier.

"You'll like her; she's a stitch," says Jiang. "And by including her in our study, we can show how handicapped people can succeed in China."

We arrive to beaming greetings by wife, husband, and their two apprentices. We chat. We drink tea, eat candy and tart early tangerines, engage in mutual photography. Ms. Wang is, indeed, a stitch, her natural merriment brimming over the veneer of formality she tries to assume in my august presence.

"Look," she says, as we rise to go, "why don't I wash your hair?"

This seems to me to be a question with only one answer.

"Thank you so much! But we can't—we have other tasks for this afternoon," I respond.

"No, really, I mean it. It won't take long, anyway. We'll give you all a wash and trim. It'll be fun."

I look around for guidance, and am surprised to see Hua, Li, and Jiang looking rather expectant. There are no other customers waiting, and, truth to tell, we have no other appointments. My hostess persists:

"Please let's do it! I've never cut naturally curly hair before. Your hair *is* naturally curly, isn't it? They told me it was, and it doesn't look like a perm. You need a haircut, you know."

Why not? I could adduce reasons. This is not an elegant salon. The clippings are swept up only once a day, the combs and brushes have been used on many scalps, the family's little boy will surely run his tricycle over my toes as I sit with my head in the washbasin. But these are trivial matters. I am focused elsewhere—on Wang's unknown level of technical expertise, and on how much dignity I am willing to sacrifice to playful pleasure. Hua is already seating herself in front of one of the apprentices. Only a very poor sport would refuse. I, too, take my seat under a tangle of blow-dryers.

Wang shampoos me, towels me off, combs me out, and commences. She is using very long shears, I observe with alarm. Perhaps she is a unique genius, a mute inglorious Milton of the mousse, hidden away in the crannied wall of Youth Street. I will emerge with the best haircut I

Hairdresser and Her Staff, 1988

have ever had, will be transformed. She will show me the secret, which I will impart to a long line of future hairdressers, and all the obeisance that men and women alike pay to beauty will be mine.

No, Wang has the technique of a hedge-trimmer. Trying to level my fractious locks, she slashes them shorter and shorter. Soon, hair that was below my shoulders now poufs out above my ears, increasingly resembling a yak mane. Like a comic carpenter cutting bit after bit off each succeeding leg of an ever-wobbly table, she will snatch me bald if I don't stop her, for she has lost her way entirely.

"You'd better stop now," says Teacher Jiang, firmly. "It's getting very short."

In mid-slash, Wang pulls herself out of her destructive trance. Lacquering the remaining stubble with a lavish hand, she glues the wildly uneven ends into a melon-shaped carapace. The others emerge looking shinier, but basically as they had when they came in. They appear to be suppressing mirth, but they are good at that. We try to pay, are elaborately rebuffed, we take more photos to commemorate our new 'dos, and we leave. It will be six months before my hair recovers.

DECEMBER 8, 1988. CHENGDU

The last phase of the fieldwork—assistants coding, me working on projects in the apartment or off running errands—is good fun. The four of us, or five, when Lu Fubuzhang drops over, take lunch in neighborhood restaurants. We eat our way through enormous meals and discuss the parallels between their bureaucratism and ours and the rollback of abortion rights in the United States. They see this last much as we would see the reinstitution of witchcraft trials. They grouse about China's economic backwardness and its causes, a topic that had been raised earlier that year in sharp and critical form in the six-part television series *River Elegy* (*He Xiang*). I quote Rosa Luxemburg on the nature of imperialism, insisting on how much better China has done from its nineteenth-century carom off capitalism than Brazil or Indonesia. This cross-cultural application of Marxism is of little interest to them. They want to talk about why *China* isn't where it ought to be: the equal of *any* country, notably my own.

Constantly, in our ordinary interchange, I give my acquaintances unintended illustrations of the gap between American and Chinese consumption. Seeing a little girl blowing bubbles in the street, a friend is charmed.

"Do children have bubble gum in the United States?" she asks.

"Oh yes. I remember when I was a little girl, my mother hated it because I blew such big bubbles that it got in my hair."

"Wouldn't you know! *You* had bubble gum forty years ago! Even in *candy* we're decades behind!" she replies in disgust.

Pictures my mother sends of the house my brother and sister-in-law are building provoke intense discussion of land values, taxes, and mortgages. A three-bedroom, two-bath ranch is a piney suburb, it is attractive, but not grand. I defend China's housing policies as best I can, pointing to their spacious and comfortable apartments, rented for only 5 percent of their incomes, and to the perfectly adequate housing of the majority of women in our sample. I tout the equality between the apartment of a provincial government official whose daughter-in-law we have visited and those of many ordinary factory workers. They point to my brother's sleek new kitchen and the trees that fill his large lot.

"Nobody can buy land like that in China! Even government officials can't own a forest!" they observe, tartly.

They remind me, too, that the government has instituted a policy to encourage more private house ownership in the city; rural people have always had private ownership. Even people who work for the state will be given incentives to buy the apartments they now rent. To get this off the ground, the government periodically announces that rents will be raised. The latest rumor sets the rise at seven times the current cost, bringing them to more than one-third of their incomes.

"Realistically, they can't do it," said the Fulian. "We couldn't afford to eat on what's left."

The program has been tried experimentally in some of the universities, however. The blow has been softened by the university simultaneously giving those receiving rent raises supplements equal to the new imposition.

"The idea is to get us used to paying high rents," a retired professor told me. "You must remember that when we tell you our salaries, that's just the base. I get subsidies for rent, oil, fuel, grain, newspapers, books . . . lots of things I can't even remember." But she lives alone, and has no dependents. Younger parents with children to educate look on the current rising inflation and the unprecedented threat of having to buy housing and pay university tuition as family catastrophes in the making.

On one awkward occasion, I buy a handsome jacket, tailored in Chengdu and very fashionable. We all try it on, agreeing it looks like a proper Paris creation. I urge the tallest of them to get one too; it is just her style, and a perfect fit. Wryly, she reminds me that it cost over twice her monthly salary, a sum that amounts to forty-five U.S. dollars at the official rate, twenty at the street value.

Foreigners complain (except when we are taking advantage) of the Chinese insistence on the open recognition of different social statuses, and the differential cost of things to people who hold them. An American told for the first time that a plane ticket will cost her twice what a Chinese citizen pays generates a level of outrage that a Chinese would save for matricide. We expect the equality of the market in economic transactions, and we prefer to paper over social inequalities with the shifty pseudodemocracy that encourages undergraduate students, for example, to call younger professors by their given names. The Chinese, who think our informality either boorish or silly, do much better in coping with the privileges—expensive coats, not having to do the coding—of rank. People have different statuses; the higher the status, the less work and the more reward. What could be more obvious? One would rather be higher in rank, and have nice coats and less boring paperwork, but little in the current system encourages one to argue that others should not. Although Chinese socialism aspires to decency, honesty, and fairness, it is also structured around a system of differential rewards to the differently situated that few seriously question.

Besides. Hua, Li, and Jiang are, quite simply, very nice women, who do not envy their friends' good fortune. As we come to know one another better during these last weeks, we move beyond courtesy into friendship. That friendship is made possible, I think, because we all have learned recognize how much the differences in our lives are due to the accidents of history. We have measured each other's strengths and weaknesses and know that the work we do together is getting done because each of us has necessary abilities that the others need. It feels interdependent, it feels egalitarian, it feels fine.

December 9, 1988. Chengdu

I am down to the wire. If the before-dawn car that is to take me to the airport arrives, if the morning is not too foggy for the plane to see its way, if I am allowed to take my field notes and computer disks through Chinese customs, if I have the cash to pay for my overweight, if I do not simply sit down and refuse to leave my lovely niche, my dear new friends—I will fly to Hong Kong tomorrow. Hong Kong will be a holiday. I will buy silk shirts and eat steak tartare and play with a Canadian contingent who also cannot tear themselves away, go home, be normal, grow up again. And beyond Hong Kong are the people I long for most. I have had such a perfectly marvelous time, and have, twenty-five years after my first fieldwork, finally done the right anthropological stuff in China. Best of all, I have left them laughing.

But, but . . . To leave my beautiful, scarlet Flying Pigeon bicycle, my hard-won knowledge of how to get to places in Chengdu, dear Professor Qin and his circle of charming relatives and friends, to leave the Fulian and the stinging food and the camellia buds that will blossom without me?

This maudlin effusion is the result, I suppose, of drink. The Fulian entertained me tonight (I entertained *them* two nights ago—*un succès fou,* as it happens) at a perfectly lovely dinner in the Jin Jiang Hotel, pouring me full of liquor in the finest tradition of Chinese hospitality. The Fulian's Director was there, an honor indeed, as this busy lady heads a unit with at least ostensible responsibility for the well-being of fifty million women. Otherwise, the guests were all women I've gotten to know in the course of the research, all smart and strong and charming in their varied ways. We'd all got dressed up—I in my chic Chengdu coat—and were wearing Fulian scarves. Our nice male driver (the only man in the unit, as far as I can tell) poured and hovered a bit. Because it was *the* final dinner, we were all on our formal behavior, putting good bits in each other's dishes, giving proper toasts, making speeches. I sat on the superior side of the table (making the correct little fuss, refusing to sit "so high," because this was a formal occasion) with the higher ranks, while my companions in the field sat at the bottom—foot soldiers in this woman's army. We had known that would happen and had made our personal speeches in advance. Rules are rules. The ethnic minority costume made for me in the mountains of north Sichuan had arrived in time, was presented, tried on, photographed. We laughed like school-girls at me in its funny, flat, goathide boater-hat; they confided that everyone at headquarters had already tried it on and had pictures taken.

I enjoyed it all the more because my dinner party for them had also been a coup. I found a restaurant where none of them had been, with a decorous floor show of traditional Sichuanese folk music (delightful) and rather odd ethnic dances. (The Chinese always have to borrow minority dances for such performances because the Han haven't danced since the Tang dynasty. Tang dances, reconstructed from tomb figurines, never seem to jell. You probably had to have been there.) My guests liked all of it, including the dinner, topped off with lots of Sichuan dim sum. There was a horrendous lot of food, so we really tucked in. The leftovers were lavish enough for me to feel that *no one* could have gone home hungry.

The next night (still not very hungry), I entertained Professor Qin and his family at a new hotel. It is extraordinarily hard to find an eating place that can offer any novelty to a senior Chinese scholar; such people attend innumerable banquets. So it was a treat to have found a new tea-house restaurant at the top of one of the highest buildings in the city. From the twenty-second floor, you can see all of Chengdu, twinkling through the fog.

The Professor's five-year-old grandson was with us. His enthusiasm for the lobby bar decorated like the Altamira caves, the long elevator ride, the fish pool and little bridge in the restaurant set us all chuckling as we toured the hotel's hot spots and photographed ourselves on the stairs by the fountain. The child gave us all near heart failure by approaching an elevator shaft casually left open above a yawning cellar, and by throwing himself gaily against the roof-top restaurant windows. The one-child policy heightens anxiety yet further at such moments. The occasion was a little too formal for the professor's witty daughter to reduce me to near-hysteria—she is a magnificent storyteller—but we all had a fine time. Dinner was delicious, ample, and fancy enough to repay in some small way the constant kindnesses of these warm-hearted, generous people. I would miss them, I told them, and it was true.

DECEMBER 10, 1988. CHENGDU AIRPORT

In the car on the way to the airport, Hua gives me an official permission to take my fieldnotes out of the country.

"Don't use it if you don't have to, if they don't ask for it. It'll just confuse things, get them thinking. If there's any problem, we'll be outside until the plane leaves, and you can send for Lu Fubuzhang to speak to them."

In the event, Sichuan customs does not give a rip about my pile of papers and notebooks, and my adrenaline level slowly declines. The employees of China Southwest Air grouch about my degree of overweight—they allow twenty kilos, I bring fifty-three. They ultimately throw up their hands and send me on my way. This waiting room, cold and cavernous, supplies its exiting denizens with a last chance to buy original landscapes and instant noodles. After a warming bowl of these, I spy a vendor selling paper cups of instant coffee from a thermos bottle. I speculate on the three Euro-Americans who dot this room full of black-haired people, but am too lazy to ask what brings them here. I am done. It is hard to leave. But—as is not always the case—I know I can come back.

城都行

June 1989–November 1991

**Stanford, Chengdu, Xiamen, Cambridge,
Mt. Pleasant, Nankang, Chengdu, Ming Shan, Chengdu**

CHAPTER FIFTEEN

城都行

Tiananmen in Chengdu

MID-JUNE, 1989. STANFORD

While the world watched this spring's contest between Beijing's people and the Chinese army for the right to speak in Tiananmen square, I was trying to keep one eye on Chengdu. How would this new climate of violence affect my Chinese friends, the economic changes I was analyzing, China's painfully slow emergence from its harsh feudal past?

Chengdu is a smaller Beijing: shortly after tanks took Tiananmen, Chengdu people took to their streets, attacking government buildings, overturning official cars, giving voice to their outrage at both the killings in distant Beijing and at their own grievances against the biggest local employer. The army responded quickly. After a few citizens had been unceremoniously shot, a sullen silence descended on the ancient city's twisting commercial alleys and broad, bureaucratized avenues.

It should not surprise me that the Sichuan military is quick on the draw. Its commanders are those who shoot up Lhasa whenever the Tibetans assert their desire for control in their own country. But though the Chengdu generals are well prepared to suppress civilian dissidence, it is still a long step from killing minorities in remote places to using guns against students in Chinese capitals.

In the tense June days after the crackdowns, I try to superimpose the televised Tiananmen scenes on my memories of the broad plaza in central Chengdu where the forty-foot statue of Mao Zedong stands. I can conjure up nothing but the streams of bicyclists I had joined every morn-

Much of the material in this chapter appeared in 1991 as "Eating for Revenge: Consumption and Corruption under Economic de-Reform." *Dialectical Anthropology* 16: 233–249.

ing en route to interviews. Six, eight, twelve riders abreast, these currents pass miraculously through each other at crossroads, ignoring the white-coated cop trying to get the East-West and North-South riders to take turns. It is not chaotic, only messy and productive of occasional small and noisy collisions. It works, partly because people like to decide for themselves how to maneuver, and partly because their lives make the Chinese virtuosi in an offhand kind of respect for other people's persons and property. The scenes of popular protest that international television failed to capture in Chengdu would have resembled the city's pattern of street traffic: apparent chaos, much unspoken agreement, and a strong distaste for pushy men in uniforms.

So much attention is paid to the few Chinese leaders who hold great power that it is easy for outsiders to miss the complex and sometimes, to us, alien popular pressures to which those leaders must respond. What led so many ordinary folk to support the students' capture of Tiananmen, to make mighty protests of their own in cities all over China? Powerful state leaders can kill and imprison those who articulate the people's visions, but in the long run, they are guided by them more than they admit. The experiment with reprivatization begun in the late 1970s was a weary yielding to the logic of low-technology production in an overpopulated country, and to the acute popular awareness of how to accomplish it efficiently. All through the Maoist years, small producers kept reinventing this form of production until their government finally got it. To learn more than we already know about polities, we must track the changing daily lives of ordinary people, find out where they want to go. These changes add and multiply, the irresistible mathematics of history. In the short run, leaders speak with guns; in the long run, people like those I met in Chengdu will whisper the future with their lives. The whispers are soft, and often confusing, so we must listen very hard to hear clearly what they say.

Despite the sometimes uneasy atmosphere in 1988, lots of people *were* having a fine time in Chengdu at what in retrospect was the apogee of small-business success. But not all. The many people who work for the state—and there are hundreds of thousands, for Chengdu has plenty of industry, including big plants run by the military—were worried about inflation, inequality, their futures, in a system being dismantled piecemeal, without clear guidelines. Owners of private capital were under scrutiny, almost attack, on the grounds of endemic tax evasion and high living. But the tensions were stronger than I guessed. I would not have predicted an uprising. Understanding China is not just a job; it is a life.

I scrounge resources and permissions, and plan to return in the autumn, when anxieties will have abated.

November 5, 1989. Chengdu

Five months after Chengdu's Tiananmen-inspired protests, the city appears almost exactly as it had when I left last December. A friend's baby is flourishing; people waltz in open-air pavilions by the Jin Jiang River on warm nights; crowds of flower-lovers visit the annual chrysanthemum exhibition in People's Park. Only one person I know has disappeared.

There are some changes. A new carpet brightens the lobby of the Jin Jiang Hotel where a protesting crowd trashed it. Shops in this and a neighboring hotel are noticeably empty, perhaps because of the looting, perhaps because of tourist boycotts. The broken glass, torn clothing, and lost shoes that littered the hotel's forecourt after the riot have, of course, long been cleaned up, as have the prostitutes with whom I sometimes shared its late-night lobby last year.

A large state department store and theater are gone, burned to the ground when fire spread from the police station that was the principal target on the night after tanks entered Tiananmen. Noticeably fewer buses now ply Chengdu's crowded streets. Crowds burned dozens of them, along with official and police cars, in protests always clearly aimed at state institutions. The city government piled up a mountain of their charred, mechanical corpses; people point out where it stood for an ominous month behind the statue of Mao Zedong, still a punitive old City God.

A doctor friend tells me that between one hundred and fifty and two hundred people were injured seriously enough in the June 4th and 5th violence to risk seeking help at hospitals. An unknown number of Chengdu people died: local estimates vary between "a few" and thirty, but Amnesty International reports over three hundred. Most died on the second night of rioting, June 5. Plain-clothes police armed with rebar beating off the charge on the hotels accounted for some of the dead. Others were shot from hotel windows. With obvious pleasure, someone recounts for me the rumors put about to confuse the police. These kept authorities concentrated in the commercial downtown until protesters had had a few good whacks at the hotels. Was it relevant that the U.S. consulate has offices in the Jin Jiang? People don't think so.

"The US had nothing to do with this; Six-Four was a purely internal matter."

The army prudently lay low, leaving crowd control to the civil police.

University security has tightened since the sustained protests. Students returned to campuses in the fall to find the small gates in their encircling walls bricked up, channeling all traffic through well-guarded main gates. A few students have disappeared into the limbo of arrest—five at one university, doubtless more elsewhere. People known to have participated in Chengdu's huge street demonstrations before May 18, when such rallies were ineffectually criticized by Li Peng, are under investigation. By July, at least two had been executed for setting fire to vehicles. Most of those arrested in Chengdu, as in Beijing, were *not* students, but rather the sort of people Chinese officials find generally troublesome: the unemployed, street peddlers, small-time hustlers of various kinds. This poorly defined category of powerless "bad elements" is almost infinitely expansible when scapegoats must be found. Their clearest identity is of those whom socialism, with its promise of meaningful work for all, has failed.

Chengdu residents are proud that their city was second only to Beijing in the spring protests. What they protested, however, is not yet clearly understood outside China, nor are the consequences of the protests. Many in the West interpret the student-led revolt as a liberal-democratic movement fueled by China's increasing openness to capitalism. I am spending six autumn weeks in Chengdu and in the Fujian city of Xiamen talking to the small businesspeople who benefited most from the "economic liberalism" of the 1980s. Their reading of Tiananmen is very different from that purveyed by the U.S. media.

The sacrifices of protesters have been met not only with political repression but, more important, with another sharp turn in the shifting course of the Chinese economy.

Did China's leaders, insulated from daily life in the "forbidden city" of Zhongnanhai, consider the effect of tanks in Tiananmen on their ability to control a private sector grown increasingly independent under the 1980s reforms? Goddesses of democracy and intellectuals' demands for press freedom and increased rule of law were, as ideology always is, tropes in a discourse on political economy. China's leaders would not have deliberately provoked uprisings in forty of China's cities; they have been too costly. But putting down a political movement has frightened people away from resisting rapid and often unwelcome economic changes. Tiananmen has enabled the leadership to reassert far more stringent controls on the private accumulation of capital than those in force during the eighties. In the fall of 1989, the proverb that captures the arbitrary imperial style—"Kill the chicken to scare the monkey"—is on everyone's lips.

The events of 1989 offer clear if disheartening insights into the latest confrontation between socialism and the petty capitalism that has been so critical to China's economy for a millennium. Since the decollectivization of agriculture in the late 1970s, China has returned to household control (if not, strictly speaking, of ownership) in agriculture and in some industry and commerce. Countryside and city, even in inland Sichuan, are dense with the sort of small producers I interviewed last fall.

Distant early warnings that leaders wished to cut back petty capitalist power were abundant in the press and on the grapevine long before the student movement gained momentum in Beijing. From September of 1988, the daily papers I consumed with my funny breakfasts were filled with discussions of how to tax and contain private businesses more effectively. Before I could eat my lunch, another of my businesswomen informants would have wondered whether the government would dismantle a system that had penetrated so many households and that made daily life so much more convenient for them. The older they were, the more clearly they remembered the dismaying series of contradictory experiments with private production the country has experienced since 1949, and the more they worried over the security of their newly acquired capital.

The political crackdown after Tiananmen was followed by a low-key but strikingly efficient economic repression aimed at disrupting the accumulation of private capital and the lowering of consumption. Direct action resulting from a State Planning Commission decision was implemented in early October. The new austerity policy was soon being described as an effort to limit the further expansion of small, uncontrollable businesses and to reinvigorate state-managed medium and large ones.

The most direct mechanism for recapturing private capital is confiscation. Firms with foreign capital are exempt, but small, local companies specializing in producer goods are especially vulnerable: many newspaper accounts refer to increased "supervision" and "consolidation" of private businesses. On my third day in Chengdu, I learn of an excellent example, a firm established in the early 1980s with family savings. With much hard work on the part of its founder, it transfers light industrial goods between Sichuan and several coastal provinces. It was seized in late July, 1989, not as punishment for tax evasion or any other definable iniquity, but because it was well worth having. Its owner has been retained as manager, but the comfortable two-bedroom apartment the family purchased with profits may also be subject to confiscation. To keep it, the owner must prove it was not bought with excess profits, "excessiveness" left undefined. The owner quotes Jiang Zemin as saying that private business families should be left, after taxation, with enough to eat, but not enough to live well or expand on. "The country is poor, so it wants us *laobaixing* [commoners] to be poor, too," the normally ebullient entrepreneur says ruefully. Others use the trite but appropriate metaphor: "They want to eat up everything we earned in the 80s."

Like Confucian officials before them, present-day bureaucrats are ambivalent toward expansionary private businesses. The taxes they generate are undoubtedly useful, but profit-making businesspeople rapidly gain social power, which Chinese officials have long seen as a violation of social order. The press is stressing that "the original purpose of developing the private economy was to encourage the unemployed to find jobs for themselves," and that "the State wants the private sector involved in food and drink, repair work, handicrafts and service industries which are not profitable for State- and collectively-run enterprises."[1]

Tax collection, and now tax reform, are powerful tools in officials' efforts to regain control of the economy. In 1988, a small restaurant or service establishment paid not only income tax but a variety of other taxes and fees: sanitation, administration, and small business tax; insurance, water, and electricity fees. These typically amounted to between twenty and thirty yuan each month, roughly half of their (additional) income tax payments. Taxes and fees for the smallest establishments thus added up to between sixty and ninety yuan a month—a range within which many workers' salaries fall. Tax rates have doubled since 1988, and new taxes are constantly added. Drivers of taxis in Chengdu pay a flat five yuan a month as a pork consumption tax.

"As if my cab ate pork," the owner says in disgust. "Even *I* can't afford to eat pork at today's prices"—a pardonable exaggeration.

During my 1988 fieldwork, tax evasion was so normal that people alluded to it with few qualms. Soon after Tiananmen, the central government began a push to capture these revenues, resulting in returns 50 percent higher for the first nine months of 1989 than for all of 1988. One authority said the amounts to be got from private businesses were "astonishing."

[1] "State to Set Private Businesses Straight," *China Daily*, November 7, 1989.

In 1988, most of my subjects paid about 10 percent of their profits in income taxes and fees; in 1989, people complain that it is closer to 30 percent. A tax of 10 percent, or even of 30 percent, by social democratic or even U.S. standards is hardly outrageous. By the standards of those unaccustomed to direct taxes since the revolution, however, it is hard to swallow. Ordinary Chinese people's conception of private property is fundamentalist: no one outside the family gets a share of its earnings. A state that taxes at all is "undemocratic." The term *"ziyou,"* translated as "freedom," figured largely in the May and June protests. The core of its meaning to most folks that I know is the absence of obligation to make involuntary contributions to a public purse.

If taxes were believed to be redistributive, people might well grit their teeth and pay up; urbanites have a well-developed awareness of the immediate and long-term utility of publically funded infrastructure, education, and the like. But businesspeople fear that the taxes extracted from them will go either into leaders' pockets or toward paying China's international debt.

"They are already borrowing to pay interest to foreign banks; where will it end?" says a savvy restaurateur.

As things are, entrepreneurs grit their teeth and try harder to protect what they have accumulated, laying plans to survive a yet sharper policy turn that may leave them with nothing to tax.

In practice, taxation—at least in Chengdu—is accomplished through a system that bears a strong resemblance to those of pre-1990s Taiwan and late imperial China. Taxes on small businesses are collected twice monthly by Small Business Association members who have been appointed by that association from their own urban districts. Groups of seven or eight tax collectors are responsible for a tax district of 700 to 800 private business households. They make themselves available to payers on the appropriate days, keep records, give receipts, and chase down delinquents, fining them "a percentage or two" for each late day. Individual tax payments for the year are some times set in meetings where negotiation is possible and sometimes simply assigned on the basis of the tax collector's guess at each firm's income. The reluctance of small firms to keep books is based, of course, precisely on this expectation. With no records, no other system is possible.

Groups of businesspeople such as the wholesalers in a large city market have a great deal to gain from solidarity. A neighboring stallkeeper watches your baby while you go to the toilet; you in return keep an eye on her inexperienced helper while she buys a *chaoshao* lunch. Small-town garment retailers hire a bus together to expedite their visits to urban suppliers. Tax collectors who are members of such informal collectives accept and report rather low rates of taxable income. As a result, everyone on the bus or in the market pays taxes lower by a factor of between three and ten times what the system in principle requires. Informal pressures can easily be brought to bear on collectors in such circumstances to collude for the common good. Similar implicit tax resistance can also occur where there are genuine emotional links, as in parts of town inhabited by families who have been neighbors for generations.

Where a collector is responsible for a dispersed group of business families with no connection to her own however, she has a much freer hand in assigning tax rates. In such tax districts, the amount collected depends more on personal relationships than on regulations or accounting procedures. The possibilities for graft are obvious, and the fear of and loathing for such unofficial officials are sometimes patent. Businesspeople angrily describing a corrupt individual sometimes direct anger as well at the shadowy, grasping state she represents. Collectors I have met through official channels are quick to insist on how honestly they fulfill their duties.

"I'm not the kind of tax collector who slips some of the money into my own pocket," said one woman. "I put it all in the bank the way I'm supposed to."

The dislike of tax collectors sometimes takes active forms. *People's Daily* reported 8,017 incidents throughout China of assault against collectors and their offices between 1986 and 1988. Seven hundred and thirteen collectors were seriously injured (twenty-six disabled); eleven were killed.

The tax system runs on payoffs and ambiguities, with almost everyone in small business implicated in practices that are dubious, if not criminal. As in so many of their relations with the state, private businesspeople depend on a network of contacts—a *guanxiwang*—of favors and services that transfer resources between socialist and petty capitalist spheres. Such transactions are popularly viewed as both legitimate and illegitimate. One *ought* to follow the system as regulated by authority in the interest of society at large; at the same time, one has a moral duty to care for one's family and improve one's child's opportunities by whatever means come to hand. The breakdown of socialism has brought this age-old Chinese moral dilemma once again directly to the fore.

People are squeezed, too, in more direct ways. In Sichuan, many state employees have long been required to use 15 percent of one month's wages each year to buy five-year government bonds. In November 1989, an additional levy of from 60 to 110 percent (varying by work unit) of that month's wages was enforced on state workers, even those in production, and bonuses were canceled. It is reported that in some regions, workers were required to buy three months' worth of bonds in 1989. The government, it is rumored in Chengdu, simply does not have the money to meet its payrolls. The government's banks are offering high interest on savings as another means of repooling capital that the eighties dispersed so widely.

I read the state's reabsorption of private surpluses as a Friedmanesque attempt at controlling inflation. But it seems punitive as well, intended to warn state employees of their vulnerability while drastically constricting the flow of cash to the family businesses that supply most small daily comforts. A high-ranking official published his opinion that tax collection must be improved to "readjust the staggering profits some private entrepreneurs make and to hold back upstarts"—an ancient term of contempt for thriving merchants. The overall effect of de-reform, motivated more by Confucian images of stability than by socialist visions of abundance, is to cut consumption even at the cost of cutting production.

Images of eating as *the* key area of consumption have always pervaded Chinese culture. People who overconsume food, especially those eating at public expense, are frequently scolded by officials. *People's Daily* carried an essay written in the hectoring tone used in such homilies:

> Owing to the current fight against corruption, banqueting at public expense has become less prevalent. But a new practice—banqueting at "private" expense—is in full swing in some places.
>
> A village Party secretary spent 800 yuan offering 10 tables of sumptuous dishes in his home to his guests in just one month. Villagers thought it was the secretary who footed the bill. But well-informed sources said that the so-called "family banquets" were actually disguised public banquets. It is a new way adopted by some to avoid the crackdown on corruption. . . .
>
> Both banqueting with public funds and with "private" funds is a disgraceful way to exploit the State. Since the practice of eating "family dinners" has newly emerged, the most urgent task is to nip it in the bud.[2]

Low-level state workers ready for lunch recite with a peculiar suppressed glee how the government forbids officials to order more than

[2] "Banquet Ruse," *China Daily*, October 28, 1989.

four dishes and a soup for public entertaining. They then order six, seven, or eight, leaving most of the food uneaten. "Eating at the public trough," to use the American metaphor, is, after all, a primary reason for entering government service. If the water and gas pressure are so low that apartment dwellers—mostly state employees—cannot wash and cook, if salaries are frozen while prices rise madly, if only businesspeople can afford the 7,000 yuan a year in fees that permit a child with average grades to enter a key middle school—why then, eat up. It's on the expense account, the only perk left.

China's leaders turn to these control measures principally, I believe, to maintain the political-economic domination over private producers that has been a major preoccupation of Chinese ruling classes for centuries. The inherent tendency of markets to generate "social disorder" or "freedom" (depending on where you stand) is well known to Chinese statecraft. Late imperial rulers and some post-1949 leaders have emphasized the negative, social disorder aspect—"*luan*," chaos, rather than the positive "freedom" aspect stressed by liberal traditions. But the phenomenon is the same.

Through the screen of Western journalism, people outside China saw the 1989 spring protests throughout China as motivated primarily by liberal values deriving from Euro-American experiences with capitalism. In part, the protests were "liberal." This does not mean, however, that the protesters themselves were demanding freedom for all forms of private enterprise. Petty capitalism embodies the personalistic relations that so easily become illegitimate. The demonstrations in Beijing, Chengdu, and many other cities were protests against corruption, calls for the restoration or creation of a clear distinction between state / public resources and household / private resources. Protesters objected to the gobbling up by well-placed leaders' households of the best bits of the collective economy, for such practices turn socialism into feudalism. They demanded the rectification or elimination of transfers between the socialist sphere—which thus loses its socialist character—and the petty capitalist sector—where the familism of even large enterprises links officials' children and street-hawkers in a common universe of (im)morality and (mal)practice. Capitalism as practiced in China by transnational corporations was never an issue.

The students who initiated the protests, and the great majority of urbanites who supported them, are on the state payroll. Much of the energy for collective action came from their anxieties about their own economic destinies, firmly rooted in the socialist political economy.

Would a student from Beijing University, China's best and brightest, have a job of the sort she thought she deserved if the leadership kept giving all the best companies to their "sons and younger brothers"? The "freedom" to criticize leaders was woven into the need to preserve a socialist mode from corrupt transfers at the top. Student and other participants acted heroically, but we should be clear about their goals and the political economic conditions that inspired them to risk their lives.

Petty capitalist participation in the uprising appears to have been insignificant in Chengdu, as in Beijing. People in the family firms I know kept their heads low during the insurrection, partly because they are not effectively organized, but primarily because the attacks on corruption smelled faintly like an attack on them.

In my 1988 interviews in Chengdu, the ambiguity of transfers between socialist and private pools of resources stood out as a critical element in the mixed economy. Many small businesses could not have been founded without appropriating forms of capital from the public domain. Workers in state food-processing plants sometimes supply their wives' grocery stores with free commodities smuggled out after hours. Or they persuade their superiors to sell them small quantities at the state wholesale price for resale in their wives' shops. As one shopkeeper noted,

> It's irregular, and we probably shouldn't do it, but I used to work in that factory before the Cultural Revolution. We were sent down for a few years. When my husband and I came back from the countryside, the factory had a job for him, but not for me. So this way the factory can help our family a little.

Men (and the rare women) who work as drivers are especially well placed to effect such transfers. They sometimes simply steal goods, or they use their trucks after hours to move, for example, their wives' factory output to the railroad station, or they rent out the truck and their services to other small businesses in need of transport.

Space is at a premium in Chengdu. A good "door room" or shophouse on a busy street rents for as much as 1,000 yuan a month, a figure few beginning businesses can afford. About half the businesswomen in my sample for whom retail location was important were renting their shops either from close relatives or from a close relative's state work unit at figures well below market prices.

"We couldn't afford to do business in this spot if we couldn't rent from my father-in-law's unit;" "This door room was a residence belonging to my mother's unit. After the new policy permitted private business again, we thought it was a waste just to live here. So I quit work at the Street factory, and now Mother and I run this restaurant."

Many elements of petty capitalism, which is by definition household-based and personalistic, are widely seen as inherently corrupt and corrupting, sometimes even by petty capitalists themselves. Pornography and prostitution are often mentioned among the natural vices the free market is heir to. A bafflingly inconsistent anti-porn campaign in the fall of 1989 provided many new opportunities for graft, without noticeably reducing its targets. Indeed, the campaign seems to have infinite flexibility: I hear its principal slogan, "*Sao huang*," "sweep away the filth," hissed at me on a Xiamen street. In Chengdu, popular hotpot restaurants, it is gossiped, owe their popularity and their association with a wicked demi-monde to their (I hope apocryphal) custom of lacing the soup with cocaine. "People who go to such bad places late at night get addicted to hotpot [fondue], and can never break away from that kind of life."

Discussions of corruption are often illustrated with references to exploitation, meant more or less in the technical sense: workers are paid less for their work than they actually produce, leaving a profit for the employer. Some forms of exploitation are egregious, condemned by nearly everyone. An ugly case of child labor broke in Chengdu in fall of 1989, drawing condemnation from Li Peng himself. The owner of a shoe factory was taken into custody and fined 62,597 yuan for a list of malfeasances including brutal mistreatment of sixty-three apprentices, eleven of whom were children. Apprentices paid fees of 300 yuan and advances of 105 yuan for living expenses; thirty-eight had already fled, abandoning their investments, unable to bear the intense crowding, hunger, and beatings the master inflicted on them.

Increasingly, China is rearranging itself into a pattern that disturbingly resembles its pre-1949 society. A ruling class of officials assure themselves of essential supplies (such as tanks) and generate social support through employing large numbers of people. These obtain job security, political protection (of a sort), and the opportunity to dip into private wealth by virtue of their role in management, tax collection, and other coercive scams. Private production is permitted because forbidding it entirely causes both enormous social tensions and, in some spheres, lowers production. It is permitted also because its revenue-generating capacities tempt bureaucrats living on slim political pickings.

As the reforms unroll, more and more rural private firms shield themselves as "township-village enterprises," "hanging a sign" that identifies them as collectives owned and run by an eponymous administrative unit. Even brief visits to such places often reveal the control their actual, private owner exercises. Owners successful in such enterprises willy-nilly position themselves to be elected or appointed to local government, and the circle between private and public neatly closes. Only the tiniest firms are truly private in Sichuan, unless their owners are shielded by bureaucratic office. On the coast, wholly indigenous private firms are permitted to grow somewhat larger, but most large enterprises are sheltered by the input of sometimes merely decorative Overseas Chinese or other foreign capital. Everywhere, at the low-middle end of the business spectrum, determining who or what actually owns / controls / can make binding decisions for a firm is open to passionate, silent struggle between bureaucrats and would-be capitalists, who are often the same person.

The current state, like most Chinese states before it, expends great and complex effort to ensure that the scale of private production units remains small. China's leaders appear to be most comfortable with a combination of large firms they control themselves backed up by a vast congeries of family businesses, tilling small plots or running workshops. These household producers feed families, generate taxes, provide entry-level jobs to the young, and remain politically passive. Officials appear to be thoroughly uncomfortable with both the accumulation of private capital (perhaps for good socialist reasons) and the energetic consumption that fuels economic expansion (perhaps through dangerous feudal prejudice). China's leaders, more Confucian than they can perhaps imagine, are not prepared to countenance a well-fed, well-dressed, well-educated, moderately cosmopolitan class of economic independents whom they would be obliged to treat as equals.

The state's de-reform policies seem to have little to do with socialism, which by definition aims at abundance through equality. The reforms of the 1980s increased inequality, and the corrupt transformation of public property into private capital is not likely to decrease it. Mrs. Wang, the frame knitter, and Miss Li, the noodle seller, are safer with each other than they are with the Bank of America or Deng Xiaoping's relatives— or so they clearly believe. With the latter in charge, they have no assurance that what is taken from their pockets will be wisely spent for the public good. Such assurances can only be given by functionaries whom people can see as representing their interests. The party did this for most Chinese in the 1940s, for many in the 1950s, but has been able to do so for only a rapidly dwindling proportion since the later stages of the Cultural Revolution.

It is difficult to imagine a simple outcome for China's deeply rooted contradictions. The Chinese appear tired of the struggle to move to a single, socialist system. Many identify private production with easier access to small luxuries, but also with efficient management of the essential tasks of life—selling the vegetables, finding shoes that fit, getting a job. Petty capitalists are sometimes condemned because they consume conspicuously, but they enable everyone else to get dinner on the table in one hour instead of three. At the same time, even the most profit-hungry petty capitalist blanches with horror at the war of all against all that they believe would ensue if no state regulated their firms, no monopolistic hand built harbors and railroads and post offices, and no leader gave moral examples, or at least moral pronouncements. Whether Western leftists like it or not, the protests of 1989 are vivid evidence for how many Chinese now want to live in a mixed economy that they can operate without corruption. As transfers between their two modes of production are frequently perceived as corrupt, this will be a very hard task indeed.

The corruption / consumption dilemma, so intimately associated with class issues, is epitomized in a newspaper account of the high-livers who rode the crest of the eighties' reforms:

> A random survey in August 1988 of 100 women who were about to marry revealed that 93 had bought one to two suits of high-grade wedding dresses and 98 were going to hold large banquets at their weddings.
>
> For an ordinary worker, one suit of such quality would cost 500 yuan or more, equal to over four months' salaries. To hold a wedding banquet might use up all the savings of the newlyweds as well as considerable support from parents and relatives.
>
> An attendant of a hotel gave a special reason for her wedding party.
>
> "Everyday, I have to serve a lot of officials eating on public funds. I want to hold my wedding banquet in the hotel because I want to show those people my disdain. I want to tell them if they're really wealthy, they should eat on their own [i.e., at their own expense]," she said.[3]

If the Chinese go on as they have been, each class eating for revenge, their future becomes unthinkable.

[3] "High Consumption Level Argued," *China Daily*, October 19, 1989.

CHAPTER SIXTEEN

城都行

Finding My Feet

NOVEMBER 10, 1989. CHENGDU

This week is too short to absorb the things my Chengdu acquaintances want to tell me, let alone to pursue all the questions and pay all the visits that my curiosity prompts. Wrenching into academic gear, I bear down on my other reason for coming here. The Fulian and I are working out an agreement for a project that will bring me back to Chengdu. With a letter from the Fulian's Vice-Director in hand, I can look for a grant to support it.

After Tiananmen, I knew that permission for research by foreigners on contemporary life would be hard to get. Worse, such research might frighten or endanger informants and colleagues. I decided, therefore, to try to answer a question that had long puzzled me and that might seem harmlessly irrelevant to suspicious authorities. Varying proportions (unknown) of women in different regions of China for centuries had bound their daughters' feet. It was a painful, sometimes crippling process that placed real limits on mobility and on the capacity for many kinds of work. No systematic information about its frequency or distribution had ever been collected.

In the political chaos of the mid-nineteenth to mid-twentieth centuries, the custom had been abandoned. In some regions, it disappeared before 1900 for all but a few fiercely traditional, wealthy families; in others, it continued as part of the common pattern for women's lives until the Communists stopped it after 1949. Many bound-footed women are still alive, though their numbers are dwindling rapidly in the areas of its earliest abandonment. It would be a fine thing to piece together the causes of both keeping and abandoning the custom while many women remained who could speak for themselves about it.

I wrote the Fulian, describing the idea. They vetted it up the chain of command, and after a good deal of wrangling (I later learned), gave tentative approval. Now, I have come to Chengdu to learn what that approval actually means.

As is customary in Chinese negotiations, the Fulian and I entertain each other lavishly, do some sightseeing, revisit old friends—our most politically reliable businesswomen—and strictly avoid coming to grips with the business at hand until almost the last moment. When our project-assessing meeting occurs, it is as though I had never raised the issue of footbinding before.

"We can't do anything like the last time, not right now," the Vice-Director cautions me. "It would make the Foreign Affairs people much too nervous to have you bicycling all over the city, going into people's houses, asking about taxes and things."

"How about something from before the Revolution? Could we interview old women about their work when they were young?"

"And how much better things have got for Chinese women? Yes! We could do that! We could go to the countryside, and work through village Fulian women."

I take three deep breaths, and, very softly, risk a face-to-face gaffe of incalculable proportions.

"Could we ask them about footbinding?"

Footbinding is long gone, but it remains a ticklish subject. Modern-minded Chinese remember it, as Americans do slavery, as a shameful aspect of their history, an example of barbarism they hate to admit was once an integral part of their culture. So many living people either have or have seen bound feet that complete denial is not possible. But its reality is vanishing into myth as the boundfooted disappear into housebound old age, and quietly die. Many people now believe that footbinding was once universal; many others are equally convinced that, per contra, it was never as common as critical foreigners reported. Sometimes a person believes both that footbinding was a rare, elite phenomenon and also that it was the unusual, rude practice of remote and backward villages. It is certainly nothing for China's official women's organization to flaunt before the world.

Footbinding is also a sexual subject, although I later learn that this was far more true for a small, literate coterie of fetishists than for ordinary men and women. Will asking elderly Chinese about footbinding be analogous to asking American small-town senior citizens about their youth-

Cadres and Entrepreneurs Pursuing Common Goals

ful experiences with breast enhancement? If so, my hopes for cooperation are slim.

The Vice-Director has been watching me, levelly, with her beautiful,
smooth face at parade rest. She sometimes needs my sloppy Mandarin
restated by Hua or someone else who has my idiolect down pat. She is
accustomed, too, to listening well and making a fully considered decision
at once. Only cadres with this talent well developed can perform their
multifarious duties with any semblance of completeness and success.

"Sure, we can ask them about footbinding. Why not?"

I breathe again. *Why* this is not a problem will be an interesting part of
the research in itself. But that will emerge in its own time. Footbinding is
OK. The project is OK. All things are possible.

"This would be different from our businesswomen interviews. Not so
long with each woman, but with a lot more women," I continue, determined to be sure that we are all agreeing to the same thing.

"How many?"

"If I can get enough money, can we interview—maybe (I stretch my mind to its numerical limit) two thousand?"

"How big a grant can we get?"

"We have a good chance at one for $25,000."

"Is that U.S. dollars?"

"Yes."

"It's hardly worth getting organized for two thousand women. Let's do about five. We can go to several different counties. It'll be good for the local cadres to get some training and make liaison with us. Do all five thousand have to be footbound? That might be hard."

"No," I gasp. "We'll want to discover the different local ratios of bound to not bound, so we'll interview all women over sixty-five in our chosen areas."

"That should be okay then. Why don't you write it up, and then we can talk about the budget."

Dear Vice-Director! The half dozen other cadres, perched on beds and chairs, beam. There will be bustle and plans and (though the travel will be troublesome) some time away from home and office, a break in routine. There will be bonuses.

I beam too. They could have said that $25,000 was just enough for two thousand distant interviews. They could have run the infuriating routine to which many China-studiers have been subjected, that $25,000 wasn't even *enough* for a survey of two thousand if it had to be done with a high-living foreigner in tow. As in our last project, they are being straight with me.

My flight is in two days. I must move on to Xiamen to make a similar but perhaps more difficult agreement with that city's Fulian. Sichuan Fulian has alerted them that I am coming, has asked them for cooperation. Now insatiable, I begin to fantasize about a thousand Fujian women's feet.

A good questionnaire must be well-targeted, free of ambiguity, and easy to administer. This one additionally must cope with a wide range of archaic rural vocabulary about work and kinship, in multiple regional dialects. At least a dozen experienced, assertive women have a piece of this action, and none of us is slow to bring forth and defend opinions, strategies, and the odd red herring. If we are to be ready to begin surveys this fall, we are going to need more meeting time to formulate our plan than I have allowed. With the golden promise of a large grant binding us in a materially based and thus truly meaningful relationship, I risk another step in my engagement with Sichuan Fulian.

"Vice-Director, I am going on to Xiamen University for a methodology conference with local scholars. We will be talking for three days about how to do field research. I really think that some of our colleagues here could benefit from the discussions. I also know that the men scholars need to be reminded of how important research on women is. Will you send Teacher Jiang, Xinghui, and Jufang with me to Xiamen to participate? Then we would also have time to develop a complete questionnaire for the survey before I leave China. You get them tickets, and I'll take care of their expenses in Xiamen."

This is pushing it; I am asking a lot from the Fulian, always cash-strapped, to buy plane tickets for three people. Will she assume that the grant can later absorb those travel costs? Can we begin to leave things like this on the basis of mutual trust?

I feel I must push, though. For the three women who worked so hard to make the first project succeed, there should be some reward, some recognition of their research competence. The Xiamen University conference will be a nice entry on their resumes. And Xiamen is beautiful, a seaside resort, a major notch on the gun of peripatetic official travelers, a vacation. One of the trio has relatives there. Leaders take care of their troops.

The Vice-Director gives me a long, thoughtful look. She is very good at this.

"They can go with you. They'll have to come back by train, though."

Too pleased with the accord to spot its full meaning, I agree, condemning my colleagues to a five-day train ride as the coda to their vacation. Caught in my own assumptions, it is not until far too late that I realize I should buy the return plane tickets myself.

NOVEMBER 15, 1989. XIAMEN

In between playing on the beautiful Xiamen beaches and eating the fishy fruits of its waters, we four pound out a plan. We will interview 250 women over sixty-five in each of twenty villages, divided among ten counties. The counties are chosen to give us a range of commercial versus subsistence production, distance from cities, and specialized women's work such as spinning and weaving, the raising of white wax insects and silkworms, the picking of tea and opium. Local Fulian women, surveying their own community elders, will supply us with enough, and good enough data to make our correlations between foot-

Socialist Feminists on a Spree

binding and economic conditions meaningful. I will interview a tenth of
the women in at least half of the counties myself to get a more nuanced
reading of women's responses to the custom and its abandonment. We
will have the survey responses computerized, and share all our findings.

NOVEMBER 25, 1989. XIAMEN

Because the Loma Prieta earthquake has dealt roughly with his Stanford
house, Arthur, my lover, has not yet arrived for critical meetings on our
joint project at Xiamen University. We will begin with a meeting on
methods, and then move to the first of a series of field trips that will take

me to a dozen Fujian villages over the next 3 years. My part of the team effort will be to explore women's work in textiles and the local distribution of footbinding.

I try to initiate the series of discussions in which the United States, Taiwan, and China colleagues will reconcile their wildly differing views of what we are to do and how much it will cost. While I see myself as Arthur's legitimate proxy in this matter, the Chinese, unsurprisingly, do not. In the formal table of organization, I am simply one of the U.S. team, and not a high-ranking one. My efforts at planning come across as presumptuous and irritating; I am a pillow-ghost.

The need to include women respondents, about which I am especially emphatic, is a particularly sore point. This project, already agreed to by numerous local officials and academics, as well as the Taiwan and U.S. collaborators, requires equal numbers of older men *and* women in thirty-six Fujian villages. Agreement or not, our Xiamen University colleagues do not want to waste time interviewing women.

"Rural Chinese women are illiterate. They know nothing but housework and childcare, so there's no point in asking them questions about culture," says the ranking local anthropologist.

With the failure of my arguments from anthropological history (remember Margaret Mead?), logic (who picks Fujian's tea, anyway?), and authority (our grant proposal says we interview women, so we interview women), I unleash the Army-trained Hua on them. Teacher Jiang weighs in with her own experience of life in Fujian and her awareness of its women's place in history. These Fulian interventions sharply curtail the open sexism. The men (there is only one woman scholar "qualified" to participate in our team) know that the socialist line is also a feminist one. Privately, however, they urge on me the irrelevance of such considerations for women who "before the Revolution" were meaningless pawns in traditional patriarchy.

By the time Arthur appears, we need all the efforts of our Taiwan and Chinese-American colleagues to mollify the thin-skinned scholars I have offended. Life has not prepared them to imagine somebody's girlfriend as their leader any more than it has accustomed them to asking old village women about work and kinship. To their horror, Arthur plumps for petticoat government, the Fulian, and the extraordinary value of female testimony to the realities of history. Li, Jiang, Hua, and I leave the field triumphant to finish our questionnaire.

The time for the Fulian to return to Chengdu is upon us. I arrange for one last treat, a seafood banquet just for the four of us at one of Xiamen's best restaurants. After writing down the long list of delicacies we have compiled, the waitress asks, offhandedly, if we want a special fish. Foolishly ignoring my companions' unease, I call airily for the special fish. The waitress brings it, live, in a pail, for my inspection—another sign that I am getting into deep culinary waters. I realize I may need another grant to pay for this fish, but guilt over my companions' railway return prevails. At its appointed time, the fish appears, small, delicate, health-giving. The bill for this treat is an additional 1,000 yuan—almost enough for three plane tickets to Chengdu.

The long waits between meetings with reluctant colleagues at Xiamen University give me time to scribble my previous visit to Chengdu into some comprehensibility. For several days, I take pen and notebook to Nan Putuo Si, a large temple to the Goddess of Mercy that stands beside the university, and climb its rocky hill. On a stone table and stool, staring over the glittering harbor toward Quemoy and Matsu, I make what sense I can of what I have seen. Passing tourists and occasional monks and nuns stop to watch the oddly rapid filling up of paper.

"That must be English writing."

"Yes, they can write much faster than we do."

"It's not very pretty, though."

"Of course not. Chinese writing is pretty; other languages only have a few characters."

In the Xiamen University guesthouse, friendly American scholars eagerly describe how Tiananmen affected other cities in which they were living this past spring. Across chipped bowls of bad rice and small, bony fish, we chew over the details of Six-Four/June 4, and prognosticate its long-term fallout. By contrast, Chinese academics, in the grip of the serious Party pressure on schools that has followed the rebellion, blandly ignore my attempts to discuss it, though they surely gossip constantly about it among themselves. On my long walks through Xiamen's old, granite city, local shopkeepers drop hints about their readings of Six-Four, happy to vent some irritation. They remain properly cautious with a strange and potentially loose-tongued foreigner. The owner of a button store sums up her political philosophy in a Minnanese proverb I learned during my language-lesson years: "People fear wealth as a pig fears fat."

Slowly, the Xiamen project takes shape. Arthur and I set off, sometimes separately, sometimes together, on a series of journeys into the tiny valleys and rough mountains of China's last-tamed province. In a climate of horrid heat and bureaucratic recalcitrance, Chengdu becomes a distant, cool memory, a place where people keep their promises, get the job done, and do not overtly despise their visitors. Covered in mosquito bites and linguistic confusion, I grow petulant and arrogant by turns, stupidly blaming my Fujian academic associates because they lack the Party-backed power of the Fulian to meet my research requirements. My notebooks are full of wonderful things from this time, but I remember virtually none of them. Too much *qi*.

JANUARY 1990. CAMBRIDGE, ENGLAND

I am settled at last for the academic year at Newnham College of the University of Cambridge. Much of the fall of 1989, Michaelmas term, was spent in Chengdu and Xiamen, in worrying about the effects of the Loma Prieta earthquake on Arthur's grand but rickety house in Stanford, and in coming to grips with the astonishing familiarity and comfort of English culture. Surrounded by the collection of books the China anthropologist Barbara Ward left to Newnham, I finish my account of Tiananmen and taxes in Chengdu, turn back to my long-delayed book, begin to write articles on women entrepreneurs, and seek far and wide for money for footbinding. For the first time in many years, I am free of other people's schedules, with weeks and months of days to rise, write, rest, write some more, potter in a library, write, and even think a bit. I know no one but Arthur here. The uninterrupted hours flow like fresh water around my tapping fingers.

Newnham is lovely, the brick halls roseate and well tended, the garden an Englishwoman's dream of wintersweet, daffodil lawns, and ornamental artichokes. Here, one can be a scholar and still be home and dry for tea. Bizarre foods, filthy privies, the exhaustion of long journeys in smoky buses are unknown to the classics people and biologists with whom I dine. At Trinity one memorable evening, I meet a don of high academic repute whose life has been spent in the study of a single dead Englishman's writing. Like his scholastic acolyte, the author in question also lived and died in Trinity; his books and papers are carefully kept in the college's exquisite library.

"Abroad?" the don answers me. "No, not *abroad*. I rarely leave Trinity. Everything I need is here, you know."

Would I be bored with an intellectual life consisting of transferring words from one already written book to a book in the process of being written? Perhaps.

I am exploring that possibility—the anthropologist's equivalent of lying around in fluffy slippers, reading trash and eating bonbons—by tunneling in the archives of Jardine Matheson & Company. Jardine Matheson made a fortune in the early 1800s smuggling opium up and down the south China coast; somewhere along the line, the records of their sustained attempt to enter the Chinese market by hook or crook have entered the Cambridge Library system. In a fine room, decently heated, with bathrooms nearby and gossipy lunch a short, pretty walk away, I read the shaky lines of Captain James Innes, penned aboard ship in the rough weather of December 1832. His journal mostly describes his difficulties in trying to sell inferior, old Patna opium to dozens of local smugglers who arrive demanding high-grade Benares. Two boats from Xiamen, with twenty buyers apiece, even ask for Turkey opium, a request he hadn't heard before. Everyone refuses to buy his woolen goods, and he has literally to give away his consignment of Bibles. He visits ports occasionally, when the coast guard of "mandarin boats" is elsewhere, sees something of the impressive local wealth and industry, and sarcastically records comparative prices for women and cattle. "At this Cup-chow a Woman costs 3$; a bullock 7$: at Fu-chu-fu, a Woman costs 1$; a bullock 21$. Thus the two commodities precisely changing value at the rate of three to one."

Captain Innes was a remarkable man. I later encounter him in the pages of S. W. Williams, a more scholarly observer of China. It seems that Innes was once trying to fix something with a bureaucrat through the mediation of Chinese merchants. When they refused to submit his petition, he sent for his bed, prepared to spend the night in front of the city gate. The bureaucrat caved. I am not at all sure that I want to return to the rigors of fieldwork, to Chengdu, or even to Michigan.

When my dishy lover appears at high table, my colleagues raise tiny questions over morning coffee the next day.

"So this is your weekend, is it? He does China too; how convenient for you."

Well, yes. Very convenient. But very inconvenient as well. Urgently but inconspicuously, I have for years sought an excuse to quit the Chinese world honorably. Early in my second marriage, I threw out my entire anthropology library, except for teaching books, bundling decades of scholarly journals into garbage bags for landfill. China—or at least Taiwan, my only Chinese reality in those days—had proven too difficult for me. Then one of the world's nastiest police states, its military police and ubiquitous informers made everyone fear strangers. The written language remained an appalling barrier that I have never properly surmounted. I hated the unbuffered Florida-like climate. I could no longer remember why I had ever wanted to get past Chinese alienness.

The conference in Taiwan to which—as the soon-to-be lover later told me—I had been accidentally invited brought us together in a place I had thought to have left behind forever. Pheromones drew me back to the Chinese when nothing else could have. I began to write again. I took to heart his encouragement, his innocent assumption that any person of substance would continue in her career. Some men ask their women to give up work, to leave the struggle with torts, or with oncology, or with a Chimu excavation. Not this man; and it made a difference. Not, I think, because he did so *very* much to help me. Still, I have gone on from success to success, from triumph to triumph, since I began sleeping in his bed. If I get my footbinding grant, he will be proud, and I will be footbound to China for years to come.

We are not living together in Cambridge. I want to soak in Newnham's esoteric culture—I have actually sworn personal fealty to Newnham's Principal and learned what it means to "send someone a birdcage." This hyper-Anglo year may be the only chance life will offer me to grow blasé about wearing an academic gown. Serendipitously, the *perfect* dress to wear under the gown for gaudies is my best silver-with-peach-chrysanthemums cheongsam. So I keep my Newnham suite, my gilded morning views of Peile Gate, my uneasy relationship with the female butler and her peculiar desserts, and resist the temptation to extend the weekends in Arthur's collegial housesit to full-time domesticity.

But we might. And, living together, we might yet marry. *Then* I'd be sinified for certain. Magnificent man; Chinese fieldwork for the rest of my days.

September 1991. Nankang, Taiwan

Last April, the Harry Frank Guggenheim Foundation funded the footbinding project under its program on the causes and consequences of violence and aggression—as the mass crippling of girl children can surely have been considered to be. I dare not begin this radically new undertaking—the size of the project is totally off my fieldwork scale—until I have cleared a few more aging commitments from my list. My never-ending book, all but finished in Newnham, needs a rewrite. Chinese scholars are publishing again, and my book has grown obese as I incorporate this warming syrup from long-frozen Chinese faucets.

Our coastal project needed tending, too. I did more penance in Fujian in the summer of 1991, this time traveling into hot fishing villages and muggy mountain valleys with some extraordinarily pleasant fellow-scholars. Dr. Zheng Ling, disregarding the pain of chronic endometriosis, took me to villages where men and women had portered cloth and salt up and handmade paper down their rugged slopes until the Communist government built them a road in the 1950s. Professor Shih Yilong maneuvered me through a careful chain of close friends into a week's stay with a large, jolly fisher family. Fujian is, actually, rather wonderful.

Most important, my partnership with Arthur has grown beyond the bounds of weekends and transcontinental commutes. Xiamen University's grotty guesthouse is an unlikely place for romance florescent. One sticky morning before eating our rice gruel, steamed buns, and instant coffee, however, we decided to marry.

We did marry, in the midst of a year of intermittent separation. During those months, Arthur taught at Stanford and I at Central Michigan. I stripped generations of prewar wallpaper to make my funky house saleable as he rebuilt a temporary bachelor apartment. He began writing up ten years of work on distinctly peculiar marriages, and I finally engaged my aging book manuscript to an honorable publisher. In the middle of the shavings and loose footnotes, on the coldest day northern California has felt in one hundred years, we were wed. Our nicest gift was a string of faux firecrackers sent by the Taiwan colleagues who had accompanied us to Xiamen, with the note:

"Congratulations on your marrying at last! We are not surprised, you know!"

In the fall of 1991, we escaped our continental commuting for coresidential research in Taiwan. The grant for Sichuan was perfectly timed. I could visit Chengdu to get things started in November, and return in April to collect the fieldworkers' surveys and do my own interviews. The Sichuan trips would be pleasant breaks in the rather routine work I had planned, and the travel costs would be greatly reduced by using Taiwan, rather than the United States, as my base. In November, I flew back to Chengdu.

CHAPTER SEVENTEEN

城都行

Roadwork

NOVEMBER 1, 1991. CHENGDU

My Sichuan seatmate on the plane from Beijing called home just before he got aboard; the weather would be sunny in Chengdu, he says. By the time we pull into the chaotically under-construction airport, however, the city is quilted in its usual fog. As I leave the baggage area, rain is falling on a crowd that clearly does not contain my anticipated welcoming party from the Fulian. I recalculate the time necessary for my letter to have reached Sichuan from Taiwan. Plenty of time for them to have received it, surely. Something has gone awry.

A knot of thugs resolves out of the gloom, laughing uproariously about the "foreign old maid" convoying two unsteady suitcases-on-a-leash. The villainous appearance of Chinese workingmen through the long period they frugally allow between haircuts has been raising the anxiety of lady travelers in China at least since Isabella Bird Bishop. Even though I know that most of them probably are fine sons and upstanding citizens, their collective rude remarks make me nervous. I remember the news report of a Swedish diplomat found dead in a Chengdu ditch not long ago. I have no wish to follow Rosa Luxemburg into a muddy tomb.

"How much to the Jin Jiang Hotel?" I demand of one of the least dubious-looking.

"We use the meter, according to the country's regulations."

Surely assassins don't bother to keep their meters in working order. I can't remember how much it *ought* to cost for the twenty minute ride to Chengdu; the Fulian usually sends a car for me. If I knew, I could haggle the asking price down to something reasonable, and also have a moment to assess the driver's character. Oh well. Whatever is on the meter will be less than the high bill likely to be presented to the average foreigner who looks as unraveled as I do just now. The driver's character will reveal itself in good time.

We shoot out of the airport, round a sharp curve, and are suddenly in a dark, narrow lane with no lights in sight.

"What's going on here!" I ask sharply. "You'd better be careful where you take me."

The driver, in the exaggerated drawl that Chinese use to show contempt, offers a plausible explanation.

"The airport construction makes the main road a one-way street. We have to go through this detour. Take it easy, miss."

Maybe. The trees unroll on both sides of a misty, gothic tunnel. There is no highway in sight. If a mugging lies beyond this lane, I have not only the precious temple of my body to worry about, but $20,000 in Harry Frank Guggenheim research funds, $10,000 of it in good American cash.

When I first entered the car, the plastic panels between me and the driver had seemed reassuring. Now, I realize that garroting the guy with my long purse-strap (self-defense step number one) is not an option. The Victorinox that peels my apples, opens my wine, and repairs my eyeglasses has never been unsheathed in anger. Is now the time?

The blade seems smaller than its three inches, but I decide that its tininess is an advantage. If a knife scares the man off, well and good. If, however, we come to a struggle, the thing will probably end up stuck in me, not him. Maybe such a short blade will miss my vital spots. Women of my generation are really not well socialized for this sort of thing. I conceal the open blade between the pages of Nolan and Dong's *Market Forces in China: The Wenzhou Debate*[1] and prepare to defend my honor.

I also review the reasons why my suspicions might be groundless. We are not, in fact, alone. Ghosts on bicycles regularly slide past the car windows. Loud shrieks to "Save life," in the Chinese phrasing, might bring aid. Or not—meddling in others' business, especially something that might be construed as male / female business, is something most Chinese will go a long way to avoid. Still, driving is a good job in China. It pays decently, and, since the only way to keep the vehicles maintained properly is to give each driver full charge over his car, it is relatively easy

---

[1] Peter Nolan and Dong Furen, eds., *Market Forces in China. Competition and Small Business: The Wenzhou Debate* (London: Zed Books, 1990).

for a driver to moonlight after hours, transporting goods for family or for fees. The man would be mad to risk such a livelihood. Too, dozens of people had seen me waiting, conspicuously foreign, alone, and unmet at the airport. Among the driver's mates, surely there is one the police can squeeze hard enough to reveal my murderer's identity.

Just as I am concluding that I have nothing to fear, the car stops. The odd lights, the young toughs swarming around the car, and especially the violent jets of water arcing through the fog make only hallucinatory, phallic sense. With (I hope) less alarm and more authority that I feel, I demand,

"What are we doing *now*?"

"The car's dirty, miss. It's a carwash," comes the bored reply. "Chengdu is competing for a national 'Hygienic City' award, so every vehicle that comes into the city has to be washed. It's a new regulation."

It looks, in fact, much like the carwash I visited a few weeks ago in Mountain View, California. The rough-looking, ill-coifed men working there were Mexican illegals, or Central American refugees, or maybe just kids from East Palo Alto, trying to make an honest buck. No matter how much my work and the thinking of generations of leftists teaches me to see working-men as existential equals, when I am alone at night, I fear them. Neither Sichuanese nor Guatemalan knows I am politically correct. If the rich—as I surely am tonight—are the enemy, as a woman I am doubly so: riding in planes and taxis with money in my pocket, a living affront to male superiority. Rape is a common answer to this insult. How to feel? How to assess this man, my fears, the knife?

The hoses spray climactically, and we are clean. We speed onto the familiar "big horse road" that leads into Chengdu. As I pay the driver, I am so ideologically embarrassed that I fail to protest when he charges me for the carwash.

The Jin Jiang lobby is one of Chengdu's sights, the kind of place people on a spree go to take each other's pictures. It glitters and shines from every surface, kept astonishingly clean and new looking in a country with little taste for maintenance. Alas, however, it has neither reservation nor room for me. My letter cannot have reached the Fulian.

I like the Jin Jiang, but in fact can stay just as well, if a bit more expensively, across the street at a newer hotel. Before I fade into the lavish comfort of a heated room, hot water *at all hours*, and fresh, abundant bedding, I open the curtains to watch the lights. Fourteen floors is high for Chengdu. I can see the still higher tower of the Economic Management Training Institute where I lived in 1988. I wish I could get on my bike and ride there, go "home." I dream of bicycles, of hissing motion through the dripping streets, of the city's invisible landscape of wet smells.

NOVEMBER 2, 1991. CHENGDU

My morning curtains part on a brilliant Saturday. The Fulian should be working at least half a day, but my repeated phone calls are unanswered. Odd. So also with my calls to the Qin family's work unit. I should hire a bike and go looking for them, but opt for playing hooky. It is far too nice a day to work.

I loaf around the neighborhood, dropping back to phone every couple of hours. No luck on the phone, but I buy some books, including a county-by-county atlas of Sichuan and three collections of photos of regional embroidery. I find a carved, antique mirror stand, minus mirror, a miniature of the large one that stands in our bedroom at home. The silk shop in the huge store behind Mao Zedong's statue is still in business. I buy enough brocade remnants for my clever-handed sister-in-law to make a patchwork quilt. Two women who run small shops I used to patronize offer me tea, tell me their children have grown, complain about taxes.

Chengdu's largest free market is full of parrot-bright chrysanthemums and tubs of pregnant "Guaranteed Genuine Zhangzhou Narcissus" bulbs. Goldfish, caged birds, old gents in teahouses, and beldames sweeping up after everyone are as I left them. The market proper is full of the foot-long red radishes that grow only in millennially-tilled soil, of an almost-romaine lettuce eaten mainly for its core, of new fall tangerines, and of pork by the slab or the morsel. Sichuan's women farmers plant, harvest, and cook pigfood so energetically that the province sells sixty million hogs annually, many of them for export to other parts of China. For the first time, I notice the butchers' complicated swivel meat hooks on which all that lardy pork dangles. Their design is handsome because simple and perfect, but saved from a Bauhaus bareness by blacksmiths who have given the long shanks a few ornamental twists. I begin to compute the cost in nuisance of taking twenty pounds of metal through airport inspections and defer the decision.

Late in the afternoon, someone at the Fulian picks up the phone. We go back and forth about who I am until something clicks.

"You're that American researcher who came here before, aren't you? I know you—I'm Driver Zhang."

Of course. Driver Zhang, with his aesthete's face, his tales of sleeping under the trucks while on Army convoy in Tibet, his (understandable) taste for *bai gar* liquor.

"They've all gone off work, but I'll let them know you're here. They'll come and see you tomorrow."

November 3, 1991. Chengdu

My letter never reached the Fulian, it seems, so my colleagues had imagined themselves with a free Sunday. In this exemplary work unit, leisure yields cheerfully to duty. They come and go all day: first my "gang of three" from the 1988 research, to pave the way; then the splendidly competent Vice-Director, who steers my projects past the cranky, unpredictable, and generally irrational Foreign Affairs people; Lu Fubuzhang as was, now director of a Women's Enterprise Institute the Fulian is setting up; a new Fubuzhang named Ruan ("Ruan by name, ruan by nature" I want to say—her name is close-to-homophonous with "soft," which she is. But I wouldn't dare, and can't anyway think of how to phrase it in clever parallel in Chinese); and two or three younger women, new to me, all startlingly chic. None of *them* ever slept under a truck.

They bring fruit, I distribute Hong Kong cosmetics, we shuffle round the seats trying to allocate the best positions to the highest rankers. The Vice-Director is our unquestioned Number One, but my status vis-à-vis Lu is ambiguous. While she insists that I am a guest and must sit in the only other armchair, I insist equally that her title, age, and status as guest *in this room* entitle her to it. I lose (I always lose with Lu), I sit. This settled, we go out for a massive lunch before getting down to cases.

As people flow in and out of the crowded room, events develop a complex recursive quality. The agenda with each newcomer (after greetings, fruit, presents, clarification of hierarchy, and mutual assurances that neither has grown gray or wrinkled since last we met) is: (1) the field questionnaire, (2) where and for how long shall we pretest it in the countryside, and (3) what is our computer plan?

We decide on a work group for the questionnaire for this afternoon and tomorrow. From Tuesday until Friday, a small group of us headed by Ruan Fubuzhang will try it out in a famous tea-picking region a hundred kilometers from here. Saturday I will consult with one of their computer contacts, and Sunday fly, as planned, to Xiamen.

The Vice-Director, Lu, and a few others leave to salvage some of their Sunday (it's a rarely fine day for laundry, and these are all women who must do their own washing); six of us remain to argue through the questionnaire. The debate carries us through the following day until the gargantuan dinner the Vice-Director has planned to celebrate our successful beginning.

I am beginning to worship our Vice-Director. My talents are not inconsiderable, but I absolutely lack administrative ability. I get fuddled about logistics and need a good deal of time to think through decisions that involve others. The Vice-Director does these things brilliantly and democratically. In our discussions, everyone contends with unexampled vigor, with no quarter given for rank. She then politely asks me what I think best, factors it in along with everyone else's—and settles the matter. As long as I have known her, she never gets it wrong. If every Party cadre (or even 10 percent of them) were of her caliber, a great many of China's problems would be sorted out. Promptly.

Just before dinner, she broaches the money question. This is a delicate matter. Our original agreement was written in an overly optimistic spirit, premised on a grant twice the size of the one I got. I informed the Fulian of this when the approval came through, of course, telling them we would need to rethink the budget. Now, I am also obliged to tell them that a (much-needed) strike by my university's overworked clerical staff has resulted in my receiving none of the other grant money I had been awarded for this year—the cash I am to live on. The footbinding research money is all I have on hand.

I spare the Fulian the suspenseful tale of how the $20,000 had come into my hands in Hong Kong: increasingly urgent telexes from Taiwan to various university offices back home in Michigan, desperate last-minute instructions to wire it to Hong Kong American Express (at which I have no account), the bemused expressions of the lacquered receptionist in that bank's massive Hong Kong headquarters, my door-to-door search through lower-ranking offices, and, at last, the fine young Johns Hopkins–trained regional manager, dealing me out a stack of U.S. 100s like a thick steak. We played "do-you-know" for a few minutes—I had taught at Hopkins—and he sent me on my way rejoicing, with four-fifths of the project's money in my old black purse.

Now, in Chengdu, I am not sorry for having an honorable excuse for giving the Fulian only a portion of the money in advance. Events far beyond their control or mine could cancel our project in midtask, as a number of academic projects have been canceled in China earlier this year. But I am glad to get rid of some of it. I turn over a little more than half of what we had agreed on, relieved that someone else will now stand guard over the lightning rod for trouble that ready money generally is. By April, if all goes well, I will bring the rest.

The Vice-Director seems happy with our transaction. She might well be; I have ferreted out enough about the Fulian budget to guess that I am bringing her department a sum equivalent to about a year's worth of wages. Money has been extremely tight, lately, in state service units like this one. Salary and other payments are often delayed up to three months. This addition to the department's cash flow should be a welcome one.

Perhaps because low-level official budgets have been so stringent in recent years, foreign researchers in China have often met with extortionate demands and dishonest practices. I am especially touched, then, when a ranking associate discreetly presses on me a wad of one thousand RMB (about U.S. $200) "so I will be sure to have pocket money on the road." A Fulian slogan is that going to Fulian is like going home to Mother's. Once, after the Vice-Director had given me a particularly long and precise criticism of part of our questionnaire, I repeated the slogan. Everyone was amused—Chinese mothers proverbially are nags. But the kindness that prompts the gift of pocket money is also motherly.

I take it, not because I need it urgently. Chengdu is behind the times in banking, but with a Visa card, a passport, some other odds and ends of documentation, and a long afternoon's wait, I could wring a few hundred U.S. dollars worth of yuan out of the Central Bank, a dozen blocks away. I take the wad to reaffirm the nature of my relationship to their group. Acceptance makes it clear that I am not buying so many filled-in questionnaires for so much money. I have given them a generous share of what our cooperation has shaken from the money tree and trust them to use it honorably in their own way. They are treating me like a member of the unit, giving me my cut. In ways we both know to be limited by who we are and what we do professionally, we are friends.

NOVEMBER 5, 1991. MING SHAN COUNTY

After a flurry of long-distance arrangements, we set off for Ming Shan County, to the southwest of Chengdu, for a four-day trial of our questionnaire. Ruan, who gets carsick, rides in front with Driver Zhang. Li, Hua, and I load ourselves, tiny traveling bags, and a goodly supply of tangerines into the remaining seats. Teacher Jiang, third member of our original group, is doing a three-month stint of Marxist-Leninist studies and cannot come. I will miss her—she enjoys explaining things to me more than the others do—but am not really sorry. Jiang is not a Sichuan person and finds rural treks less of a pleasure than the rest of us do.

The trip starts with gleeful discussion of several dozen traffic offenders who are being punished by standing all day on the midline of one of Chengdu's busiest streets. They look woebegone and embarrassed enough to have learned their lesson. We catalog the various irreverent sobriquets applied to Mao's immense statue that looms up behind them; I add the foreigners' standby pun for this hand-on-high pose: "the permanent wave." We peel fruit for each other. We compare episodes of carsickness. After we are well out of town, the other women settle into serious naps while I peer along the road at Sichuan's interminable string of villages and at the multitudes of Sichuanese who are walking slowly among them.

Carrying their vast crop of fall vegetables in pack baskets, on bicycles, and on tractor-pulled carts, urging water buffaloes to the plough, then attacking the ploughed clods with heavy mattocks are millions of villagers. The excellent earth, made generous by the sweat of their ancestors, does not need them all, despite the immense labor necessary to garden the landscape from horizon to horizon. Yet here they are, a thousand people in work clothes visible at any moment—surplus, superfluous, not according to plan. Those without work lounge in the simple open-air teahouses, or cluster at corners, or sell one another small bits of local produce at local markets that seem to be organized more to break the routine than from any hope of profit. The number of people in relation to available resources is appalling.

They are, by any Western standard, so very poor. The men we pass driving power-tillers-turned-truck own only two suits of clothes at best; the girls punching seeds into tilled earth will never wear the fancy bras or panties sold in Chengdu. Farmer's daughters may, someday, buy chic, high-heeled shoes (hard as boxes), but in the long chilly season will have to wear them with hose drawn up over lumpy long underwear, as their urban cousins do. They eat adequately, they are clothed decently, but they are not yet world citizens who define themselves by their consumption of comfort, convenience, pleasure. They are only villagers.

This throng of Sichuanese emerges from trees and ditches and sheds and the fog that lingers in the distance—the dragon's teeth too thickly sown. There is nowhere for them to go—no country or continent could

Main Street, Ming Shan, 1991

absorb an emigration of the half of a quarter of the world's population that it would take to lessen the pressure of Chinese on Chinese. Skillful in surviving on rice, radishes, tobacco, and good humor, Sichuanese could not be translated to Teaneck or Toronto in numbers large enough to affect the tableau vivant outside the car window. They must struggle on, and somehow learn not to perpetuate the ancestral Ponzi scheme of more and more filial children caring for exhausted, used-up parents.

I expect the population density to go down as we near our mountainous goal. It does not. The hills are terraced to their tops, patches of brush and wildland are measurable in meters, not miles, and the procession outside the car windows does not slacken. Girls carry haystacks of grass cut from roadsides for their animals; old women backpack huge baskets of potatoes or shelled corn; men and boys carry everything from trussed pigs and bouquets of live ducks to broken tractor parts. No one hurries. All plug along, working if only by moving the endless things that must be moved if all are to be fed.

We pull into a small town, which Driver Zhang announces is the county seat. An official gate appears:

"Yamen, yamen," everyone choruses—using the term for an imperial county magistrate's combined residence, judicial office, tax bureau, and jail. I would not have ventured to initiate the comparison; we all know this historical allusion is naughty. Properly labeled or not, the Ming Shan County Guesthouse stands within its walls, ready (or not) to receive us.

This county has never had a foreign visitor before. The guesthouse has bought me brand new towels, packets of toothbrushes and miniature toothpaste tubes, and about twenty pounds of fruit: good local apples and some very shopworn Yunnan bananas. Its manager has not thought to have the bathroom cleaned in any but a theoretical sense; all the fixtures are crusty and discouraging. Hua warns me:

"When the hot water comes on tonight, wash under the taps, *but don't fill the tub and get in.*"

CHAPTER EIGHTEEN

城都行

Still Looking

NOVEMBER 8, 1991. MING SHAN

The interviews, once begun, are a comedy of errors. We are directed to a village that has had no warning of our arrival, while the one that got our message cools its heels. It pours rain and is profoundly foggy on the day we climb the scenic tea-producing mountain, but turns sunny as we trudge around the commonplace county seat. We find we need long conferences on kin terminology with the local Fulian to accommodate regional dialect. In the meantime, our informants get bored and wander off.

Nonetheless, we talk to plenty of women, some of them amazing. We call first on Mrs. Li, a one hundred-year-old matron, who is mother, grandmother, great-grandmother to dozens of progeny, and who still stitches the finely sewn shoe insoles on which she once supported her children. She speaks softly, modestly, but only a fool would miss the steely leadership she still exercises. Half a dozen elderly sons and daughters-in-law show me the family's youngest baby and "Five-Good Family" awards with pride, though no one can remember what all the five "goods" are. This household, boasting many government workers, is the modern equivalent of the grand Confucian family. Counting the baby, they literally house five generations under one roof, depending on a judicious mix of the old, elaborate courtesies and sharp-edged authority to hold them all together.

The paying-a-call performance, with the dowager playing matriarchal virtue to her chorus of admiring progeny, and myself playing the traveler-from-afar come to seek cultural enlightenment, hits a snag as we are about to move on to more average households.

"You said you wanted to interview women over sixty-five!" the old lady's elderly daughter quavers, in obvious agitation. "What about me? Here I am, seventy-eight years old, and *still* nobody treats me like a senior, because she's still alive! She's bossed me around my whole life! What about interviewing *me!*"

Of course, we do interview her and, yes, her mother does correct her on numerous points of fact and opinion about the life that is still not her own to tell.

Wang Duli, Buddhist Spinster. Ming Shan

At the opposite end of the scale from Old Lady Li stands Wang Duli, a spinster of seventy-four years. Small, neat-faced, wearing bobbed gray hair and sleeve protectors over her high-collared gray jacket—she greeted us courteously, but coolly, with joined palms and a Buddhist "Omitofo." In the small courtyard she shares with several families, we find bamboo stools enough for Li Jufang and the local Fulian, me, her, and an old friend. Neighbor women perch on stone steps and bits of household equipment, expectantly.

"I hear you want to ask me about footbinding. I don't want to talk about that. We don't need foreigners taking ideas like that back home so they can laugh at us Chinese. Footbinding's over, it was never a good idea. Besides, I was never bound," Wang begins with some asperity. Turning to my associates, she continues,

"You shouldn't help foreigners to ridicule us. The past is past."

Li and I leap into the breach, as does the local Fulian, all talking at once, all insisting:

"This is about women's history! She's not going to make bad propaganda against us. She's come all the way from the US, and the Fulian is helping her! It's OK, really."

Despite the cacophony, my fluency in Chinese draws her attention on me, and the others let me take over.

"Mother-in-law Wang, really, I am not laughing at Chinese women. Look at all they accomplished even though the old society limited them so much! Besides, we are studying not just footbinding, but also women's work-lives, how women contributed to their families, and sometimes even supported themselves. I hear that you were able to do that. We really want to interview you as an example of a strong, independent Chinese woman. I am really sincere," I argue, softly.

"It's true, she's a friend of China, not an enemy. The Provincial Fulian has worked with her before," says the local cadre.

Wang downshifts, struggles with reticence and pride of accomplish- ment, relents.

"Well, ask then. I have nothing to hide. But I don't know about all that feudal nonsense about feet. My family was an enlightened one."

In an hour or so of talking about a life that has been both single and sin- gular, Wang Duli comes close to turning my mental world upside down.

I became an anthropologist principally because I shared with the anthro- pologists who first taught me a basic assumption. We did not believe in "culture." That is to say, we did not assume ideas to be active agents, exist- ing Platonically outside human selves, "causing" the events that make up societies. "Cultural" arguments were the stock-in-trade of the schoolteach- ers, clergymen, and patriots charged with explaining behavior and society to small-town Canadian youth: we go to war because we love our country; we give money to the church because we believe in God; and the like. In my family's bosom, another truth reigned: Fathers go to war because the alternative is prison; we attend church because our presence there enhances Father's professional credit. Simply by listening to Grand- mother, we could learn that ideas changed when the old ways of living disappeared, and new ways promoted new values. When I entered uni- versity, I learned that anthropologists were as good at this sort of ideolog- ical deconstruction as my skeptical parents. Ethnographies extended my social horizons, offering elaborate and exotic evidence for the proposition that, if I were to find myself in the external circumstances of a Trobriander or a Nuer, I would come to think like one. As training took me, body and mind, into the Chinese world, I learned that the proposition was true.

In the 1980s, many anthropologists changed their position on this crit- ical issue. Like so many school principals and preachers, they resusci- tated culture, then crowned and anointed it. They asserted, often in ugly, involuted language, that ideas shape our experiences totally; that people of different societies inhabit different, utterly incommensurable worlds. It was small-town epistemology all over again, even less palatable because warmed over.

Rooted in the earlier vision, I assume that we come to have certain ideas *because* of our experience in the world as it exists outside our minds. That the world is perceived through cultural lenses, and that peo- ple sometimes hold ideas fast in the face of evidence that they no longer make sense are obvious enough. In the run of time longer than an individual life, however, ideas brighten, flicker, and disappear like shadows on a wall. They *are* shadows: reflections of a material reality that may change, but not merely because we change our minds.

In assessing the strength or feebleness of ideas, I often think of my mother's mother. Dying near ninety in the mid-1950s, her early life had been lived in England under Queen Victoria. "The old queen," or, sometimes "the good queen" was, through Grandmother, a figure in our lives. Grandmother was literate only to the extent of simple Bible reading. She never questioned the profound inequalities that existed between her and my grandfather, or between them and people of a higher class. Hierarchy, beginning with that between the sexes, and epitomized in the grand gaps between herself, Victoria, and the Lord, was the guiding principle of her life. She spent that life first as a maid in a small Lancashire inn, and then as the personal body servant, or wife, to as unreconstructed an old tyrant as Dickens ever drew. I am not sure divorce had ever occurred within her circle, except for that of the terrible Mrs. Wallace Simpson, who robbed young King Edward of his birthright through her shameless public misconduct in marrying him.

Leading my later, different life, I have trampled on every virtue my Grandmother held to be essential. Divorced, remarried, childless by willful choice, an atheist analyst of religion and a radical critic of social hierarchy, I am her moral antithesis. Even my job would have troubled her. While she, like most women, had to "work out," she would have found my persistently peripatetic career not only incomprehensible, but vaguely immoral, and certainly not respectable. Two generations in my, and most Americans' lives, uproot a millennium of feudalism, putting new, capitalist bedevilments in its place. Such change happens visibly in North America, under the double impetus of technological change and immigration.

Anthropologists (my kind) conclude that a people whose population remains stable, who are not visited by sudden ecological change or pushy neighbors, and who achieve a reasonable degree of equality among themselves, can keep their old ideas intact for generations, recreating them continuously out of unchanging need. They serve; they wear well. With such folk, there is no good way to tell whether ideas cause behavior or behavior causes ideas. People easily assume that ideas are our principal guiding force, without much fear of contradiction.

When literacy, travel, and a modicum of logic give us systematic comparisons of peoples over time and space, however, this lazy, easy assumption is no longer tenable. The lives and thoughts of Inuit and !Kung, Kazakh and Maasai, Chinese peasant and Mexican campesino show powerful parallels born of the fact that peoples in each pair get their livings in similar ways.

That our thoughts spring from our actions is even clearer in places where life is changing rapidly, as in North America. My grandmother— rest her soul—would be shocked at my life; I view hers with something of the same ethnographic detachment I bring to those of the elderly Chinese women I interview. I must work hard to understand Grandmother's life clearly, a life which in its restraints seems deeply alien. My grandmother's thoughts are closer to those of spinster Wang than to mine. For women of their time, Ming Shan and Lancashire had much in common.

But that is not the reason that my Ming Shan informant left me nonplussed. Here was a woman whose entire life was testimony to the shaping force of a religious belief, a set of ideals held to in the teeth of patriarchy, Communist revolution, and the flesh.

I was born and grew up in Chengdu, in an artisan family with many children. As a girl, I became very religious, and when I reached marriage age—I was fifteen—I made a firm decision. Preserving the purity of the body and dedicating myself to a spiritual life seemed the right path for me. If you marry, you cannot do these things, or not until you are old. So I told my parents I did not want to marry.

My parents did not oppose me, for my mother especially believed that virginity and singleness were a woman's right if she chose them both. My mother was Cantonese, and Cantonese women are very strong Buddhists. My parents explained to me that if I chose celibacy, I was also choosing the responsibility of maintaining myself. If I did not go to a husband, my natal family could not support me. Mother had taught me to read scriptures, and to sew, and my body was strong and healthy, so I thought I could take care of myself. Friends helped me to find work as a maidservant in a rich merchant family, and I stayed with them for twenty years.

Soon after the revolution, everything changed. I had a little money saved, so I set out for Ming Shan, planning to support myself by sewing. On the road, I met three other women with the same purpose. We joined forces, rented a room together in Ming Shan, and lived as a family of sisters for many years. We shared work, expenses, and life's ups and downs. We ate vegetarian food, and helped each other puzzle out the scriptures. We also taught other women to read and recite Buddhist sutras. The women who came to learn from us were wives and mothers, without much time, but still devout. We helped them to grow in Buddhism, and they brought us occasional presents. With the sewing, we had enough to live on, though we lived very simply. Vegetarianism is good for the health, it purifies, and makes our single life easy and natural.

Up here in Ming Shan, I adopted a little girl to raise as a daughter, taught her to read and sew. When she grew up, she wanted to marry, so I let her marry. She seems to have a happy life, a good job, and four children. As you see, I have lots of neighbors, and we Chinese are very neighborly, if anyone needs anything. My old living-companions are all dead now, but a few friends who still live in their own homes spend most of their time over here, sewing. It's peaceful, and we talk. I have had a very fortunate life; I made the right choice to remain single.

Had we more time, and fewer onlookers, I would try harder to reconstruct her move, to discover why she chose this out-of-the-way town for her idiosyncratic household. It *was* idiosyncratic, certainly; she says she never met anyone else who had done this except for her Ming Shan companions, even though "At home, none of the girls wanted to marry. They just had to."

My guess about her choice of Ming Shan is only a guess: Immediately after Liberation, in 1949, life did not change greatly for the big Chengdu households that employed servants like Wang. By the mid-1950s, when she left the city, however, such households were disintegrating as the businesses on which they depended were collectivized. Party workers may have offered Wang no substitute job, or none she cared for. They may have urged marriage, disapproving of Wang's "feudal" views.

But why Ming Shan? Her religious commitment suggests an answer. The tea slopes of this mountain were formerly occupied by large Buddhist temples, each a major pre-revolution landlord. The lives of monks and nuns living there must have been changing, too, by the mid-1950s; the clergy pushed out into secular life. At least in Ming Shan, celibate, independent women were no novelty, for it was an area where the relative freedom of a Chinese nun's life had long been accepted. Perhaps Wang had heard of the mountain as a place where women like herself came and went without causing social ripples. Perhaps, indeed, one or two of her companions were former nuns.

Though her Buddhist laywoman life is highly unusual in Sichuan, such lives were common enough before the revolution, particularly along the southeast coast. In Guangdong, many women—we will never know their numbers—by custom chose celibacy and thus independence as either nuns or laywomen. Both Buddhism and Daoism supported this alternative to marriage.

When jobs for women were abundant, more of them could model their lives partially on those of celibate, self-supporting nuns, even if they did not become full-time religious. In one part of Guangdong, during the late-nineteenth- and early-twentieth-century boom in export silk production, women earned enough at the delicate, demanding work of unreeling cocoons that substantial numbers delayed or even refused marriage. Their tradition of female celibate independence persisted when the silk market crashed during the depression of the 1930s. Then, some traveled, alone or in groups, to Hong Kong and Southeast Asia, working as servants, and living with each other.[1]

From her mother, who was, perhaps, a part of this exodus, Wang inherited a view of a society that had a place for the self-supporting woman. Here, it seemed, was "culture" in action: ideas prompting behavior that moved a single woman against the strong current of Chinese expectations.

For a few nights, I worried that I had been utterly wrong about the power of culture. Maybe it did float around, like a genie in a lamp, eternal, nonmaterial, but still capable of making us take action. Yet as I mulled over her words, her life, and her links back through her mother to the independent, sisterly spinsters of Guangdong, I saw things more clearly.

Here, in a tiny stone courtyard on a back street of an impoverished Sichuan county town, Wang's tradition ends. Her daughter has followed her husband; the friends who come to chant sutras from her books are as elderly as herself, preparing for the final independence of death. No sisters will pass the secrets of autonomy down in Ming Shan. Cut from its social and economic roots, belief fades quickly. None of my associates could understand her motive for living "so unnatural" a life, and all wondered at her ability to support herself in a society whose economic deck is so stacked against women.

Listening to Wang Duli, I remember a "vegetarian hall" in Xiamen, on the coast, where last year I interviewed half a dozen women like her. The youngest was in her thirties, with a modern factory job that gave her the freedom to choose her traditional path. Only in places where girls are

[1] Important anthropological research on these silk-reelers and their subsequent exodus to Southeast Asia has been done by Janice Stockard, in her 1989 book *Daughters of the Canton Delta: Marriage Patterns and Economic Strategies in South China, 1860–1930* (Stanford, Calif.: Stanford University Press) and by Andrea Sankar, in her 1978 Ph.D. dissertation "The Evolution of the Sisterhood in Traditional Chinese Society: From Village Girls' Houses to Chai T'angs in Hong Kong" (University of Michigan).

paid directly, where they have many workmates among whom to find those of like mind, and where collages of old beliefs lie to hand or new ones can be assembled can this indigenous liberation for women persist.

I tell Wang what I know about Chinese celibate women—the Guangdong spinsters of her mother's time, the Xiamen factory worker. She is pleased: "The Buddhist religion is very powerful; when we believe in it, it helps us to lead pure, good lives." For her, the link is still the power of ideas. Preferring my own view, I settle back into a familiar materialism, relieved not to have to refurnish my entire intellectual house.

NOVEMBER 13, 1991.

We do a dozen solid interviews in our four days in Ming Shan County. It is a sketchy introduction to the area, but enough to amend our questionnaire and get on companionable terms with our future work-team. We sit in farm courtyards with the wizened subjects of our peculiar inquiry, a Fulian cadre filling in the forms. I focus on understanding the difficult local dialect, interject follow-up questions as women drop the amazing into the matter-of-fact, and take notes on what I see.

Chickens pass through, checking dirt floors for tidbits, recently married brides bounce babies in backslings, whispering over my clothes and skin. Women in their forties, not old enough to have daughters-in-law to help them, are busy ghosts on the periphery, washing clothes, chopping pigfood, trying to keep a little order in households where everyone spits ad libitum, where men drop clothes, dirty dishes, cigarette butts, and their tools wherever the whim takes them, and where babies relieve themselves through split pants with equal freedom. It is astonishing how clean the houses are (if you overlook the chickens), and how healthy the people. I rarely see skin diseases and infections that signal real uncleanliness, though there is plenty of superficial dirt acquired only today or yesterday. I drink tea at every house from cups that have never seen soap, and am never ill.

Nothing surprising happens. Perhaps I have grown unsurprisable by tales of childhood misery, overwork, and loss. Our questionnaire contains a long list of female relatives whose feet the informant is asked to identify as bound or not. Perhaps one-third of the women cannot remember this visible fact about their own mothers and grandmothers. Women died young, orphans were almost the norm.

As we work, but also at meals and in our bouncy rides through the countryside, I watch Ruan Fubuzhang. My initial impression is correct.

In mid-Michigan, this round, pouty woman would play bridge, eat too much chocolate, and keep a nasty, yipping, fluffy dog. She admires pretty, but is too lazy to try for beautiful. She decries her fatness as she reaches for yet another stuffed bun. Unsupervised, she will be a disaster as a fieldworker, hurrying through the work so as to get back quickly to the comforts of home. Her perception of the distance between herself and the common folk we visit leads rarely to sympathy or even curiosity, but often to contempt. She will bully them, and they will, wisely, plead ignorance of everything but their own names.

In short, Ruan is an average low-level Chinese government worker, an Everycadre. I consider my luck in having a whole set of capable and vigorous Fulian women—including, thank heaven, Ruan's boss, the many-armed Vice-Director—to counterbalance her. Can my gang of three keep her at it? Quietly, privately, in tactful words, each assures me that she will do her damnedest.

Poor Ruan. Her motives for being here are so feeble, her taste for walking through mud and excrement in high heels so ill developed. She is like one of those unfortunate sinologists' spouses, dragged off to Chinese cities that, while treasure-houses to their academic partners, are bedlams to them.

Back at the guesthouse, I try to improve our relationship, remembering to use her title, to offer her fruit, and to insist that she dip first into the dishes that come to our table. I admire and praise what I can about how she has managed our trip. I keep my barbed tongue to myself. Like a sensible Chinese, I work around her as best I can, and will remember to cast an especially skeptical eye over data from the counties she has personally supervised.

We break our drive home at a roadside tangerine market. Trucks come here to load up for state stores and work units, and for the occasional large private sale. We bargain for fifty kilos to split among ourselves. Gentle Li turns out to be a ferocious haggler, practically turning the tangerines inside out, and insisting on weighing the carrying basket on two different scales so as to subtract accurately from the final price.

"I grew up in the country, you know," she reminds me.

She is in no hurry about this, so Ruan and I, arm in companionable arm, look over the pigs' feet being sold a few paces up the road. To me, there does not seem to be much difference among them, but we inspect them all, snorting in amazed contempt at their many defects. Ruan buys several kilos, greedily pleased that they have cost her 20 percent less than in Chengdu. She describes lingeringly the delicious things she will do with them.

Her tangerine deal concluded, Li wants to tour the pigs' feet too. Li, so decisive about fruit for our collectivity, gets cold feet when it comes to a private purchase. Should she have some, or which, or none? Driver Zhang's horn makes the decision. Li scrambles, fruitless, into the van, and we roar back to the city.

The computer expert I meet the next day is less expert than we had hoped. Or perhaps my capacity to deal intelligently with an unfamiliar computer program described in heavy Sichuanese is at fault. With luck, however, I will see a working database when I return. We wrangle cheerfully over a long list of last-minute changes to the questionnaire—I am still having last gasps of insight into its improvement in the car on the way to the airport—but the hard work is done. I invite the Vice-Director and a dozen colleagues to Sichuan dim sum in the fancy restaurant at the top of my hotel. She invites us all to a hotpot dinner in the provincial government headquarters. As usual, she has outdone herself. The ingredients of the elegantly presented banquet include: rabbit ears, pig brains, duck tongues, goose shins, cow dewlap, pig tripes, duck blood cubes, small whole fish, and a magnificent array of vegetables.

"It's a very special meal," says Hua.

Meal by meal, meeting by meeting, China replaces some of the Anglo atoms and assumptions from which I was once entirely constructed. It is easier to encompass Chineseness by absorbing and digesting, perhaps, than by seeing, listening, and writing. As I fall asleep still gurgling with hotpot, I remember a three-month-old infant recently drenching my trousers with an unexpected explosion of baby poop. This innocent excretion, derived in the last instance entirely from the nursing mother's own heavily seasoned diet, smelled principally of fragrant Sichuan pepper. Having taken in *huajiao* with his mother's milk, this baby will follow a more direct route than I can to Chineseness. Our Vice-Director's festive meal of peculiar parts is informative—of China's need for extreme frugality, combined with the culture's unexpected penchant for the outré—but I must go on tasting new dishes, meeting more people, looking for insight from my ground-level perspective. Especially, I must learn China as women learn it; from them, as out of their babes, come the unexpected truths.

The political map of Sichuan is a patterned patchwork of men's communities that reveals very little about the ways women's marriages, adoptions, work, and friendships stitched discrete settlements into a distinctive, female topology. A man often dies in his birthplace, having lived his entire life there; a woman almost never does. Talking to women

Renmin Road just East of Mao, 1993

who have lived their married lives in one village, or in one city neighborhood draws a sample of people who have also lived a decade or two in other places. Chengdu threads lead to Ming Shan, to Le Shan, to Laijiang, to the other counties of our footbinding study. Generations of sisters and daughters have embroidered a woman-to-woman pattern over the underlying masculine patchwork.

In the spring, when the Fulian has done its best, I will return to follow some of those threads. At its beginning, I saw this retrospective footbinding study as quite separate from my 1988 pursuit of small business-women under post-Mao economic reform. Now, the lines between them blur. When I sit on the flowery slopes of Emei Shan next year, unraveling lives and discovering feet, I will still be looking for Chengdu.

城都行

November 1996

Shanghai, Chengdu

CHAPTER NINETEEN

城都行

Coda

NOVEMBER 29, 1996. SHANGHAI

Even at three A.M., Shanghai mutters in its sleep. Wide awake in the YMCA, I listen to the city-sound of cars, and karaoke, and the occasional crying baby. Too prudent to go out exploring, too lazy to read any of the tomes I've brought for academic friends, I down some melatonin and wait for second slumber.

Shanghai has grown on me in recent visits as I have walked more of its shopkeepers' streets and ventured into its industrial labyrinths. It is only a base for the rural sorties of the current project, however; I've done no interviewing here. Having no fully funded excuse to breach their privacy, I still follow narrow alleys leading to the villagelike clusters at the core of most city blocks, still peer up the black stairwells that lead—I know—to comfortable homes. My high hotel perch gives views of backyards—potted plants, hand-washed laundry, and all. Inside, beyond the big-street facades, it probably looks like Chengdu.

My last Sichuan project, begun with high hopes in 1994, was a fizzle. The Women's Fed and I had set up an elaborate survey tracking how households sent daughters into the expanding labor market. I got a start-up grant, we tested it on 1,200 households, each fieldsite more problematic than the last, and finally our hoped-for main grant fell through. Even the work we accomplished was disappointing. Local officials fended us off rudely, obnoxious policemen convoyed us everywhere that we bullied our way into, we were all anxious and jumpy. The bureaucratic wind toward rural research had shifted, perhaps because Sichuan had seen dramatic peasant riots over economic mismanagement in recent years. On my return to Stanford, already knee-deep in unanalyzed data from another project in Fujian, I let the migrants slide.

Now an excuse to indulge my taste for things Sichuanese has surfaced. Six months ago, I rashly printed out my accumulated travel journals, edited and numbered the pages, and found myself with a picaresque to publish. After submitting it to the criticism of friends and a few less-biased sources, I wanted to let my Chengdu colleagues have a whack at it. Will the Fulian want their countrywomen and themselves portrayed in everyday dress by even a sympathetic foreigner? Once, a Women's Fed colleague showed me a *Reader's Digest* article, a real cold war, anti-Chicom hatchet-job, in which some kindly treated stranger let loose all his ignorance and prejudice, blasting his Chinese guides by name.

"Don't ever do this to us, OK?" she said. "This sort of thing makes big trouble for people. Travel guides, and people like us in the propaganda section are supposed to give foreigners a good impression of China, not make propaganda for China's enemies." I promised.

I think my journal conveys not animosity, but truths that China's friends need to tell: truths about common humanity, about the individualism of Chinese (neither more nor less than ours), about the difficulties and successes of leaping a cultural gap. But I am not yet convinced that our Vice-Director and all the rest would read it in the same way. I have always acknowledged the formal research we have done together as a joint effort, listing individual colleagues as well as the Fulian as a unit—both responsible and deserving of credit for our work. *Looking for Chengdu* is different. In its pages, they are not observers *with* me, but observed *by* me, in ways none of us had assumed would be made public. Like any subject of anthropological inquiry, they have been included in a process for which it is extremely difficult to obtain fully informed consent.

All anthropologists face this dilemma, and we face it with perpetual uncertainty. Before leaving on this trip, I obtained a copy of the "Draft American Anthropological Association Code of Ethics," which I have pondered on the plane to Shanghai. The code stresses not only my professional obligations to science, but my obligations to everyone from Chairman Jiang Zemin to all "persons or animals" with whom I work. Its preamble concludes:

"In a field of such complex involvements and obligations, it is inevitable that misunderstandings, conflicts, and the need to make choices among apparently incompatible values will arise. [Anthropologists] are responsible for grappling with such difficulties and struggling to resolve them in ways compatible with the principles stated here." This is all very Protestant, and it is not much help.

As I grapple, I am reminded of another social analyst of China, Roxane Witke. Witke, while setting up a political science project in 1972, was summoned by Jiang Qing, Mao's wife, to write her memoirs. Jiang, then an immensely powerful figure, told Witke insider stories and revealed her lavish lifestyle. By 1976, with the "fall of the Gang of Four," Jiang was in jail, and Witke's book, published in 1977, was rumored to have played a role in her capital conviction as "giving state secrets to the enemy." When the "informed consent" of China's de facto Empress becomes an act of sedition, should I even try to obtain it from village grandmothers? If the political wind blows too hard, might my friends not be better off claiming ignorance of my purposes and denying everything? "Good God, was *that* what she was up to? We had no idea! How like a lickspittle capitalist running dog to so twist our words and abuse our hospitality!" Given what has often happened in Chinese political life, that's what I'*d* say.

Don't ask, don't tell may be a better guide for anthropology in authoritarian regimes than anything the AAA's handwringing Code suggests. But here I am, unable to resist the temptation to ask the lively, capable Fulian women face to face if they can bear to be written about.

December 6, 1996. Chengdu

The Shanghai–Chengdu contrast is 1990s China in microcosm, especially as regards road traffic, which may be the quickest possible source of insight into any industrialized culture. I took cabs seven times in my Shanghai week; we were stopped and fined by police for minor infractions on two of those occasions. Another three times, the cabbie refused to take me exactly to my destination, because his license number was odd (or even), and he couldn't drive certain streets on even- (or odd-) numbered days. All three graciously took small change off the fare. Traffic cops were everywhere, and cars, bicycles, even people, stopped for red lights. The broad new streets on the east side of the Huangpu River—Pudong—and the just-opened toll road to the airport were marked with international highway signs in conventional symbolism and coloring. In Shanghai, we are in the great world, following a (perhaps slightly hypertrophied) rule of law. Shanghai's socialist heritage of industrial discipline and collective action merges smoothly with cosmopolitan expectation.

Then I arrive in Chengdu.

As the first and only foreigner to disembark, I am swept up by the most entrepreneurial of a crowd of taxi drivers, who seizes my bag and steers me rapidly through the parking lot. And past the parking lot, into a small street, behind a bank.

"What's all this? Where's the taxi?" I demand, gruffly. "I don't want any trouble here."

The young man looks around uneasily.

"It's all right. My sister will drive you. She's a woman," he offers, soothingly.

And then the sister appears, with her little, red—and obviously private—car. I can handle this. I jump in.

We chat as she roars onto the toll road for the twenty-minute trip from airport to city center. We chat, but we do not communicate. She has never spoken to a foreigner before and cannot easily overlook my linguistic ineptitudes. I have not heard this rich Sichuanese dialect in over two years and must rustily reconstruct algorithms that translate the tonal system of my northern Mandarin into her southern version.

The trip does not take twenty minutes, as it did when the new road was still lined with radish fields and underemployed youths selling raw pork. Colorfully tiled villas have sprouted, factories are a-building, neon signs offering the delights of karaoke punctuate the emerging suburbs. Most of these structures have been built on spec, and stand empty, awaiting a new turn in the real-estate crap-shoot that fuels the "development" that innocent foreigners so admire. But they have given work to brick-layers and electricians, profits to contractors and realtors, and pay-offs to the officials who have stamped all of their permits and licenses. Money has changed hands, and Chengdu is, I doubt not, grateful.

I ask, as I have been asking everywhere in Shanghai, whether she knows any workers who have been laid off. All over China, government enterprises are trying to downsize themselves out of long-term commitments to workers, to restructure so as to provide only wages rather than the former socialist mix of subsidized housing, health care, education, and other benefits. Women are especially vulnerable since their former package also included maternity rights, child care, and the costly obligation of large enterprises to monitor their reproductive trajectories. Shanghai shed 13,000 women cotton-mill workers this week, not the first, and surely not the last of this former labor aristocracy to be dumped on the market.

Chengdu, it seems, is much the same as Shanghai in this respect, at least. My driver's younger sister has just been pink-slipped, also from a textile factory, and now gets thirty *yuan* a month not to come to work. This is not enough to buy her food, and she is desperately looking for work. Women like her are not going to be snapping up empty suburban villas. I miss a lot of the detail of this story, but the distress comes through unfiltered.

"They take the factory money and invest it in Guangzhou or even Hong Kong, then don't have money to pay the workers. I have a job in the post office, but who knows how long that will last. Workers in government services are better off than state industrial workers, but it's getting very tight. We just have to think of ways to make it." She pats her steering wheel, and lapses into what, for her, must be a lengthy silence.

The invisible motion of contemporary Chinese political economy suddenly resolves itself into a multidimensional, material reality. We are stuck in traffic. My driver, following the principles of "cockroach capitalism" (their phrase, not mine), seizes an opening to advance our immediate interests. She moves over into the oncoming traffic lane. When that too clogs, she moves left yet again into the other (oncoming) lane. Behind us, real daredevils weasel into the (oncoming) bicycle / tractor lane. In graceful synchrony, drivers coming toward us have done the same thing. Headed north are six lanes of traffic; headed south six lanes confront them. In between revs a mass of hundreds of trapped cars, trucks, buses, and people trying to get live pigs to market, centered on a handful of hysterical cops. The efficient, modern, state-funded infrastructure of highways, tollgates, and exits is less passable than any muddy country road. China in a nutshell.

DECEMBER 13, 1996. CHENGDU

It proves to be a pleasant and rewarding week. My Women's Federation associates laugh at my prepublication scruples, suggesting that I keep names to a minimum "because good Communists" one says sweetly "don't seek personal publicity." They want to talk about setting up a new project, for which they have already established bureaucratic ground. Next year, if I can get the funding, we will interview women who have been laid off in their thousands by state enterprises. The state-sponsored socialist affirmative action that gave them and our entrepreneurs their education and social experience now trickles away before their eyes. Laid off, pushed into retirement as early as forty-five, or, as young school-leavers, refused jobs on the grounds of gender, women in still-elite, still-valued state employment are growing vanishingly few.

The project is eminently fundable for academic reasons and because the Women's Federation officials can use our results to push for gender equality in work. It sounds a bit dull, but thoroughly worthy. When I make the trip back to the airport, I ride a comfy legal cab with a boring, accentless driver, and the trip takes only twenty minutes. I send up a small prayer for surprises, and open my notebook.